"In *Racism in the Neoliberal Era*  well-researched and argued racism-centered analysis of the origin, growth, and consequences of American neoliberalism. Its insights are especially relevant in explaining the convergence of today's perfect storm of covert institutionalized racism, white nationalist politics, the control of all levels and branches of government by the economic elite, and rampant racial and economic inequality."

Noel A. Cazenave, University of Connecticut, USA and author of *Conceptualizing Racism: Breaking the Chains of Racially Accomodative Language*

"Randy Hohle traces the ways in which neoliberalism recast the culture of racism, allowing white elites to limit blacks' voting rights and access to social benefits, while reinforcing de facto segregation and subjecting blacks to random and lethal police violence. This book is timely and important."

Richard Lachmann, State University of New York at Albany, USA

"Randolph Hohle provides great insight into how elite white oligopoly capitalists (aka neoliberals) use white-racist framing to con white Americans into accepting large-scale austerity and privatization schemes (public = black/bad, private = white/good) that maintain or increase racial and class inequalities. Since the 1960s civil rights movement this white male elite has thereby schemed to weaken meaningful racial desegregation and firmly maintain their centuries-old control over US society."

Joe Feagin, Texas A&M University, USA and author of *Racist America*

"For those wondering how social divisiveness and wealth inequality have gotten so out of control in the U.S., Randolph Hohle's latest book provides a much needed explanation. Providing something of a revelation for all those interested in social problems and social justice, Hohle ties the abandonment of support for minorities, the poor, and the education of children to the hegemonic takeover of public policies by neoliberalism at all levels of the State. Hohle's connection between the decline of American democracy and Neoliberal social policy requires us all to pay attention before current social cleavages become irreversible."

Mark Gottdiener, University of Buffalo, USA

Racism in the Neoliberal Era

Racism in the Neoliberal Era explains how simple racial binaries like black/white are no longer sufficient to explain the persistence of racism, capitalism, and elite white power. The neoliberal era features the largest black middle class in US history and extreme racial marginalization. Hohle focuses on how the origins and expansion of neoliberalism depended on language or semiotic assemblage of white-private and black-public. The language of neoliberalism explains how the white racial frame operates like a web of racial meanings that connect social groups with economic policy, geography, and police brutality. When America was racially segregated, elites consented to political pressure to develop and fund white-public institutions. The black civil rights movement eliminated legal barriers that prevented racial integration. In response to black civic inclusion, elite whites used a language of white-private/black-public to deregulate the Voting Rights Act and banking. They privatized neighborhoods, schools, and social welfare, creating markets around poverty. They oversaw the mass incarceration and systemic police brutality against people of color. Citizenship was recast as a privilege instead of a right. Neoliberalism is the result of the latest elite white strategy to maintain political and economic power.

Randolph Hohle is an associate professor of sociology at Fredonia, SUNY. His previous books include *Black Citizenship and Authenticity in the Civil Rights Movement* (Routledge, 2013) and *Race and the Origins of Neoliberalism* (Routledge, 2015).

New Critical Viewpoints on Society Series
Edited by Joe R. Feagin

For a full list of titles in this series, please visit www.routledge.com/New-Critical-Viewpoints-on-Society/book-series/NCVS.

Racism in the Neoliberal Era: A Meta History of Elite White Power
Randolph Hohle (2017)

Violence Against Black Bodies: An Intersectional Analysis of How Black Lives Continue to Matter
Edited by Sandra Weissinger, Dwayne A. Mack and Elwood Watson (2016)

Exploring White Privilege
Robert P. Amico (2016)

Redskins? Sport Mascots, Indian Nations and White Racism
James V. Fenelon (2016)

Racial Theories in Social Science: A Systemic Racism Critique
Sean Elias and Joe R. Feagin (2016)

Raising Mixed Race: Multiracial Asian Children in a Post-Racial World
Sharon H. Chang (2015)

Antiracist Teaching
Robert P. Amico (2014)

What Don't Kill us Makes us Stronger: African American Women and Suicide
Kamesha Spates (2014)

Latinos Facing Racism: Discrimination, Resistance, and Endurance
Joe R. Feagin and José A. Cobas (2014)

Racism in the Neoliberal Era

A Meta History of Elite White Power

Randolph Hohle

NEW YORK AND LONDON

First published 2018
by Routledge
711 Third Avenue, New York, NY 10017

and by Routledge
2 Park Square, Milton Park, Abingdon, Oxon OX14 4RN

Routledge is an imprint of the Taylor & Francis Group, an informa business

© 2018 Taylor & Francis

The right of Randolph Hohle to be identified as the author of this work has been asserted by him in accordance with sections 77 and 78 of the Copyright, Designs and Patents Act 1988.

All rights reserved. No part of this book may be reprinted or reproduced or utilised in any form or by any electronic, mechanical, or other means, now known or hereafter invented, including photocopying and recording, or in any information storage or retrieval system, without permission in writing from the publishers.

Trademark notice: Product or corporate names may be trademarks or registered trademarks and are used only for identification and explanation without intent to infringe.

Library of Congress Cataloging-in-Publication Data
Names: Hohle, Randolph, author.
Title: Racism in the neoliberal era : a meta history of elite white power / Randolph Hohle.
Description: New York, NY : Routledge, 2017. | Series: New critical viewpoints on society series
Identifiers: LCCN 2017027291 | ISBN 9781138682139 (hardcover : alk. paper) | ISBN 9781138682092 (pbk. : alk. paper) | ISBN 9781315527499 (ebook)
Subjects: LCSH: Neoliberalism—United States. | Racism—Economic aspects—United States. | Race discrimination—Economic aspects—United States. | Elite (Social sciences)—United States. | United States—Race relations.
Classification: LCC HB95 .H645 2017 | DDC 305.800973—dc23
LC record available at https://lccn.loc.gov/2017027291

ISBN: 978-1-138-68213-9 (hbk)
ISBN: 978-1-138-68209-2 (pbk)
ISBN: 978-1-315-52749-9 (ebk)

Typeset in Adobe Caslon Pro and Copperplate Gothic
by Apex CoVantage, LLC

Dedicated to Maxime, Gage, Henry, and Shea

CONTENTS

ACKNOWLEDGMENTS   XI

INTRODUCTION: THE TRICKS ARE NEW,
BUT THE BAG IS THE SAME   1

1   CITIZENSHIP AND SYSTEMIC RACISM   28

2   PIECEMEAL BLACK DISENFRANCHISEMENT:
    DEREGULATION AND THE VOTING RIGHTS
    ACT IN THE NEOLIBERAL ERA   52

3   PRESERVING THE WHITE ECONOMY AT ANY COST   78

4   SOCIAL WELFARE AND THE SEGREGATED
    WELFARE STATE   108

5   THE NEOLIBERAL METROPOLIS: RACIAL SEGREGATION,
    SUBURBANIZATION, AND GENTRIFICATION   138

6   RACISM AND THE NEOLIBERAL CRISIS IN
    AMERICAN EDUCATION   165

7	WHITE-PRIVATE VIOLENCE: POLICE BRUTALITY AND MASS INCARCERATION	191
8	DIVERSITY AND FUTURE TRENDS IN RACIST NEOLIBERAL GOVERNANCE	222
	REFERENCES	249
	INDEX	263

ACKNOWLEDGMENTS

This was an ambitious project from the start. I'd like to thank Joe Feagin, who encouraged me to expand on the theory and ideas I originally developed in *Race and the Origins of American Neoliberalism*. I was fortunate enough to have colleagues and friends with expertise in urban sociology, finance, policing, and social welfare. So thank you, Mark Gottdiener, Shannon Monnat, Michael Aiello, Mary Carney, Cassandra Daniels, and Allen Shelton. Thanks to Richard Lachmann for teaching me about historical sociology and elites. Thanks to Ronald Jacobs and Steven Seidman for teaching me about cultural sociology all those years back. Thanks to the anonymous reviewers for their feedback and suggestions on how to make this a better book. I had no research assistants or any course releases from the institution that employs me to help me write this book. But I did have a lot of help from my family.

INTRODUCTION
THE TRICKS ARE NEW, BUT THE BAG IS THE SAME

Let's start with the murders of two young boys. On 22 November 2014, 12-year-old Tamir Rice went to a local neighborhood park, Cudell Park, on Cleveland's west side, to play. Cudell Park sits on Detroit Avenue, a 16-mile road that parallels Lake Erie, bending northeast as it heads toward downtown until it ends on the banks of the Cuyahoga River. November 22 was one of those late-fall days in Cleveland when a light dusting of snow covered the grass but the sidewalks were still warm enough to melt the snowfall. It was the type of winter day you could leave your winter jacket unzipped. Rice slowly walked back and forth between two picnic tables under the gazebo with his toy gun, a black plastic replica of an 'airsoft' gun. Rice pulled the toy gun out of the waistband of his pants. He put it back in and took it out again before pointing it at no one. He may have been playing the sort of imaginary games young American boys have played for generations, games such as cowboys and Indians, Star Wars, or cops and robbers. He may have been fantasizing about getting revenge on the kids who bullied him at school. A call came into the 911 dispatch about someone at the park who was "probably a juvenile" pointing a gun at people that was "probably fake." The 911 dispatcher alerted the police.

A police car carrying two officers drove up on to the grass between the gazebo and line of white concrete pillars that divided the park from the sidewalk. The police car was perhaps 15 feet from the sidewalk and 10 feet from Rice. A white police officer named Timothy Loehmann jumped out of the car with his real gun, a Glock handgun loaded with 9mm ammunition issued to all Cleveland police officers. He pointed his gun at Rice. At 12 years old, Rice would not have had any experience with police pointing guns at him. He was scared, silent, and grabbed for his shirt to show the police that the toy gun was in the waistband of his pants. Loehmann shot him twice, once in the chest and once in the pelvis. It was not a point-blank shot. Loehmann shot Rice at what is considered contact distance because it was far enough for the bullet to be tugged by gravity and angle its entry point. The bullets struck major vessels, intestines, and other organs. Rice collapsed on the cold concrete floor of the gazebo. The sound of the plastic toy gun hitting the cement pad would have echoed under the gazebo roof if it weren't still in the waistband of his pants. The sound of flesh of a five-foot-seven-inch, 195-pound body hitting the concrete pad was a thud. It did not echo. His body lay on the ground for 12 minutes before the ambulance arrived.

The time between when police arrived at the park and when Loehmann shot Rice was two seconds. Cleveland's deputy police chief claimed that the police ordered the boy to raise his hands and that Rice pointed the toy gun at Loehmann. The police chief said the gun's bright-orange tip, indicating that the gun was a toy, had been removed. The murder captured on video shows that none of the events the police said happened. There was not enough time between the police exiting the car and the shots fired for a police officer to issue an order to Rice to raise his hands and for him to pull the toy gun out of his pants and point it at the officer. Rice was not Billy the Kid. It was impossible for the officers to know that the toy gun was missing its orange tip. It was still in his pants—between the bullet hole in his chest and the bullet hole in his pelvis.

Two other measurements of time in this story also matter: 4 minutes and 2 minutes. Rice's body lay on the cold concrete floor under the gazebo for 4 minutes before a second set of police officers arrived and administered first aid. Loehmann's partner stood there dazed as Loehmann hobbled to the other side of the patrol car out of view from Rice's hemorrhaging body. Roughly 2 minutes after the shooting, Rice's

INTRODUCTION 3

14-year-old sister ran toward her brother, only to be tackled, handcuffed, and thrown into the back of the patrol car. Her crime? Being black and upset at the sight of her little brother lying on the ground dying. Two separate investigations, one by a special prosecutor from Colorado and another by a former FBI supervisory agent, claimed that Loehmann "acted reasonably." Timothy McGinty, the Cuyahoga County prosecutor, recommended to the grand jury that they not bring charges against Loehmann, a curious move since prosecutors don't typically side with the defense. Loehmann was eventually fired in May 2017 for lying on his job application.[1]

Gunshot victims fall down and die in the movies and on television shows. Ballistic science indicates that a gunshot victim will seldom die from a bullet becoming lodged in or hitting a major organ. Gunshot victims die from suffering an infection by bacteria entering the open wound, or they simply bleed to death. Tamir Rice bled to death. His autopsy report indicated that he died as result of a hemorrhage at the base of the mesentery, body tissue that contains veins and arteries that circulate blood to the intestines. All that was left in his intestines was 75 ml of body fluid and two surgical sponges. He was officially pronounced dead at 12:54 a.m., 9 hours after he was shot.[2]

Now let's compare Rice's murder to the murder of a 14-year-old boy almost 60 years earlier, Emmett Till. In mid-August of 1955, Till came to Money, Mississippi, from Chicago to spend the summer with his extended family. Using some money they earned working in the cotton fields, he and his cousins went to Bryant's Grocery and Meat Market store to by candy and soda. Till bought a pack of gum and flirted with the store clerk, a 22-year-old white woman named Carolyn Bryant. While standing outside the store, Till wolf-whistled at Bryant as she walked away. Till's cousin Simeon Wright stated, "Whistling at a white woman in Mississippi? Oh no, it's better to play with a rattlesnake." Whether Till was serious about his sexual advances toward Bryant or he wolf-whistled to impress his cousins is unknown. Till openly bragged about his white girlfriend back home in Chicago. Till liked to stand out from other blacks in Money. Instead of overalls and bandanas, he wore stylish clothes that local blacks considered flashy and that local whites considered uppity. Till refused to wear shoes without socks. Despite the

1954 *Brown v. Board of Education of Topeka, Kansas,* ruling that separate and equal was unconstitutional, Mississippi continued practicing Jim Crow laws in their schools and public spaces and Jim Crow customs in their social interactions. Till broke a Jim Crow custom and paid for it with his life.[3]

Two local white men, Carolyn Bryant's husband, Roy Bryant, and his half-brother J. W. Milam stood trial for the murder. More men helped in the abduction, including local black men who understood the general danger of breaking Jim Crow customs to the black community, even if it mean helping Bryant and Milam murder a young boy. Bryant and Milam murdered Till in a ritualized killing that was more reminiscent of Europe's Middle Ages than postwar Mississippi. In addition to pistol-whipping Till, Bryant and Milam gouged out his eyes with a nut picker, lopped half his right ear off with a hatchet, anchored him to a 70-pound cotton gin fan by wrapping a piece of barbed wire around his neck and the fan, shot him in the face, and then threw his body into the Talla-hatchie River. There is some debate over when they shot Till in the face: while he was being tortured or right before they threw his body into the river. There is no debate that he suffered a slow and painful death that started at 2:30 a.m., after the men took him from his great-uncle and aunt's house, and lasted well into dawn.

Two boys found Till's naked, swollen body while fishing 3 days after he went missing. They would have most likely found his body face down in the river. In the *Adventures of Huckleberry Finn,* Mark Twain writes how Huck hid on Jackson's Island as a ferryboat shot cannonballs into the Mississippi River in an effort to bring his presumed drowned body to the surface. Science tells us that the bacteria found in the stomach and intestines produce methane, hydrogen sulfide, and carbon dioxide, which inflate the body like a balloon, causing the body to float to the surface face down. Mississippi's August heat would have made the Tal-lahatchie River ideal for bacterial growth. Till's body should have remained submerged because of the weight of the fan, but the combina-tion of the inflation and the river's current pushed Till's body onto the river's bank. The cotton gin fastened around Till's neck most likely kept his skin on. Recovery divers have experienced pulling drowned bodies out of water only to have the skin slip off the body, like removing a sock. Till's mother opted to have an open-casket funeral for her son to show the world the horrors of the ritualized style of murder known as lynching. The mortician removed Till's eyes and swollen tongue and stitched his head back together. Tens of thousands of people attended his funeral. Chicago's black newspaper, the *Chicago Defender*, published a photograph of Till's mutilated body to rally blacks to take political action. Till's murder was one of the key events that helped start the black civil rights movement. Bryant and Milam were found innocent of Till's murder.[4]

The murders of Till and Rice are eerily similar, yet the contexts of their murders indicate some major differences. Jim Crow laws are no longer on the books, but where we live, go to school, and work is still racially segregated. Racism and segregation in Till's time differed by the urban north and rural south. America was in the midst of an economic and demographic transition in the first half of the 20th century. The Great Mississippi Flood of 1927, which flooded some 23,000 square miles, killed 250 people, and left more than 200,000 blacks displaced from their homes, prompted many blacks to migrate from the Delta to Chicago in search of jobs in the factories. More southern blacks followed this migration route as the mechanization of agriculture and drop in global agricultural commodity prices eliminated the black agricultural labor market. The median income for blacks in Chicago was about twice the national median income for blacks, reflecting Chicago's nuanced political and economic white-black relationships designed to keep blacks in the south side but still loyal to the white democratic machine politics. Till was murdered in Mississippi, where elite whites openly sanctioned and ignored white-on-black violence.

Rice's neighborhood paints a different portrait of where and how we live today. Although 36% of the households in Rice's neighborhood made less than $25,000 a year in 2013, the median black household income was $45,461. The neighborhood was about 38% black. In fact, lower-income whites are more likely to live in middle-class neighborhoods than affluent blacks or Hispanics are. Since the 1970s, a narrow slice of racially nonthreatening blacks have acquired a middle-class status and moved out of the urban ghettos. Blacks are more likely to live in the suburbs today than the cities. Yet, as Elijah Anderson stated, contemporary segregation "co-exists with an ongoing racial incorporation process that has projected the largest black middle class in history." The movement of middle-class blacks from the communal ghetto has created what sociologists have dubbed the "hyperghetto" or "American Apartheid": single class and single race, or simply the concentration of poor and black.[5]

There is another difference between then and now: the strategies and exercises of power of the elite white power structure. It's the small differences in the murder of these two young boys that highlight some very big changes in the reproduction of elite white power.

One of these small differences is how white violence has moved from the margins of the white community to the core of the state. State violence has become systemic and rational. The spectacle of black murder by white mobs has been replaced by the rational killing of blacks by the police backed by the legitimacy of state power. According to a study published by colorlines.com, from 1980 to 2005, police killed about 9,500 people nationwide. Blacks and Latinos were more likely to be killed by police than whites. At the time of Rice's murder, the Cleveland police department was under investigation by the US Justice Department for the "unreasonable and unnecessary use of deadly force," and the Justice Department found that "the use of excessive force by CPD officers is neither isolated, nor sporadic." The incident that triggered the US Justice Department's investigation was a high-speed car chase that ended when Cleveland police officers fired 137 shots into the car, hitting the driver 23 times and the passenger 24 times. Patrol Officer Michael Brelo fired 49 shots, including 15 shots as he stood on the hood of the suspects' car and fired through the windshield. Since the 1980s, American cities have enthusiastically adopted racist police strategies, such as 'zero tolerance' and 'broken windows,' popularized by the conservative think tank the Manhattan Institute, former NYC police chiefs William Bratton, Raymond Kelly, and Bernard Kerik and Rudolph Giuliani's global security consulting firm, Giuliani Partners. By 2012, 1 out of every 15 children had had a parent in jail. For black children, it was 1 out of every 9.[6]

White violence moved from the margins to core of the American state in relation to the increased white racialized insecurity of public life. Jim Crow laws legally segregated public transportation, schools, parks, diners, and swimming pools. Jim Crow customs racially segregated everyday life to limit interracial social interactions taking place on public sidewalks and to ensure that the limited interracial relations reflected the white/black racial hierarchy. Erving Goffman called the latter min-strelization, in that blacks had to perform the role of subordinate to ensure their safety, even though it meant reinforcing the racial hierarchy they despised. Emmett Till refused to play the minstrel role. Rice never had the chance. Elite and ordinary whites were threatened by integrated public life. As the civil rights movement succeeded in securing protective legislation to eliminate legal forms of segregation and discrimination, elite whites rightly identified that their historic control over black labor, the economy, and the state was at stake. In turn, elite whites adapted their strategies to regain control.[7]

One strategy was privatization. Privatization replaced Jim Crow as the preferred elite white strategy to control public life. Between the end of Jim Crow and the rise of neoliberalism, a cultural thread organized around a language of white-private/black-public emerged from the fusion of the elite white business community and segregationists. Public life was recoded as black, while private life was recoded as white. Public spaces and public life haven't fully disappeared. In part, they were simply made unwelcoming for blacks and those on the margins, as new forms of police surveillance, such as security cameras, dotted the urban land-scape. But most of public life as Americans in the 1950s knew it was privatized. Play was privatized in the form of backyard play sets, and private backyard pools replaced public pools. Public shopping in down-town shops was privatized in the form of suburban shopping malls, where shoppers abandoned public transportation in favor of the private car to carry them back and forth from their private homes to the private shopping centers. As the historian Kevin Kruse noted, once whites stopped using public amenities, they stopped funding them with their white tax dollars.[8]

The examples of how state violence toward blacks became more rational and systemic and the rise of privatization to manage racially integrated space are just two features of racism in the contemporary neoliberal era. I define neoliberalism as the political project designed to create the conditions for capital accumulation based on the upward distribution of resources and an ideological adherence to meritocratic notions of individual success and personal responsibility. The policy side of neoliberalism is organized around four issues: privatization, austerity, deregulation, and tax cuts for the wealthy. Instead of a smaller state, the combination of neoliberal policy provides elites with maximum control over the state. This includes controlling where public money is spent and who gets tax cuts and tax credits, creating elite-led private-public partnerships, and altering the regulatory field to benefit businesses over citizens.

In the pages and chapters that follow, this book will provide a meta history of the most important changes and continuities of elite white strategies to maintain power that began in the 1980s. Rather than a sharp break from the past, I argue that neoliberalism is just the latest elite white strategy that uses racism to preserve elite white political and economic power. The origins and continuity of American neoliberalism are sustained by racism. Racism allows elite whites to secure support from other whites, primarily the white middle class, who identify as good whites first and as part of a social class second. Paradoxically the diversity of elites masks elite white power, as elites point to token forms of inclusion as proof that the status quo works, that racism no longer exists, and that poverty is the unfortunate outcome of bad decisions, or simply a "state of mind."[9]

Scholars generally begin the story of neoliberalism in 1979. The year 1979 is the moment that the neoliberal project moved from the business community to the core of the American state. According to this story, elite whites took advantage of the OPEC oil embargo of 1973, which triggered an economic condition known as stagflation. Stagflation occurs during a time of high inflation and high unemployment. However, the original attempt to combat rising inflation came in 1971, as Nixon took the US dollar off of the gold standard. This didn't cause inflation to subside. In 1973, the dominant oil-producing nations in the Middle East limited the number of barrels of oil they sold on the international market. This drove up prices and spurred more inflation. Elites shuttered unionized factories in the northeast because of rising labor costs and international competition. They relocated their factories down south to union-free 'right-to-work' states and replaced workers with computers.

David Harvey identified Jimmy Carter's appointment of Paul Volcker as the chairman of the Federal Reserve in 1979 as the key moment that elite whites reclaimed control over the economy. Volcker figured that the Federal Reserve could either fight inflation or promote full employment, but not both. Volcker chose to fight inflation. Inflation hurts elites because it erodes the value of wealth. Inflation can actually help the poor and working class because it makes paying off existing debts easier. In order to limit inflation, the Federal Reserve increased interest rates as high as they legally could. This curbed demand for housing and automobiles because loans carried interest rates close to 20%, while increasing the yields on bonds. America's white elite could rest easy at night, knowing that their money was safely growing in the hands of bond portfolio managers. The rest of America didn't sleep so well as the country entered a severe economic recession.[10]

The global and domestic economic events of the 1970s are only one part of the general story of the rise of neoliberalism. The other was the role of ambitious politicians who were eager to please the elite white power structure by championing a neoliberal agenda of tax cuts, austerity, and deregulating the financial industry. For example, Jack Kemp, a former quarterback who played for the NFL's Buffalo Bills in the 1960s and preached the gospel of tax cuts for the wealthy during his playing days, and William Roth, who would also sponsor legislation that led to the creation of the Roth IRA in 1997, a private retirement account that allows for tax-free gains on withdrawals made during retirement, set out to cut taxes for the wealthy. The result was the Economic Recovery Act of 1981, popularly known as the Kemp-Roth tax cuts. The 1981 Kemp-Roth tax cuts lowered the tax bracket for the wealthiest Americans from 70% to 50%. It also cut estate taxes and corporate taxes. The top tax bracket was lowered again from 50% to 28% in a Reagan's signature piece of neoliberal legislation, the 1986 Tax Reform Act. In both cases, ambitious politicians pushed for tax cuts much larger than even Reagan wanted. Inspired by the 1980s' tax cuts and backed by more ambitious politicians, President George W. Bush signed the 2001 Economic Growth and Tax Reconciliation Act and the 2003 Jobs and Growth Tax Reconciliation Act, affectionately known as the 'Bush tax cuts'. The Bush tax cuts slashed taxes across

10   INTRODUCTION

the board, with high-income earners paying a tax rate of 35%, and the lowest income bracket paying 10%.

American neoliberalism is not the property of one political party. Republicans and Democrats have both championed neoliberal policy, albeit with some minor differences. Democratic presidents have been more apt to raise taxes on the upper classes than Republicans. Nevertheless, Democrats, also backed by the elite white business class, have advanced neoliberal policy reforms. William Jefferson Clinton backed policy to deregulate many markets, including health care. His signature piece of deregulatory legislation was the Financial Services Modernization Act of 1999, also known as Gramm-Leach-Bliley. Banking deregulation removed the protective barriers in place that separated commercial banking, investment banking, and insurance. This empowered large banks over local regional commercial banks, which large banks promptly acquired. The result was the consolidation of a banking sector into a few very large banks too big to fail. Although popular sentiment claims that subprime mortgages caused the collapse of the financial industry in late 2008, which ushered in the Great Recession, it's not quite that simple. Now that banks are able to be commercial banks making loans and investment banks buying and selling securities, they are susceptible to taking on too much risk and fluctuations in the market. When the financial system predictably collapsed, the state bailed out the banks by giving them no-interest loans. While the 2010 Wall Street Reform and Consumer Protection Act deregulated the financial field by mandating banks hold minimum reserves to withstand market swings and created new federal offices to monitor the amount of risk bankers take, it did not deregulate the field in a way that would have restored the principles of Glass-Steagall, which mandated boundaries between commercial banks, investment banks, and insurance companies after the financial collapse and fiscal crisis that caused the 1929 Great Depression.

Despite his entire presidency having been played out in the shadow of the Great Recession, Barack Obama still embraced neoliberal policy, even if he did not do so as enthusiastically as his predecessors. Obama allowed the Bush tax cuts to expire for top earners but did not advocate for reestablishing a real progressive tax structure. Rather than reinstate Glass-Steagall, he recruited the aforementioned Paul Volcker to chair his economic advisory board and supported the Dodd-Frank amendment. Obama's signature piece of policy, the 2010 Affordable Care for America Act, is a privatized system of health insurance. The state subsidizes private health insurances and private citizens who make up the health-care insurance exchange. The Affordable Care Act made health insurance mandatory. This tilted the advantage toward private health insurance firms over citizens because citizens are now compelled by the state to purchase private insurance or face a monetary fine.

The typical story told of the rise of neoliberalism I just reviewed was told through the lens of a racially neutral political framework dominated by elites and large organizations. A problem of looking at politics and economics from this viewpoint is that it tends to downplay the social conditions that gave rise to and sustain neoliberalism. I'm not disputing the advisory roles of economists or the impact of ambitious politicians looking to advance their careers and make their mark on history. They are obviously important. My issue with the standard account of American neoliberalism is that racism is conspicuously absent. Racism and capitalism were intimately linked during modernity and have continued to change in tandem. As the system of slavery gave way to elite white ownership of black labor, elites relied on a system of state-supported racism to extend minimal benefits of capitalism to white ethnics. This state-racism system, more commonly known as Jim Crow, legally restricted the expansion of the early welfare state to whites. Although the civil rights era severely weakened elite white control over blacks, the elite white response to the civil rights movement emphasized a new form of the racism-state relationship called neoliberalism.

The story of American racism is actually older than America. Racism was a product of European modernity. European racism was constructed during the formation of the world capitalist system, as slavery became the key source of labor to extract commodities such as sugar, cotton, and tobacco in the Americas. In order to justify slavery in the time of enlightenment, and by extension Europeans' view of themselves as the only civilized people on the planet, dark-skinned people were recast as a biologically inferior and uncivilized other. To paraphrase W. E. B. Du Bois, the Europeans discovered whiteness the moment they discovered the New World. The American Revolution for independence from the

British Empire created the world's largest democratic experiment at the time. It broke from Europe's political framework, which was defined by feudalism and monarchies. It helped legitimize democracy and the modern nation-state. It did not change the existing racist structure. Too much of the embryonic American state's economy was dependent on slaves. Wealthy slave owners, like George Washington and Thomas Jefferson, remained wealthy slave owners as they moved from elite political revolutionaries to America's first elite white social class. African slaves picked the American cotton supplied to the textile mills at the heart of global industrialization, including those in the United States, Britain, and France. Although the American Civil War ended slavery in America, racial oppression and the escalation of capitalism via the Industrial Revolution cemented America's racial and class structure. Elite southern whites responded to southern reconstruction with Jim Crow laws, while elite northern whites continued to profit from exploiting immigrant and black labor. Agriculture depended on cheap black labor until the 1950s, when the combination of industrial-grade pesticides and the mechanization of agriculture made black agricultural labor obsolete.[11]

It was during the 19th and early 20th century that a new elite white class formed around finance and industry. Elite white men tightened their grip over the state, which handed over 246 million acres of land for free or at a very favorable price to white families and a favorable tax structure for industrial elites that ignored taxation on income. Even when black families could take advantage of the 1866 Homestead Act, which authorized the transfer of public land to farmers, black farmers were left with land comprised of poor soil and were at the mercy of white-controlled finance and trading networks. The level of wealth in America during the second half of the 19th century was not only unprecedented; it was without peer. America was the only western state that witnessed the growth of large corporations like US Steel and Standard Oil. It was the only western state to have "robber barons," like J.P. Morgan, Andrew Carnegie, and John Rockefeller. Warren Harding won the presidency backed by elite whites who had soured on the Progressive Era's emphasis on antitrust laws and progressive taxation. After the Progressive Era, elite white interests meant austerity and lowering taxes for the rich. During his acceptance speech to become the Republican presidential nominee in 1920, Harding emphasized the need for austerity to protect elite white interests: "We will attempt intelligent and courageous deflation, and strike at government borrowing which enlarges the evil, and we will attack the high cost of government with every energy and facility." Harding appointed Andrew Mellon, the robber baron banker and monastic disciple of *laissez-faire* economics, as secretary of the treasury, establishing a clear link between elite white financial interests and national economic interests.

Elite control of the state wavered for a bit during the middle of the 20th century. A few cracks in America's racist structure appeared in relation to the Great Depression that spanned the entire decade of the 1930s. A combination of labor union challenges and growing black demands for equality provided the background for Franklin Delano Roosevelt's New Deal. Much of the New Deal focused on white labor, as policies designed to create a national minimum wage and the Social Security Act did not really help blacks confined to the agricultural sector. The Fair Employment Practice Committee (FEPC) desegregated the military and the federal workplace. Yet, the US government's forced relocation of over 100,000 Japanese Americans living in California into internment prison camps lingers over discussions of FDR's antiracism. Blacks did not benefit from New Deal policies. As Bruce Shulman argued, the New Deal was based on a flawed logic that "economic progress either required or was certain to accomplish some changes in race relations." Black war veterans returned home to find the system of racial segregation they left still existed. A new white power elite emerged as power was centralized into the presidency, joints chiefs of staff, and American CEOs, in spite of the New Deal and token forms of racial integration. Elite whites patched up the cracks in the racist structure after World War II.[12]

In Jim Crow America, whites did not have to worry about being white on an all-white public stage. This time period was also defined by white class solidarity that demanded an expansion of the welfare state. Whites could think of themselves as belonging to social classes or geographical status groups, such as farmers or blue-collar or white-collar workers because public life and political struggles were white. Political movements in the Jim Crow era, such as the progressive movement, the populist movement, or the farmer-industrial worker coalition behind the New Deal, were white struggles to redistribute public resources and build a better public infrastructure for whites. Southern populists were electing governors who promised to tax the rich to pay for better public schools, road infrastructure, and pensions, as the Supreme Court debated *Brown v. Board of Education*. Southern white populists elected governors like "Big" Jim Folsom in Alabama and Huey Long in Louisiana, who promised to sock it to the rich. Don't let their populist leanings fool you. These guys were still racist. But since public life was basically the exclusive province of whites, there was no need to worry about blacks benefiting from the redistribution of public money. Once public life and the state were no longer racially segregated, elite whites responded by defunding and privatizing public amenities.

The black civil rights movement transformed public life into a field of political struggle just by removing the legal barriers that supported racial segregation. But the civil rights movement could not do anything about the economic aspects of elite white power. As I have shown elsewhere, the seeds of neoliberalism were sown in the field of a racially integrated public. The elite white response to the black civil rights movement fused the business community and segregationists. In the process, normative meanings of white-private were embedded into concrete social policy, such as taxation and deregulation, while normative meanings of black-public were embedded into privatization and austerity. The conversion of generic working class values like hard work into a racialized discourse of personal responsibility silenced racism in the rationale for continued neoliberal reforms. Basically, once the civil rights movement racially integrated public life, the white-public era, defined by increases in public benefits, progressive taxation to pay for pensions and public services, and breaking up monopolies in the name of the white-public collective good, disappeared. The question is how did elite whites secure more control over the economy when their hold over the state temporarily weakened?

Although scholars have documented the role of racism driving modernity and capitalism since the 17th century, the role of racism in shaping political and economic policy somehow disappears after the civil rights movement. Instead of racism driving neoliberal policy, racism is recast as the study of racial inequality. Racial inequality is portrayed as a side effect of a major economic shift that left job skills outdated. Racism becomes the property of poor whites that are in dire need of more education. In other words, racism is understood through the lens of neoliberalism rather than as its own causal variable. A much different story of the neoliberal era unfolds when racism is understood as a driving force behind the assemblage of the neoliberal project. Racism explains how neoliberalism got here and why it won't go away. Thus, in order to understand elite white power in the neoliberal era, we first need to construct a working theoretical framework that explains the relationships between racism, capitalism, elites, and culture.

Sociologists have developed a handful of theoretical models to explain racism's stubborn persistence. The earliest models, developed in the 1950s, explained racism and prejudice as individual attributes. Individuals held racist views. A minority of racist individuals was responsible for racial violence. What we commonly call society, the collection of social institutions like the state, economy, schools, military, criminal justice system, and religion, to name a few, are understood to be impersonal and objective forces incapable of bias. In this line of thought, racism is an irrational force in the modern world because it mucks up an otherwise rational society.

Individual-level explanations of racism are comforting to the idealists in society. It provides them hope that individuals can outgrow racism, that we can educate ourselves out of racism, and that marginalized black and Latino people can better their lot in life by working hard and obtaining college degrees. It's also a comforting framework for white conservatives and white liberals who want to think of the world as colorblind and postracial because the ascendance of some blacks into positions of power indicates that racism could not possibly be systemic. Let's go back to the example of the murder of Tamir Rice. If we try to understand his murder through the lens of individual racism or prejudice, we are directed to questions such as the police officer's inexperience on the job, his inexperience interacting with poor blacks, his stress level, or some sudden movement Rice made that triggered this specific event. It transforms his murder from a racially driven act into a psychological drama. Instead of situating Rice's murder within a pattern of the thousands of blacks killed by police over the last decade, individual-level explanations repeat the criteria to explain each specific murder as an independent and unconnected phenomenon. Racism does not just take up residence in the mind.[13]

Understanding the relationship between racism and capitalism starts with two theories: racial formation theory and critical race theory. In *Racial Formation in the United States*, Michael Omi and Howard Winant outlined a theory to explain the social construction of race. In contrast to biological and essentialist accounts of race that explain racial identities as rooted in our DNA, racial formation theory explains how political and economic forces socially construct racial identities. This means that what it means to be black, white, or Latino/Latina is unstable. Racial identities are completely dependent on the political context in order to be salient. For example, as racial identities became a meaningful social category during modernity, black bodies were racialized. To be racialized meant that Europeans took visible differences between them and the rest of the world as a starting point to embed negative meanings into bodies of color. Subsequent black resistance for freedom and equality had to challenge and go through these racial identities. Thus, what it meant to be black during slavery is different from what it meant to be black during the civil rights era and is different from what it means to be black in the neoliberal era.[14]

Racial formation theory established race and racial identities as their own field of inquiry rather than a by-product of the class struggle or part of a broader socioeconomic status. Racial identities organize social institutions and guide social interactions on the basis of racial difference. Although racial formation theory provides an excellent analysis of the making of racial identities, it has no account for the concrete material advantages that provide the backbone of elite whites, nor does it account for unintended consequences of racial movements for equality and civic inclusion.

The second theory is critical race theory. Eduardo Bonilla-Silva has advanced critical race theory as one of the dominant sociological theories on racism. Critical race theory captures the structural and material aspects of racism. The central theme of critical race theory is the reality of competing racial group interests over material resources. In contrast to

Marxist accounts of competing group interests based on social class, critical race theories emphasize how racism produces its own racialized social structure. There is an asymmetrical relationship between racial groups that is intertwined with class but not wholly dependent on class interests. It can be difficult to separate race from class when we look at racism and capitalism from a structural viewpoint. However, if race and class groups are considered on equal grounds, then the logic of the theory is clear. The key point for critical race theory is how racism and capitalism are sustained by the connection between the material political, economic, and ideological worlds and their corresponding cultural practices. In other words, the reproduction of social structure guides us all to be complacent in reproducing racial domination.

Critical race theory differs from racial formation on one key point: the importance and role of culture. When racial formation theory explains the social construction of racial identities, it explains culture as the outcome of power. In contrast, the account of culture in critical racial theory relies on ideologies to subdue racial groups and legitimate racist social structures. For Bonilla-Silva, "racial domination would not be possible without ideology." Because culture and ideologies are flexible, whites are able to adjust and adapt to resistance from blacks and anti-racist whites. Bonilla-Silva and Lewis defined the era after Jim Crow as the era of new racism because the emphasis on color-blind and racially neutral terms replaced explicit racism. Color-blind racism is simply a racist ideology used to reproduce elite white power.[15]

Critical race theory's emphasis on and the incorporation of the materialist aspects of society is a good starting point to understanding racism in the neoliberal era. It's how they conceptualize culture that makes me pause. Critical race theory has not developed an adequate cultural component to complement its material side. The sole emphasis on ideologies rooted in material interests generalizes and conflates elite whites' interests with all white interests, despite very different material interests within white groups. This type of generalization cannot explain empirical realities that inequality within racial groups is wider than inequality between racial groups. It cannot explain why some blacks can achieve civic inclusion while other blacks cannot walk down the street without suffering from police harassment. If elite white power is rooted in ideology that's tethered to material interests and elite whites still monopolize wealth in America, then why do elites need color-blind racism? Why do companies and universities practice racial realism and emphasize diversity to enhance their public image if all whites are racist and universally reject racial civic inclusion?

The limitations racial formation theory and critical race theory are found in their strengths. Both are very good at explaining the production and subsequent reproduction of racism in lieu of antiracist political challenges. But each is limited to theoretical explanations of the reproduction of racism, racial identities, and white power by homogenous racial groupings. In order to understand the relationship between racism and neoliberalism, we need a theory that explains how racism can tie otherwise disparate and heterogeneous aspects of the state and the economy together. We need to understand how challenges to racial oppression and the subsequent elite white response create new representations, racial identifications, and elite white political strategies. In short, to understand racism in the neoliberal era, we need a theory that explains the long history of and systemic relationship between racism and capitalism and how the contested terrain of culture produces changes in criteria for civic inclusion, which in some cases may actually hinder subsequent efforts to achieve racial equality and social justice.

The theory of systemic racism is part the umbrella of critical race theory. Joe Feagin developed a comprehensive theory of systemic racism to explain the central role that racial oppression plays in sustaining the racial *and* wealth hierarchy in America. Rather than an automatic reproduction of racism, systemic racism helps us explain how elite white strategies to maintain their power ushered in strategies and, inadvertently, new forms of capitalism. The main aspects of systemic racism is that racial oppression is at the core of US society, a series of interlocking white institutions and frameworks reproduce elite white privilege, and the long-term historical patterns of power and resistance between elite whites and racial groups explains the assemblage and organization of society. The theory of systemic racism has much in common with Bonilla's critical race theory. Both theories emphasize the historical, structural, and material aspects of racism. However, systemic racism's analytical focus is on the symbolic and material networks between heterogeneous white groups that sustain power in spite of antiracist social movements.[16]

Systemic racism helps us understand how racism shapes the networks between social institutions and our identities. In *The Power Elite*, C. Wright Mills mapped out overlapping elite networks to show how the centralization of power in the middle of the 20th century focused on a narrow segment of elite American society. Elite whites are defined as the narrow social group that has an extraordinary influence over society and continues to win despite political opposition. Elites have maintained their grip on social power by creating a bounded social network of other elites. Through select boarding schools and social clubs, elites essentially grew up together and married one another. This allowed for CEOs to network with US senators and the joint chiefs of staff and vice versa. Because wealth is overwhelmingly acquired through inheritance, there weren't too many sharks in the gene pool. Whereas elite boarding schools groomed and socialized young elites to be entitled, and later on privileged, elite social clubs were the private spaces where elites could hash out business and politics. Access to this private world of elites required a membership card and the right familial networks.[17]

Based on theoretical principles of systemic racism, we can now theorize that the foundations of a meta history of elite white power are found in their extraordinary control over political and economic power. Elite whites obtained political and economic power through the material relations between capitalism, the state, and racism: the combination of owning and then controlling black labor, the upward redistribution of state resources, and control over key political institutions. However, before moving on, we need to answer one more theoretical question: How have elite whites regrouped and withstood challenges to their power? To answer this question, we have to fuse critical race theory and systemic racism with an account of culture that 1) illustrates the independent power of racism sans economic and political structure, 2) shows how cultural change emerges at the limits of existing forms of power, 3) distinguishes between the intentional and unintentional effects of black struggles for equality, and 4) explains the legacy of these cultural networks and structures in assembling multiple forms of racial inequality.

At the same time Mills was documenting the centralization of power in the American state in the 1950s, the fragile network between white populists, segregationists, and agrarian elites was crumbling. Mills overlooked the rise of the southern white business class, who mobilized against the black civil rights movement. For example, the Young Men's Business Community (YMBC) was an influential local business association in Birmingham, Alabama, from the 1950s into the 1980s. They led a successful legal battle to deregulate state apportionment in Alabama that gave more power to the urban business class over the state. They also led the fight to replace Eugene Bull Connor during the 1963 Birmingham movement with a moderate racist, Albert Boutwell, who was known for his work in the state senate to privatize Alabama's public school system in the aftermath of *Brown v. Board of Education*. The YMBC was one of a handful of private business associations restricted to white men that began writing economic policy around corporate tax cuts, business tax credits, and privatization. The example of the YMBC is noteworthy to the extent that the black struggle for citizenship rights and civic inclusion exposed cleavages between white groups and prompted a new array of elite white strategies to preserve their power during the civil rights era. The liberalism of white unions and the white middle class stopped at the door of racial integration. This new arrangement not only preserved elite white power, but it also introduced a new culture to assemble the neoliberal project.

Culture is generally defined as the intangible beliefs, values, and social norms that organize how we understand ourselves to be part of social groups, as well as the corresponding corporeal behaviors and practices. Over the past several decades, this understanding of culture has broadened our understanding of how social actors create meaning and act strategically within various social contexts. Instead of viewing racism as culture, that is, as a set of beliefs and corresponding practices, it's more fruitful to understand how racism is aligned with other cultural and material attributes. Racism has its own independent features and must be linked with material structures, cultural practices, social institutions, forms of knowledge, and influential political actors. Thus, a sufficient account of culture is needed to explain how the links necessary to assemble a series of otherwise heterogeneous elements that comprise

INTRODUCTION 21

neoliberalism into a coherent racially driven and geographically patterned political economy are forged, severed, and maintained.

The cultural approaches to the study of racism rely on the concepts of boundaries and frames. Researchers have shown how whites strategically deploy racist tropes to secure political power, police group boundaries, and mask otherwise racist claims. This is generally broken down into a structural (or macro) camp and a social-psychological (or micro) camp. The structural approach to culture focuses on dominant racist ideologies that sustain the material advantages enjoyed by elite whites. The social-psychological approach analyzes how racism shapes how individuals learn to identify with a social group. According to this approach, racism is rooted in negative black stereotypes. Negative black stereotypes are beliefs like blacks are lazy, blacks are unwilling to work, blacks are violent, and so on. Since making overt racial statements in public is no longer considered acceptable, whites code their racial statements in race-neutral values and race-neutral ideologies rooted in the tradition of liberalism.[18]

The work on racial boundary formation bridged the macro-micro cultural approaches to stereotypes and prejudices. Whereas the social-psychological approach focused on prejudices, boundary formation focuses on how groups draw from symbolic resources found in larger cultural structures, like narratives and cultural repertoires. Michele Lamont defines symbolic resources as the cultural traditions and interpretative strategies involved in how we make conceptual distinctions of others as good or bad. Whereas the social-psychological approach focuses on in-group/out-group distinctions, boundary formation focuses on the collection of subtle differences social groups emphasize to define themselves as good. For example, Lamont shows through a large sample of in-depth interviews that working white men emphasize generic structural values like hard work and personal responsibilities, whereas black workers emphasize generic values of taking care of and protecting their families. Thus, the combined macro-micro perspective connects the construction of prejudices with larger cultural structures.[19]

Although the persistence of negative black stereotypes, color-blind racism, and understanding how groups define the moral criteria for group membership are obviously important, they do not address the relationship between elite white power and neoliberalism. For one, the emphasis on color-blind language fails to say how and why certain terms are race neutral and others are color-blind. Nor is color-blind racism a new feature in the post-civil rights or neoliberal era. Color-blind racism existed in the 19th century. Southern lawyers and other state bureaucrats wrote the 1890s state constitutions that ended the period of reconstruction in a way that did not contain a single reference to blacks. Southern states that privatized public education in the mid-1950s in an attempt to get around the *Brown* decision were also void of explicit racial statements. Second, in order to account for culture in the relationship between racism, elites, and neoliberalism, we need a theory that explains the process of how elite whites can extend the framework of what it means to be white across class boundaries. Boundary formation theories explain that racism is a by-product of a larger set of moral sensibilities. It's an excellent theory to explain the production and reproduction of racial group membership by contexts such as occupation or neighborhood and the micro variances that lead secretaries to construct boundaries between themselves and custodial workers. But it cannot explain how racism can assemble heterogeneous groupings that cut across and between social groups to sustain elite white power.[20]

A starting point to theorize the relationship between elite white power, racism, and neoliberalism is Feagin's concept of the white racial frame. The white racial frame is an overarching "white world view" that "encompasses a broad and persisting set of racial stereotypes, prejudices, ideologies, images, interpretations and narratives, emotions, and reactions to language accents, as well as racialized inclinations to discriminate." The white racial frame helps a majority of whites maintain a white identity in relation to their complex, layered, and contradictory experiences with racial minorities, politics, and their own social class. Whereas boundary formation theory explains the maintenance of group membership by creating boundaries around perceived differences, the white racial frame explains how the historical stubbornness of racism unites whites from different ethnic, religious, and class backgrounds into a coherent white identity in spite of perceived and real material differences. The white racial frame also functions as a cultural framework that guides how racial minorities seek civic inclusion. The process of seeking civic

INTRODUCTION 23

inclusion rather than structural change keeps the racial structure intact by emphasizing diversity and ignoring the role of wealth in maintaining this elite white network.[21]

My theoretical and analytical approach starts with the basic tenets of the white racial frame and extends it by two ways. The first is an analytical strategy I borrow from cultural sociology that emphasizes the cultural autonomy of the white racial frame. To say that the white racial frame enjoys cultural autonomy allows me to analyze how elite and nonelite whites construct discourses and narratives that divide the world into normative semiotic categories of not just white and black but good whites, bad whites, good blacks, and bad blacks necessary to understand the nuanced dimensions of racism in the age of neoliberalism. The second extension is to add the analytical framework of assemblages from Bruno Latour. The assemblage of heterogeneous elements means that social and material aspects of society link together to form what we know of as society. Racism and racial identities are social. The material includes commodities like cotton and oil, the police officer's handgun, organizational think tanks, and the bodies that sit in front of computers keeping the engines of financial capitalism churning. Rather than use history to break down or 'deconstruct' the origins of elite white power, the analytical framework of assemblages allows me to understand how something like the white racial frame operates like a web of racial meanings that connect social groups with economic policy, geography, and police brutality.

I use the above analytical framework to construct a theory I call the language of neoliberalism, or white-private/black-public. The language of neoliberalism refers to the racial assemblage of language around the signifiers of white, black, public, and private. In this case, white is recast as everything good, black as everything bad, public life is the state, and private life refers to everything conceptualized to be outside the state, such as the economy. Rather than divide the world into simple black and white categories, the form of racism that sustains neoliberalism is best analyzed through the assemblage of a sequence of signifiers that begin white-private and black-public. It's better to think of each assemblage as a distinct thread rather than an overarching binary or grand narrative. Elites weave together a thread of white-private taxes to distort the perception of who 'owns' public resources and white-private security to define who is comforted by an expanded police and military presence. On the flip side, elites weave a black-public taxes thread to define who benefits from public resources and establish a basis for rejecting social welfare. The theory of white-private/black-public states that increases in racial integration activates white support for neoliberal policies. This also means that the activation of austerity and privatization is less likely to occur in all-white areas and public-social institutions disproportionately benefiting whites.

After the nationalization of the neoliberal project in 1979, we find elites drawing from white-private/black-public to expand austerity, privatization, and deregulation away from its racist origins. Whereas black-public regulations referred to the rejection of social regulations that promoted racial equality, white-private-regulations refers to the rejection of economic regulations. For example, bad white-public regulations refer to the rejection of financial regulations and progressive taxation that is harmful to elite whites like entrepreneurs and CEOs of large corporations. Good white entrepreneurs are recast as *the job creators*, and imposing unfavorable regulations on the job creators is bad for all whites. Good white-private draws from the cultural associations of personal responsibility to expand the privatization of insurance, retirement, water, seeds, and even core state functions, such as the court system. As we will see in Chapter 7, white-private has led to the privatization of arbitration between employers and employees. Unlike public arbitration, the employer gets to pick the private arbitrator, whose decision is not eligible for appeal. The language of neoliberalism now indirectly expands the neoliberal project through the expansion of white-private.

The language of neoliberalism expands in a nonlinear fashion, existing at the center of a web of meanings connecting racism with deregulation, privatization, austerity, and taxation. Racism is not just an ideology playing a supportive role to neoliberal policy. Through the process of struggling for civic inclusion into a society still organized around racism, blacks create nuanced racial representations, such as 'racially threatening' or 'racially nonthreatening,' which in turn create new links between racism, diversity, racial realism, and elite white power. The expansion of the white racial frame reconciles the internal contradictions in neoliberalism,

INTRODUCTION

such as the need for strong state regulations to enforce specific forms of deregulation and the need for increased spending to offset the problems with selective austerity. More concretely, we see this in how white-private links austerity with increased police spending and the privatization of prisons. Yet, this web of meaning is not contained to direct linkages but also expands outward in an indirect manner, where the privatization of prisons expands into the privatization of parole and into the privatization of arbitration. Each indirect sequence away from the initial white-private link further hides the causal role of racism in neoliberal social policy and social institutions until it's virtually impossible to trace its direct causal sequence.

The language of neoliberalism is based on an expansion of the white racial frame and is compatible with the basic premise of critical race theory outlined above: Elite whites obtained political and economic power through the material relations between capitalism, the state, and racism that gave them the combination of owning and then controlling black labor, the upward redistribution of state resources, and control over key political institutions. The emphasis on the white racial frame's cultural autonomy and the causal impact of white-private/black-public to create direct and indirect links between the social and material world indicates how elite white power remains consistent across different economic and political contexts. The elements that bind actors together are not just regular ties, and therefore, traditional boundaries that distinguish an 'us' from 'them', or just black from white, do not hold up. The definitive pattern in the neoliberal era is the expansion of white-private/black-public as elite whites respond to resistance and struggles for racial and class equality. In the end, elite whites are still in power. The more things change, the more they stay the same.

Notes

1. Mitch Smith, "2 Outside Reviews Say Cleveland Officer Acted Reasonably in Shooting Tamir Rice, 12" *New York Times*, 10 October 2015, located at www.nytimes.com/2015/10/11/us/2-outside-reviews-say-cleveland-officer-acted-reasonably-in-shooting-tamir-rice-12.html?_r=0; Elahe Izadi and Peter Holley, "Video Shows Cleveland Officer Shooting 12 Year Old Tamir Rice within Seconds" *Washington Post*, 26 November 2014, located at www.washingtonpost.com/news/post-nation/wp/2014/11/26/officials-release-video-names-in-fatal-police-shooting-of-12-year-

26 INTRODUCTION

old-cleveland-boy/; Timothy Williams and Mitch Smith, "Cleveland Officer Will Not Face Charges in Tamir Rice Shooting Death" *New York Times*, 28 December 2015, located at www.nytimes.com/2015/12/29/us/tamir-rice-police-shootiing-cleveland.html

2. Patricia J. Williams, "How Could Tamir Rice's Death be Reasonable?" *The Nation*, 2 November 2015, located at www.thenation.com/article/how-could-tamir-rices-death-be-reasonable/; Cuyahoga County Medical Examiner's Office, Tamir Rice, located at www.scribd.com/doc/249970779/READ-Full-Tamir-Rice-autospy-report

3. Sandy Alexander, *The Properties of Violence: Claims to Ownership in Representations of Lynching* (Jackson, MS: University of Mississippi Press, 2012); Ryan Loughlin and Joie Chen, "Emmett Till's Cousin: Murder Never Crossed My Mind after He Whistled" *America Tonight*, 26 August 2015, located at Aljazeera.com

4. Mark Twain, *The Adventures of Huckleberry Finn* (New York: Penguin Classic Books, [1884] 1999), Chapter 8.

5. US Census Bureau, 2009–2013, "5-Year American Community Survey, Census Track 1017" Cuyahoga County; Elijah Anderson, "Emmett and Trayvon: How Racial Prejudice in America has Changed in the Last Sixty Years" *Washington Monthly*, January/February 2013; Loic Wacquant, *Prisons of Poverty* (Minneapolis, MN: University of Minnesota Press, 2009); Douglas Massey and Nancy Denton, *American Apartheid: Segregation and the Making of the Underclass* (Cambridge: Harvard University Press, 1998).

6. "Killed by the Cops", located at www.colorlines.com/articles/killed-cops; The United States Department of Justice Civil Rights Division, United States Attorney's Office Northern District of Ohio, "Investigation of the Cleveland Division of Police" 4 December 2014, located at www.justice.gov/sites/default/files/opa/press-releases/attachments/2014/12/04/cleveland_division_of_police_findings_letter.pdf; Wacquant, *Prisons of Poverty*; David Murphy and P. Mae Cooper, "Parents Behind Bars: Happens to Their Children" ChildTrends.org, October 2015, located at www.childtrends.org/wp-content/uploads/2015/10/2015-42ParentsBehindBars.pdf

7. Irving Goffman, *Stigma: Notes on the Management of a Spoiled Identity* (New York: Simon and Schuster, 2009); Joe Feagin, *How Blacks Built America: Labor, Culture, Freedom, Democracy* (New York: Routledge, 2016).

8 See Kevin Kruse, *White Flight: Atlanta and the Making of Modern Conservatism* (Princeton, NJ: Princeton University Press, 2005).

9. Black conservative Ben Carson described poverty as a state of mind, Yamiche Alexander, "Ben Carson Calls Poverty a 'State of Mind' Igniting a Backlash" *New York Times*, 25 May 2017, located at www.nytimes.com/2017/05/25/us/politics/ben-carson-poverty-hud-state-of-mind.html?mcubz=1&_r=0

10. There are plenty of good sociological works on neoliberalism. For a general historical account of neoliberalism sans racism, see David Harvey's, *The History of Neoliberalism* (New York: Oxford University Press, 2005). Monica Prasad, *The Politics of Free Markets: The Rise of Neoliberal Economic Policies in Britain, France, Germany, and the United States* (Chicago: University of Chicago Press, 2006) zeroes in on the role of political elites and takes a cross-national comparison of neoliberalism but also does not mention race or racism. In fact, she goes out of her way to downplay the importance of race in favor of rogue elites. For an approach that emphasizes the role of neoliberal think tanks and ideas that emerged at end of the golden era of capitalism and created

INTRODUCTION 27

various crises via the perceived breakdown of institutions, see John Campell and Ove Pederson's, *The National Origin of Policy Ideas: Knowledge Regimes in the United States, France, Germany, and Denmark* (Princeton, NJ: Princeton University Press, 2014).

11. W. E. B. Du Bois paraphrase taken from Joe Feagin, *Racist America: Roots, Current Realities, and Future Reparations, 3rd Edition* (New York: Routledge, 2014), p. 29; Sven Beckert, *Empire of Cotton: A Global History* (New York: Vintage Books, 2014).

12. Bruce Shulman, *From the Cotton Belt to Sunbelt: Federal Policy, Economic Development, and the Transformation of the State* (New York: Oxford University Press, 1991).

13 A classic study on viewing racism from a social-psychological and individual level is Howard Schuman, Charlotte Steeh, and Lawrence Bobo, *Racial Attitudes in America: Trends and Interpretations* (Cambridge, MA: Harvard University Press, 1985).

14. Michael Omi and Howard Winant, *Racial Formation in the United States, 3rd Edition* (New York: Routledge, 2014); Howard Winant, 2000, "Race and Race Theory" *Annual Review of Sociology* 26: pp. 169–185.

15. Eduardo Bonilla-Silva, 1996, "Rethinking Racism: Toward a Structural Interpretation" *American Sociological Review* 64 (June): 465–480; Eduardo Bonilla-Silva, 2015, "More Than Prejudice: Restatement, Reflections, and New Directions in Critical Race Theory" *Sociology of Race and Ethnicity* 1 (1 January): pp. 73–87, 77.

16. Joe Feagin, *Systemic Racism: A Theory of Oppression* (New York: Routledge, 2006).

17. C. Wright Mills, *The Power Elite* (Oxford: Oxford University Press, 1956); For examples on how education reinforces elite power see Pierre Bourdieu and Peter Collier, *Homo Academicus* (Stanford, CA: Stanford University Press, 1990); Shamus Khan, *Privileged: The Making of Adolescent Elite at St. Paul's School* (Princeton, NJ: Princeton University Press, 2012).

18. See Lawrence Bobo and Cybelle Fox, 2003 "Race, Racism, and Discrimination: Bridging Problems, Methods, and Theory in Social Psychological Research" *Social Psychology Quarterly* 66 (4 December): pp. 319–333 for an overview on the social psychological approach to studying racism.

19. Michele Lamont, *Dignity of Working Men: Morality and the Boundaries of Race, Class, and Immigration* (Harvard: Harvard University Press, 2002); Michele Lamont and Virag Monlar, 2002, "The Study of Boundaries in the Social Sciences" *Annual Review of Sociology* 28: pp. 167–195.

20. Ibid; with the notable exception of Mara Loveman's work on race in Latin America, boundary formation theory does not have much of a historical context, see Mara Loveman, *National Colors: Racial Classification and the State in Latin America* (New York: Oxford University Press, 2014).

21. Joe Feagin, *The White Racial Frame: Centuries of Racial Framing and Counter-Framing* (New York: Routledge, 2013), p. 3.

1

CITIZENSHIP AND SYSTEMIC RACISM

On the third Monday of every January, America celebrates Martin Luther King Jr. Day. Americans don't celebrate MLK Day the same way they celebrate other civic holidays like Memorial Day, the Fourth of July, or Labor Day. There are no barbecues or picnics or fireworks or commemorative parades of contemporary civil rights activists to help us remember the fight against racial inequality. I'm sure many whites don't celebrate MLK Day at all. But whites in the public sector will get a day off of work in any case. School children also get the day off, but they have to endure a civics lesson on why we celebrate King's birthday. Unfortunately, MLK Day has been reduced to a sanitized story of a man who had a dream, how unfair it was to have segregated drinking fountains, and how the civil rights movement was successful because it was nonviolent. The entire holiday illustrates the power of the white racial frame on US history, even by whites who are genuinely sympathetic and supportive of racial equality. There was nothing distinctive about blacks using nonviolence in the civil rights movement. Blacks were nonviolent prior to and after the civil rights movement. King was nonviolent, but so was Malcolm X. Whites and the police were the primary violent actors before, during, and after the civil rights era. The 1964 Civil Rights Act and 1965 Voting Rights Act helped to expand the black middle class, but we still live in a world characterized by extreme racial inequalities. So why do we celebrate King's birthday?

One big question we have to answer is how it is possible for extreme racial inequality to exist side by side with increasing racial civic inclusion in the neoliberal era. In order to answer this question, we have to start with the history of systemic racism and citizenship. The civil rights movement fundamentally changed our understanding of American citizenship. Its impact was more than just obtaining protective rights to vote and laws against economic and housing discrimination. I'll show throughout this book that elite whites have always gotten around pro–civil rights legislation by deregulating specific fields or by pursuing privatization. For now, we have to focus on the two things that must occur for legal citizenship rights to be converted into substantive citizenship rights. One, elites and state officials must enforce protective rights through administrative means, and two, all citizens must be deemed worthy of these rights. The latter informs the former. And while the civil rights movement changed what counts as good citizenship to obtain protective rights, they were unable to make inroads in the administration and enforcement of rights. Herein lies the clue as to how systemic racism shapes both civic inclusion and multiple forms of civic exclusion in the neoliberal era.

The black civil rights movement created a rupture in universal notions of white-public citizenship. Elites assembled white-public citizenship after the end of slavery to create a white-first identity necessary to sustain an imagined white America. The combination of the end of slavery, black reconstruction, immigration, labor movements, and legal challenges on who counted as white were real threats to elite white power. Elite whites used the state to defeat the labor movement with violence, ok'd pensions to white veterans, gave away land to white homestead families, and used the Supreme Court to safeguard a white-only racial composition of public life. The rupture in white-public citizenship severed the link that tied white with good citizenship. In its place was a new understanding of racial difference. Racial differences were no longer whites and then everyone else. Racial differences were reassembled based on notions of what counts as good and bad citizenship. To be a good black citizen means to be racially nonthreatening. Unfortunately, good black citizenship created an unintended system of color-blind racial exclusion necessary for the neoliberal turn.

The elite white response to the black civil rights movement ushered in the neoliberal era. Elite whites used their control over the state to protect the basis of their power: the white-private economy. They did so by devaluing racially integrated public life. Yet, the neoliberal turn needed a new ideal of the good white citizen to reestablish the imagined white community. Only, in this case, the imagined white community was an imagined *private* white community. Elite whites recast good white-private citizens as moderate on racial problems and economically, politically, and personally responsible. They cast off poor and overtly racist whites, sacrificed in the name of racial progress. And although opportunities for racially nonthreatening, good blacks were there, especially if they did not threaten the stability of the new white-private economic order, marginalized blacks became the public face of the underserving bad citizens. The splintering and then subsequent reassembling of difference along lines of good and bad citizenship make systemic racism and diversity compatible in the neoliberal era.

Good Citizens and Bad Citizens

In theory, being an American citizen comes with a lot of privileges and benefits. America is a wealthy nation. Its wealth originated in its abundance of valuable natural resources, such as oil and natural gas deposits, timber, aluminum, nutrient-rich soil, a diverse climate, and access to fresh water. America's abundance of natural resources gave it a unique advantage during modernity: the duality of independence and being situated in a key position of a global trading network. This unique structural advantage set the stage for American economic prosperity via the Industrial Revolution. Today, millions of people collectively produce goods and provide a range of services to generate America's wealth. Yet, all of this collective wealth is concentrated in the hands of a small minority of elite white families.

The same thing can be said about the privileges and benefits of American citizenship. Despite its vast wealth, the United States has not developed a comprehensive social welfare system to ensure its poorest citizens' social rights are met. Yet, social welfare policies that help the

CITIZENSHIP AND SYSTEMIC RACISM

middle class, like old-age insurance and Medicare, are dubbed the 'third rail' of American politics: touch them, and your political career is dead. Despite its ideological and symbolic doctrines of freedom and independence, America's actual history is characterized by the tension between who was included and who was excluded. As a status marker, citizenship is the ultimate measuring stick for who is included, while slavery serves as the ultimate measuring stick of exclusion. The American story of exclusion versus inclusion pivots around the question of who and what counted as good white citizenship.

At the nexus of the state, the market, and civil society sits the concept of citizenship. Citizenship is a juridical-normative designation of what it means to be a member of a nation-state. The juridical component of citizenship captures how citizens have legal rights. Citizenship rights set limits to state power and protect citizens from the ravages of a free market. As European states formed in the 16th and 17th centuries, elites and state rulers exchanged citizenship rights for military service and loyalty to the nation-state. Citizens generally have two fundamental sets of rights. The first are political rights: the right to vote and the right to hold office. Political rights are necessary for democracy. Without political rights, the state would be omnipotent and despotic. The second set of rights is economic rights. Economic rights are basically the right not to be a slave and to sell one's labor in exchange for a wage. Economic rights also shape a regulatory field that protects vulnerable citizens from exploitation by the market, such as minimum wages, a 40-hour workweek, and laws against race, age, and sexual discrimination. Whereas political rights are necessary for democracy, economic rights are necessary for capitalism.[1]

T. H. Marshall added a third set of citizenship rights that he called social citizenship rights. Social citizenship is the right not to starve or be homeless, in short, the right not to live in destitution. Marshall understood that citizenship served as the architect of social inequality by legitimating social differences and that social welfare and charity reinforce the existing ideas of deserving and undeserving citizens. Nevertheless, social rights are fundamental for civic inclusion and universal systems of social welfare and, in turn, are the most contested rights. Fraser and Gordon argued that the gendered and racialized realities of citizenship created a tension between social rights and civil rights, simplified through the difference between contract or charity: "discrete contractual exchanges of equivalents juxtaposed against unreciprocated, unilateral charity." The neoliberal era solved this tension by privatizing charity, reserving the redistribution of public resources for elite and middle-class whites and placing the contractual aspects of citizenship front and center.[2]

An important theoretical and practical question remains regarding the contractual understanding of social citizenship: how can society remain together if all human relations are converted to economic relations? The answer is found in the cultural and normative dimensions of citizenship.

The normative dimensions of citizenship are the cultural aspects of citizenship that shape an understanding of what and who constitutes good citizenship. It's a necessary component to facilitate civic and social inclusion. The cultural aspects of citizenship include a common language, media, and the collective remembrance of holidays and traumatic events. The cultural aspects of citizenship create links between citizens. The links between citizens subsequently shape the degree of civic inclusion necessary to make the legally held rights into substantive rights. Citizenship requires a national identity that supersedes if not outright replaces group identities. For a multiracial society like the United States, a national identity is problematic. Other citizens judge social groups and individuals as being worthy of citizenship on the basis of race, ethnicity, gender, and social class. Who and what counts as good citizenship captures why all citizens are not treated equally despite having legal citizenship rights. After all, has there ever been a phrase as hollow as 'equal before the law'?[3]

The presence of the normative dimension of citizenship alongside legal rights elevates good citizenship from an idealized practice to a core marker of civic inclusion. There are two components of good citizenship. One is an old notion of active citizenship that dates back to antiquity. Good citizens are involved in their community. They join civic groups, participate in block clubs, and volunteer for military service. In short, active citizens do more than just vote. However, blacks, Latinos, immigrants, and poor whites have historically done all the things that indicate active citizenship and still face discrimination. Active citizenship is built on assumptions of elite white males who have unfettered access to public life because someone else, almost always a woman, is burdened with responsibility of taking care of the home. The conditions necessary for active citizenship are also a marker of inequality.[4]

Symbolic citizenship is the second and more significant component of good citizenship. Symbolic citizenship captures how a notion of idealized citizenship underpins access to citizenship. Idealized citizenship refers to how a nation prefers to see itself in relation to romanticized cultural values, beliefs, and its history. Idealized citizenship is used to justify the inclusion of some into the core of society and the exclusion of others on the margins. Good and bad citizens are defined by the degree they reflect idealized citizenship. The degree that one reflects idealized citizenship determines if one is worthy of state benefits and public resources. This includes which groups get tax cuts, which budgets are subjected to austerity, and which groups benefit from deregulations. The white groups that have historically supplied the dominant image of the good citizen have varied, ranging from Midwestern farmers to soldiers to the white middle class. Nevertheless, the beneficiaries of good citizenship are white.[5]

Social groups highlight the various lines of difference as they make claims for civic inclusion. The lines of difference are drawn on the basis of links between racism, xenophobia, and the economic needs of elites. It's what stipulates which groups and how many of them are allowed to immigrate to the United States. It also shapes which social groups are worthy of civic inclusion. Racial and ethnic groups must contest what and who counts as good citizenship while simultaneously reflecting good citizenship. This was the paradox captured by good black citizenship. Good black citizenship is the racially nonthreatening political representation of black citizenship. The civil rights movement had to debunk harmful black stereotypes that blacks were violent, emotional, dumb, dirty, and diseased. They did so by disciplining and shaping black bodies to appear racially nonthreatening while protesting and speaking to the press. On the one hand, this worked. Sympathetic whites joined the black struggle and pressured the federal government to pass the 1964 Civil Rights Act and the 1965 Voting Rights Act. On the other hand, the elevation of good black citizens necessitated the exclusion of bad citizens of all races.

The unraveling of whiteness from good citizenship opened up new channels for civic inclusion and civic exclusion. One unintended consequence of good black citizenship was legitimating a set of bad social practices associated with bad black citizenship. Bad black citizens were deemed racially threatening and unworthy of citizenship. Another unintended consequence of the unraveling of whiteness from good citizenship is that it set the stage for the neoliberal turn. The language of white-public helped sustained simple binaries like black versus white or the deserving versus the undeserving poor as markers for civic inclusion. Racism in the neoliberal era weaves through the representations of good whites, good blacks, bad whites, and bad blacks. Even though good black citizenship represented a narrow slice of black life in the civil rights era, elite whites used them as proof that equal citizenship was something that was achieved rather than given. What was the basis of achievement? Look no further than elite white businessmen.

Elites define good citizenship in the neoliberal era in terms of one's ability to be successful economically. Margret Somers has appropriately characterized citizenship in the neoliberal era as becoming contractualized and commodified. Building off Fraser and Gordon's claim that the social rights pivot on the distinction between the contract and charity, Somers argued that citizenship has become a privilege and something earned based on one's ability to exchange labor or produce surplus value in the market. When we link white-private with good citizenship, then the banker, the businessman, and the entrepreneur emerge as the representation of good citizens. Good white-private citizens are the job creators. Contemporary political rhetoric that we need to 'run government like a business' and 'welfare is an incentive not to work' illustrates how neoliberal social policy pivots around good white-private citizenship. Generic values, such as personal responsibility and independence, are redefined in terms of economic success. Good citizens are successful because they are personally responsible and play by the rules. Bad citizens lack personal responsibility so they deserve whatever economic hardship or poverty they endure.[6]

Good white-private citizenship in the neoliberal era goes to great lengths to mask its systemic racist origins. The idea of an achieved or earned citizenship appears to be racially neutral and open to everyone. White-private citizenship is a new assemblage of neoliberal citizenship, where diversity within the same social class reinforces the social mirage of meaningful civic inclusion. After all, the paradox of racism in the neoliberal era is how additional rights have increased black civic inclusion while amplifying racial inequality across wealth, employment rates, local elites, imprisonment rates, where we live, and where we send our children to school.

American Citizenship: Elite White Men and Their Exclusions

The state of New Hampshire became the ninth of the original 13 states to ratify the US Constitution on 21 June 1788 and thus, ushered in the start of the American government. Rhode Island held out until 29 May 1790 over issues of currency and slavery. The first ten amendments to the Constitution ratified in 1791 are known as the Bill of Rights. The Bill of Rights does not mention the word *citizenship*. In fact, the first mention of the word *citizenship* in the US Constitution does not occur until the 14th Amendment, the amendment that abolished slavery and was ratified in 1868. It's fitting that who was legally a citizen was known but unspoken until the abolition of black slavery. Before we get to the lasting impact of slavery on American citizenship, we have to ask the obvious question: were all whites considered citizens? The short answer is no.

In America, the process of extending legal rights to marginalized groups began in the late 18th and early 19th century. Only elite white men enjoyed the designation of American citizens after the states ratified the US Constitution. Or more precisely, only elite white men enjoyed the privileges of American citizenship after *they* ratified the US Constitution. The right to vote and participate in government was based on whether or not you owned property. The US Constitution should be considered a feudal document, where rights were based off of property ownership in a time where owning property was the basis for generating wealth and elite social status. This did not change until New Hampshire became the first state to eliminate property ownership as a condition for universal white male suffrage in 1792, a year after elite white men made all the important decisions regarding the establishment of a government. A broader movement to remove property ownership requirements began after the War of 1812, as poor whites demanded citizenship rights based on their military service. North Carolina was the last state to remove the property requirement in 1856.

The definitive other to elite white citizenship was the African slave. In addition to the economic dimension of property ownership, the cultural aspects of early American good citizenship included linking enlightenment values of freedom and liberty with bourgeois values of decency and civility. As Feagin noted, "One irony of the slavery system was the accent these 'gentlemen' and 'ladies' put on values such as chivalry and personal honor, even as they practiced social barbarism." The contradictions inherent in elite white citizenship were made possible by the formation of the first white racial frame. By the mid-1600s, Europeans drew from folk theories, religious dogma, accounts of merchant travels, and science to assemble the first white racial frame. The first white racial frame justified colonialism and the slave trade. Europeans depicted non-Europeans as exotic, dangerous, and closer to animals than humans. American elites inherited this white racial frame from their European ancestors, emphasizing the difference in physical appearances between blacks and whites. Early American elites used the white racial frame to cement all undesirable and unwanted cultural traits on the most powerless members of society—slaves.[7]

Two numbers capture how elite whites valued African slaves. The first is the number three-fifths. Slaves were counted as three-fifths of a human being in the American census. In addition to defining blacks as 60% human, the three-fifths count lowered the amount of taxes slave owners owed to the federal government. The infamous "three-fifths compromise" between northern and southern elites defined how the first US government counted blacks to determine the electoral representation of whites. What little southern planters gave up in political power, they made up for in economic power. And since the United States as a whole relied on slave labor for its economic prosperity, southerners did not lose much political influence, if they lost it at all. The second number is $200 million: the value of African slaves used as collateral to secure the loans and financing necessary for the

CITIZENSHIP AND SYSTEMIC RACISM   37

expansion of America's cotton empire. Human slaves were private property that generated wealth for their owners. They were bought, sold, bred, and used as collateral no differently than the cattle or hogs or the cotton that they harvested.[8]

America's elite white power structure was built on racism and slavery. While slavery has existed in various forms throughout world history, American slavery was central to the assemblage of the world capitalist system. Why? The answer is found in the complex social relations surrounding cotton. Historian Sven Beckert's book *Empire of Cotton* traces how capitalism resulted from the explosive growth of the global cotton market. Cotton requires a certain temperate climate. Cotton will not grow if the temperatures dip below 50 degrees Fahrenheit. Cotton will not grow in Europe. But cotton could grow in the American colonies. Three years before Eli Whitney introduced the world to his mechanized cotton gin in 1793, America produced 1.5 million pounds of cotton. This number increased to 167.5 million pounds by 1820. Cotton accounted for more than half of all US exports between 1815 and 1860. A system of cotton cultivation required more than a warm climate and nutrient-rich soil. It also required a state with the power to coerce and discipline labor. As Beckert argued, "What distinguished the United States from virtually every other cotton-growing area in the world was planters' command of nearly unlimited supplies of land, labor, and capital, and their unpatrolled political power." The land came from Native Americans, the labor came from African slaves, and the capital came from American and English banks.[9]

American slavery was a large-scale commercial and capitalist market-place supported by the state. This meant that a series of interlocked institutions kept the system in place 60 years after the closing of the international slave market. Some of the institutions were specific to slavery: slave traders, slave transport ships, slave pens, slave auctions, slave guards, and physicians who specialized in inspecting the slave body to determine a slave's monetary value. The rest of the institutions are the main institutions that collectively make up society, such as the family and the state, that were responsible for the consolidation of elite white power. Elite plantation-owning families intermarried and networked with cotton merchants to create a monopoly over cotton production and distribution. Elite slave-owning families became part of the state. There were slave-holding presidents, congressmen, and Supreme Court justices. They set and enforced the laws sanctifying slavery. They redistributed public resources to benefit plantation-owning families by building rail lines and canals to connect isolated cotton plantations with the slave ports in New Orleans.

The plantation was the economic engine of early America and the site where labor, discipline, and slavery came together to define the two poles of American civic inclusion. The plantations produced many of the raw materials necessary for American textile factories to operate. The plantations were larger than factories and organized around an ironclad hierarchy of the elite white slave owner and the black slave worker. In the middle were ordinary whites who relied on the plantations for work. In *Discipline and Punish*, Michel Foucault showed how disciplinary power sorted out and classified 18th-century populations in order to define and produce an idea of the good soldier, the good worker, or simply, the good citizen. In the age of slavery, disciplinary powers worked through the bodies of ordinary whites to make them into good white citizens. Disciplinary power connected the social importance of the plantations with the mines and factories. All whites who did not own property or were sharecroppers had to do to learn the value of being white was look over their shoulder. The incentive to be a good white was threat of slavery.[10]

Although the Civil War ended the system of African slavery, slavery continued to shape the process of American civic inclusion. The two markers that defined noncitizens—slavery and the not-owning property— were no more. The elite white response to citizenship resulted in a new assemblage of white-public citizenship. White-public citizenship emphasized mobilizing the state to redistribute resources to all whites, albeit in different quantities. The Homestead Acts of 1862 and 1866 resulted in the transfer of 246 million acres of land at low or no cost to about 1.5 million homesteads, almost all white. Black homesteaders received land in the parts of the South where the land was not good for farming. Even then, white merchants and bankers forced black and poor white homesteaders to leverage their land and future crop yields in order to obtain high-interest loans. Black farmers needed access to upfront capital

CITIZENSHIP AND SYSTEMIC RACISM 39

to operate the farm. The banks sent their accountants or ledger men to the farms to count the yearly yield and collect payment. Eventually, the ledger man simply became known as 'the man'. For Native Americans, the man was President Andrew Jackson, a noted racist, xenophobic, anti-Catholic populist. The public lands the United States transferred to white homesteaders came from Jackson, who oversaw the relocation of native peoples and indigenous tribes out of the South and to the flat and dry Midwest.[11]

Elite whites struggled to maintain their imagined white community in the face of 19th- and early 20th-century immigration. They used every means of authority available to them through the state to preserve their imagined white community. Max Weber defined the state as the ultimate end game of politics. Controlling the state grants the dominant social group access to a host of monopolies: the monopoly of violence, the monopoly of taxation, and the monopoly of writing laws. The easy part was getting other white immigrants to assimilate. As the Irish, then Italian, then Polish, and then other ethnic whites from Eastern Europe arrived in America, they identified with their national origins of Irish or Italian or Polish or Hungarian and so on. These white ethnic groups also formed civic organizations to advance their claims that they were good whites who deserved civic inclusion. The Irish formed the Knights of Columbus to fight America's anti-Catholic sentiment. Italians picked up on the romanticism that surrounds Christopher Columbus and eventually made the Knights of Columbus and Columbus holiday their own, in spite of its anti-American-Indian overtones. The hard part for elite whites was keeping nonwhites out—physically, legally, and symbolically.[12]

Elite whites worried about the quality of the racial stock of immigrants, even though they were completely dependent on immigrant labor to lay the rail lines, cut down the trees, dig the mines, pick the cotton, and work in the factories. The 1790 Naturalization Act granted citizenship to whites of 'good character' after 2 years of residence. It also stipulated that only white immigrants could be naturalized citizens. Subsequent naturalization acts lengthened the residency time but kept the whites only sign hanging on America's front door. A debate over who was white emerged in relation to the increase of immigrants from

Asia and persons of mixed-race ancestry. The most famous case of defining someone as not white was the *Plessy v. Ferguson* decision. Although the decision is famous for legalizing the clause of separate but equal, the case is also important for legally defining any individual of mixed race as not white. Homer Plessy was seven-eighths white and one-eighth black. The Supreme Court continued to restrict the legal definition of who was white in the early 20th century. Bhagat Singh Thind, an elite Indian Sikh who immigrated to the United States, sought naturalized citizenship on the basis that he was white because he was not of African ancestry. Thind claimed that elite Sikhs were conquerors, just like Europeans. Nevertheless, in the 1923 ruling *United States v. Bhagat Singh Thind* the Supreme Court ruled that Thind was not white by any common standard known by the "average" white man.

The black struggle for civic inclusion faced both legal and cultural obstacles that prompted a new set of struggles that wavered between W. E. B. Du Bois' Talented Tenth and Booker T. Washington's hard-work approach. Du Bois thought the best way toward equal citizenship was to highlight the best of the black community to debunk negative black stereotypes. Members of the Talented Tenth should return to black communities not just to educate but also to improve the character of poor blacks. Washington thought the best path toward black civic inclusion was working hard to debunk black stereotypes that blacks were lazy. Washington thought blacks could earn citizenship through hard work, even though blacks already worked hard. Du Bois through his involvement in the formation of the NAACP, much more than Washington's political influence around Tuskegee, created a political black network capable of mounting a legal challenge to black civic exclusion. Along with the black church, local NAACP offices were the staples of black civil society. The NAACP and a young Thurgood Marshall, who would become the first black Supreme Court justice, successfully argued that the separate but equal clause of *Plessy v. Ferguson* was unconstitutional. This was the broader social and legal importance of the 1954 *Brown v. Board of Education*. However, the struggle for black civic inclusion would be led by the next generation of black activists demanding substantive citizenship rights.

Black Civic Inclusion and New Divisions in the Civil Rights Era

Social movements do not struggle for civic inclusion without changing the composition of what counts as good citizenship. The civil rights movement targeted the normative meanings behind who counted as a good citizen in order to change what counts as good citizenship. Since American citizenship was always racialized as white, blacks had to deracialize citizenship. Once blacks were no longer universally defined as bad citizens and whites were no longer universally defined as good citizens, whites could no longer morally justify universal forms of racial discrimination. The part of the civil rights movement affiliated with King, what I call the liberal project, targeted the link between whiteness and citizenship. The liberal project presented the black body in such a way as to appear racially nonthreatening to whites. To be racially non-threatening does not mean 'acting white'. The notions of acting white or acting black are based on essentialist and biological understandings of race. The only genetic difference between human races is the genetic sequence for skin tone. To be racially nonthreatening meant eliminating or limiting the physical markers that reflected one of the many black stereotypes whites used to justify exclusion. The physical markers included outlandish styles of dress, such as old zoot suits, but also styles of dress associated with rural poverty. It included the pace and decibel level of black speech. It included not showing any emotions of anger or distress even when these emotions would seem justified, like during a police beating. These were the embodied qualities of good black citizenship.

There were many marches, boycotts, and protests during the civil rights era. Some, like the Montgomery Bus Boycott, the black student lunch counter sit-ins at Woolworth, and the march on Selma are well known. Others, like pool swim-ins to protest segregated hotels in Florida are less well known but still important. What they all have in common is protesters went through some type of training to ensure that they could reflect good black citizenship before participating in the protest. Local civil rights affiliates of the Student Nonviolent Coordinating Committee (SNCC) or the Southern Christian Leadership Conference (SCLC) held role-playing scenarios to see if activists could withstand physical and verbal harassment without losing their cool. SCLC adopted the Highlander Folk School's "citizenship schools" to train activists and ordinary blacks on how to be racially nonthreatening. The citizenship schools involved lessons on handwriting, literacy skills around a civic vocabulary, and word pronunciation. Leaders of the movement urged blacks to dress like they were going to church while protesting. This had the obvious symbolic benefit of creating the public representations of good black citizenship. Wearing a suit also had a very practical benefit: the multiple layers of clothes and shoulder pads helped soften the blows from police batons and violent white onlookers.[13]

How the liberal project created the political representation of good black citizenship illustrates the performative aspects of racial group formation. The performative aspects of racial group formation include the repetitive bodily acts and presentation of self to project a meaningful political identity. It also includes various audiences, local and national, white and black, occupational and family, which confirms the successful performance through the presence of rewards and sanctions. The rewards can range from access to employment or housing in desirable neighborhoods—the types of things white citizens may take for granted. The sanctions range from ridicule to discrimination to police brutality. Reflecting good black citizenship does not guarantee blacks a life free from racial discrimination. But the presence of rewards and sanctions does create opportunities for good blacks to enter elite white networks. Thus, there is considerable pressure on blacks to reflect good black citizenship.

Good black citizenship was not the only black political representation to emerge from the civil rights era. A second form of black political representation emerged at the limits of good black citizenship. The liberal project strove for equality by obtaining protective rights through judicial and legislative change. The legislative gains did not translate into improved conditions for blacks at the local level. The lifting of voter restrictions also allowed for more whites to get on the electoral rolls than blacks and thus nullified the potential for any sweeping political changes in the Deep South. Local elite whites simply ignored the school desegregation rulings until subsequent federal mandates in the 1970s. As I will show in more detail in Chapter 3, local and national elite whites mainly began to rely on the market to enforce segregation. The market was the one thing that they exclusively controlled because the market was conceptualized as existing external to the state. At the nexus of the limits of legal rights and the white response to the civil rights movement, we find the reboot of black nationalism and black authenticity.

Malcolm X rebooted black nationalism in the 1960s. He was never politically active in the sense that he organized protests, ran for office, or even had a coherent political platform. But his writings and speeches outlined a political representation of blackness designed to address the needs of blacks on the margins. I call the black political representation associated with the black nationalist project 'black authenticity'. Black authenticity refers to the embodiment of black citizenship based in relation to rejecting whiteness, being racially nonthreatening, and black stereotypes, on the grounds that all three were legacy performances of slavery. Because slavery eliminated black historical and cultural ties to Africa, black authenticity was the invention of new black political agency based on the politics of the civil rights era.

Black authenticity was the outcome of a different racial performativity than good black citizenship. The racial performativity of black authenticity organized a set of cultural singularities, dogma-like political practices that sought to cleanse internal differences. The reason was simple: to create a single unified black political identity that could supersede internal differences along the lines of class, rural versus urban, and North versus South. For example, the performativity of black authenticity eliminated all physical and cultural markers broadly associated with slavery and contemporary racial colonialism. These physical markers included relaxing the hair to straighten it out and using skin-lightening products to make black bodies reflect white bodies. The cultural markers included rejecting Christianity and changing one's name because both came from European colonialism and slavery. Put it all together, and black authenticity meant a way of making claims for civic inclusion that was racially threatening to whites.

Black authenticity became racially threatening once civil rights groups began organizing their political claims around black nationalism. Although Malcolm X had a lot to do with the articulation of black authenticity, it was the civil rights groups that began working in the urban areas who put black authenticity into a political context. SNCC was the first group to recognize that racial integration was not enough to alter the structural components of systemic racism and citizenship, which included wealth and access to the state. Removing voting restrictions did not change anything in rural Lowndes County, Alabama. Thus, Stokely Carmichael, who would later change his name to Kwame Ture, organized the Lowndes County Black Panther Party in order to run black candidates for political office. In the spring of 1965 in Atlanta, Georgia, SNCC formed the Atlanta Project to fight urban poverty alongside Julian Bond's struggle to obtain his democratically elected seat in the Georgia State Assembly after the state legislature refused to recognize his electoral victory. The struggle against urban poverty included a fight against slumlords who refused upkeep on their buildings, resulting in buildings without heat or running water and where residents suffered rat bites. SNCC also addressed police brutality and the US government drafting blacks into the Vietnam War. The protests were typical of the kinds of marches and rallies used throughout the civil rights movement, except that leaders like Bill Ware wore African-inspired clothing and were not shy about yelling at the police when they grabbed and shoved black protesters. The Atlanta Project created a tent city as an alternative to living in urban slums. Thus, in every meaningful way possible—in style, in substance, and in the types of claims for civic inclusion—black authenticity was very different from good black citizenship, except for one: neither was violent.

The civil rights movement loosened elite whites' choke hold on defining good citizenship. One form of power that the civil rights movement tapped into was how exercising power over the self produces change in others. Good black citizenship achieved substantive citizenship rights because they changed how whites viewed some blacks. Not all whites were hardened racists. Many ordinary whites were somewhat ambivalent to the civil rights movement as long as the demands for integrated schools and neighborhoods didn't affect them. Elites highlighted their newly discovered progressive values on race by marginalizing bad whites as the bearers of racism, and by extension, bad white citizenship.

Good White Citizenship in the Neoliberal Era

The ascendance of a new white elite accompanied a new representation of good white citizenship that ushered in the era of neoliberalism. The new white elite that rose to political prominence in the 1970s was the liberal business class. I define them as liberal to capture both their moderate racial views and emphasis on hyperindividuality, or simply, crediting and blaming the self for all economic successes and failures. The normative image of the good white-private citizen in the neoliberal era is the white businessman. A vague image of the white male in a suit and tie or perhaps khaki pants and a long-sleeved light-blue shirt, short hair parted to the side, and no sideburns accompanies the representation of good white citizenship. Marketers and fashionistas call this look 'normcore'. Queer theorists would identify this as part of a social performance that reinforces heteronormativity. However, good white citizenship is not just an image that whites use to communicate to other whites that they are good citizens. Good white-private citizenship is assembled through the mastery of the social practice of moderation: moderation in personal spending in order to invest and avoid debt and moderation in politics to avoid rocking the boat. Moderation is what communicates to others that you are successful because you are personally responsible. It organized the mind-set that a white person was middle class regardless of income and wealth. Good white citizenship hides social class and racial privileges that many good white citizens are born into. It also hides the fact that Americans took on unprecedented levels of personal and consumer debt starting in the 1980s and 1990s to reflect good white-private citizenship.

The idealization of the businessman is not entirely new. From Benjamin Franklin to Andrew Carnegie to Sam Walton, a certain mystique surrounds the elite white men who can make a lot of money and create jobs in a capitalist economy. What is different about the businessman as a good white-private citizen in the neoliberal era is that good white-private citizenship generalizes the relations between pro-business deregulations, limited public spending on the poor, and elite tax cuts as beneficial to all whites. As a central part of the white racial frame, good white-private citizenship is the glue that binds diverse white social groups into a unified sense of whiteness.

The passage of the 1964 Civil Rights Act inadvertently made it possible for the rise of the liberal business class. The original liberal business class comprised local and state elites in the South and the West, who made their money in the service sector industries of banking, insurance, and real estate. They were political rivals to the entrenched agrarian and industrial elites, who did not want change. The old white elite enjoyed relations with longtime senators and congressmen who chaired congressional committees and wrote laws to protect elites' special interests. The liberal business class positioned themselves between the civil rights movement, the segregationists, and old white elites as the moderate alternative to racism. Their ascendance to power was uneven and typically due to the weakness of agrarians in the South and the industrialists in the North. Elite whites tried to block the passage the 1964 Civil Rights Act by arguing that whites would be the real victims of regulations that made residential segregation and redlining illegal. Elite whites singled out how white bankers and entrepreneurs would no longer be able to conduct business in a fair and profitable manner. For example, Robert Ashmore, a Democratic congressman from South Carolina, stated,

> It's unbelievable that a banker, a man who operates and owns, or controls a bank or federal savings and loan institution, if he should deny employment, or if his bank should deny a loan or a line of credit to someone, then he would have to show that he did not deny this loan or this credit, line of credit, because of the man's race.

For Ashmore and other elite whites, regulations stipulating racial equality were reverse discrimination. They were black-public regulations. Elites stoked the flames of racial insecurity among the white middle class to rally them against Lyndon Johnson's Great Society, America's last real attempt at creating a fair and just society.[14]

The liberal business class became the dominant political group in the Republican and Democratic Parties by the start of the 1980s. On the Democratic side, the liberal business class was known as the "new politics" Democrats. A cohort of Democrats from the South and West, including Jimmy Carter, Bill Clinton, Gary Hart, and Jerry Brown, were slowly supplanting the old New Deal liberals, like Ted Kennedy, Tip O'Neill, and Walter Mondale. In the Republican Party, they were simply known as Reaganites. White-private was the tie that bound the liberal business class across political parties. White professionals turned their backs on union members, casting them aside as greedy and bad whites. This was never more evident than when Ronald Reagan fired 11,345 air traffic controllers, federal employees who walked off work over a labor dispute and refused to return to work. The federal government decertified the Professional Air Traffic Controllers Organization. Reagan is credited with the start of union breaking and throwing the support of the federal government behind white-private employers over union members.

The start of the 1990s and the Clinton era extended the idea of good white-private citizenship to embrace what he called a third way politics: "The liberal left parties in the rich countries should be the parties of fiscal discipline. It is a liberal, progressive thing to balance the budget and run surpluses if you're in a rich country today." Research behind the theory of systemic racism indicates that economically conservative politics are incompatible with socially liberal values of equality. Racial inequality is sustained by a combination of ideology and the social advantages of wealth. What the third way of politics illustrates is how a white-private politics of moderation champions diversity instead of structural change. Since diversity is limited to the incorporation of good black and good Latino citizens, racial and ethnic inclusion happens without changing the basis of elite white power. Elites flaunt their personal support for diversity to prove that racism no longer exists or that we have entered a postracial society.[15]

The third way of politics folded into the notion of compassionate conservatism at the turn of the 21st century. Compassionate conservatism was President George W. Bush's political philosophy: "It is compassionate to actively help our fellow citizens in need. It is conservative to insist on responsibility and results. And with this hopeful approach, we will make a real difference in people's lives." Whereas the third way of politics stressed austerity and moderation for good white-private citizens, compassionate conservatism stressed personal responsibility for good white-private citizens: "We are using an active government to promote self-government." In this case, it was a government actively supporting elite whites via tax cuts and wartime public spending. Good white-private citizens don't need or rely on the public sector to be successful or to help others. White-private citizenship reached its cultural apex in the Bush era.[16]

The normative dimension of good white citizenship in the neoliberal era indicates the changing expectations and obligations that exist between the state and the public. The realignment of white-public to white-private and black-public has devalued the expectations of the state to solve social problems. Obligations toward the self have replaced obligations toward other citizens and the collective good. There is one caveat to the simple devaluing and revaluing binary of the public I just set up. Whites still support and demand public services when public services benefit whites. Only when public resources become associated with blacks, whether it's a threshold associated with the number of minorities at public parks, beaches, or shopping centers, or if social welfare services are perceived as benefiting minorities more than whites, is the language of neoliberalism activated. Good white-private citizenship *needs* a bad black citizen. Without a bad black citizen, the neoliberal project falls apart.

Conclusion

A historical overview of the relationship between systemic racism and citizenship highlights how elite whites have adapted to minority group challenges for equality and civic inclusion. Throughout the 19th and early 20th century elites opened up access to the state for whites. The era of white-public featured the formation of a comprehensive social welfare system, the funding of public schools, and the elimination of restrictive voting laws that increased white civic inclusion while shoring up elite white power. Divisions between elite and ordinary whites still existed. Neighborhoods were still stratified by social class and ethnic identities, and unions struggled for better pay and safer working conditions. Elites reluctantly supported the expansion of social rights when they benefited white citizens. White-public laid the foundation for the construction of a white-public welfare state and economy. The black civil rights movement ended the era of white-public when they severed the relationship between whiteness and good citizenship. Elite whites responded to the racial integration of schools and neighborhoods with privatization. They responded to the Civil Rights Act and Voting Rights Act with a combination of deregulations and privatization. The new good white-private citizen did not need or use public resources. The pivot from the Keynesian political project to the neoliberal project pivoted on the figure of the good white-private citizen.

By breaking citizenship into its legal and symbolic dimensions, we can see how changing laws to guarantee formal legal equality is not the same as guaranteeing substantive equality. Substantive equality is tied to the symbolic aspects of citizenship. The representations of good and bad citizenship are powerful indicators of who has access to and benefits from distribution of state resources. Symbolic citizenship helps us understand how the contested and splintering definitions of racial group membership create opportunities for some and not others. It explains how a contradiction between diversity and racism exists in spite of legal rights and the liberalized attitudes of whites. It explains the dual development of a growing black middle class and extreme racial inequalities. Although good white citizenship binds elites and ordinary whites from a variety of backgrounds into a coherent political identity, it also willingly groups and discards marginalized whites as bad citizens. As I will show throughout the book, elite whites deregulate various laws to guarantee elite advantages over ordinary Americans. Elites' ability to drum up support for deregulations is tied to their ability to produce a bad black-public citizen.

White-private citizenship dictates the terms of civic inclusion in the neoliberal era. It masks its racist criteria for civic inclusion by marking good citizenship as achieved status and individual achievement open to all. Somers argued that citizenship has become something that is earned in relation to one's market value. White-private citizenship pits economic rights against social rights. The implication of white-private citizenship is that it undercuts the protections inherent in citizenship rights. Whereas Marshall saw citizenship rights as providing the basis of exclusion while supporting equality, white-private citizenship provides the basis for limited inclusion while creating social cohesion between elites and ordinary whites. The neoliberal turn needed good white-private citizenship to propel ordinary whites to turn their backs on the black-public welfare state and, by extension, to reject social citizenship as black-public citizenship.[17]

The end of slavery, the establishment of legal citizenship rights for former slaves, and the period of reconstruction did not end systemic racism. The landmark desegregation cases, Civil Rights Acts, and the 1965 Voting Rights Act that define the civil rights era did not create wholesale change in lives of black America. Racism adjusts and is adjusted by institutional variables like good citizenship and the entrance of new social groups into the political arena. Economies change. States change. But the relational nature between white and black citizenship as the benchmark for civic inclusion and exclusion has not.

Notes

1. Richard Lachmann, *States and Power* (New York: Polity Press, 2010).
2. Nancy Fraser and Linda Gordon, "Contract Versus Charity: Why There Is No Social Citizenship in the United States" pp. 113–127 in *The Citizenship Debates*, edited by Gershon Shafir (Minneapolis, MN: University of Minnesota Press, 1998), p. 115.
3. On the various uses of citizenship, the relationship between citizens, and between citizens and the state see Benedict Anderson, *Imagined Communities: Reflections on the Origin and Spread of Nationalism* (London: Verso, 1991); Eric Hobsbaum, *Nationalism and Nationalism since 1780:Programme, Myth, Reality* (Cambridge: Cambridge University Press, 1990); Roger Brubaker, *Citizenship and Nationhood in France and Germany* (Cambridge, MA: Harvard University Press, 1992); Paul Licterman, *The Search for Political Community: American Activists Reinventing Commitment* (Cambridge and New York: Cambridge University Press, 1996); James M. Jasper, *The Art of Moral Protest: Culture, Biography, and Creativity in Social Movements* (Chicago: University of Chicago Press, 1997); Sarah Waters, 1998, "New Social Movements Politics in France: The Rise of Civic Forms of Mobilization" *West European Politics* 21 (3): pp. 170–187; Pascale Casanova, *The World Republic of Letters* (Cambridge, MA: Harvard University Press, 2004); David Gilpin Faust, *The Republic of Suffering: Death and the American Civil War* (New York: Knopf, 2008).
4. Ruth Lister, *Citizenship: Feminist Perspective* (New York: MacMillan Publishing, 1997); Randolph Hohle, *Black Citizenship and Authenticity in the Civil Rights Movement* (New York: Routledge, 2013).
5. Jeffery C. Alexander, "Citizen and Enemy as Symbolic Classifications: On the Polarizing Discourse of Civil Society" pp. 289–308 in *Where Culture Talks: Exclusion and the Making of Civil Society*, edited by Marcel Fournier and Michele Lamont (Chicago: University of Chicago Press, 1992); Steven Seidman, *Beyond the Closet: The Transformation of Gay and Lesbian Life* (New York: Routledge, 2002).
6. Margaret Somers, *Genealogies of Citizenship: Markets, Statelessness, and the Right to Have Rights* (Cambridge: Cambridge University Press, 2008); For an overview of the discourse of personal responsibility see Loic Wacquant, *Punishing the Poor: The Neoliberal Government of Social Insecurity* (Durham, NC: Duke University Press, 2009).
7. Joe Feagin, *Racist America: Roots, Current Realities, and Future Reparations, 3rd Edition* (New York: Routledge, 2014), 40; Joe Feagin, *The White Racial Frame: Centuries of Racial Framing and Counter-Framing* (New York: Routledge, 2013), pp. 49–53.
8. See Beckert, *Empire of Cotton*, Chapter 5 on the relationship between cotton, banking, and American slavery.

9. Ibid., p. 105.
10. See Judith Shklar, *American Citizenship: The Quest for Inclusion* (Cambridge: Harvard University Press, 1991) on how slavery hovers over claims for civic inclusion.
11. Lawrence Goodwyn, *The Populist Movement: A Short History of the Agrarian Revolt in America* (Oxford: Oxford University Press, 1978).
12. Max Weber, "Politics as a Vocation" pp. 77–128 in *From Max Weber: Essays in Sociology* (Oxford: Oxford University Press, 1958); On how Irish and Italian Catholic groups used Columbus Day to fight anti-Catholic sentiment see Timothy Kubal, *Cultural Movements and Collective Memory: Christopher Columbus and the Rewriting of the National Myth* (New York: Palgrave Macmillan, 2008).
13. On the SCLC's Citizenship Schools see Hohle, *Black Citizenship and Authenticity in the Civil Rights Movement* and Randolph Hohle, 2009, "The Body and Citizenship in Social Movement Research: Embodied Performances and the Deracialized Self in the Black Civil Rights Movement 1961–1965" *The Sociological Quarterly* 50 (2): pp. 283–307.
14. Robert Ashmore quote located in Randolph Hohle, *Race and the Origins of American Neoliberalism* (New York: Routledge, 2015), pp. 41–42.
15. James K. Galbraith, "The Economy Doesn't Need the Third Way" *New York Times*, 24 November 1999, located at www.nytimes.com/1999/11/24/opinion/the-economy-doesn-t-need-the-third-way.html
16. "Fact Sheet: Compassionate Conservatism", located at https://georgewbush-whitehouse.archives.gov/news/releases/2002/04/20020430.html
17. Somers, *Genealogies of Citizenship.*

2

PIECEMEAL BLACK DISENFRANCHISEMENT

DEREGULATION AND THE VOTING RIGHTS ACT IN THE NEOLIBERAL ERA

In 2013, the Supreme Court did the politically unthinkable when it deregulated the 1965 Voting Rights Act.

Elite white men like to tinker with the rules of democratic elections. Their control over the political process is fundamental to their ability to exert extraordinary influence over general public policy. It started when they restricted the right to vote to property-owning white men. It continued when they placed a series of legal and administrative barriers on the black vote toward the end of the 19th century. It continues today in debates over congressional redistricting, voter ID laws, and the white-private financing of political campaigns. Voting is such a fundamental duty and basic right in a democratic society it's hard to fathom why anyone is against it. I take that back. It's actually quite easy to understand this as soon as we examine the relationship between racism and electoral politics.

Elite whites found little political support in outright eliminating the Voting Rights Act. In the 1970s, regional elites were split between ideological adherence against federal oversight of the states and a pragmatic desire to increase the number of minorities in the Republican Party, especially as the black and Hispanic population grew in northern cities. Southern Democrats supported a national expansion of the Voting Rights Act to expose the national myth that racism only existed in the South. Elite

PIECEMEAL BLACK DISENFRANCHISEMENT   53

whites did find support in deregulating the Voting Rights Act. Since they couldn't eliminate it, they picked away at the various sections that constitute the Voting Rights Act. Deregulating the Voting Rights Act minimizes the political influence of minority voters. It does not eliminate a minority's right to vote. The focus on deregulation allows elite whites to dress in the sheer gowns of color-blind racism, signalizing to ordinary whites that they support blacks' and Hispanics' voting rights while actively restricting minority voting rights in the name of voter fraud.

The legal challenges to the Voting Rights Act came from unlikely places, like Pasadena, Texas, and Shelby, Alabama, far from the think tanks and lobbyists on K Street in Washington, DC, but elite whites still finance the cases that make their way to the Supreme Court. It's not where the challenges to the Voting Rights Act emerge from that matters but why these challenges emerge. Voting represents a material and measurable aspect of black civic inclusion. We can quantify black civic inclusion by the proportion of voting-age eligible blacks who are registered to vote and cast a ballot and the number of black candidates running for and winning elections. American democracy is also mediated through a racially divided two-party system. Lyndon Johnson was the last Democrat to be elected president with a majority of the white vote in 1962. As the Democrats have become the party for groups of struggle, racial and ethnic minorities, feminists, members of the LGBT community, white liberals, and the working class, the Republican Party has become virtually all white and all middle class. Elites still manage both party platforms, differing only on a handful of social issues. Black civic inclusion is directly related to the racial segregation of political parties.

This chapter asks the question of why the right to vote has come under attack in the neoliberal era. The question of the right to vote raises the larger question of meaningful political participation in lieu of an increasingly racially and ethnically diverse polity that cannot easily be quantified. Why did elite whites abandon a strategy of repealing the Voting Rights Act in favor of a strategy to slowly deregulate the rules that ensure substantive citizenship rights? How does the Voting Rights Act sit at the nexus between the ongoing white response against the black struggle for equal citizenship and the white-private neoliberal project? Or more precisely, I want to know how the piecemeal deregulation of the Voting Rights Act is central to new assemblages of the neoliberal project. Neoliberalism is not a uniform political project. The initial white response to the black civil rights movement is very different to the white response to the increase of black and Hispanic elected officials in the 1990s. Since neoliberalism is driven by the elite white response to black civic inclusion, how have different points of black civic inclusion led to the multiplication of white-private strategies all aimed at limiting the black vote?

The 1965 Voting Rights Act

The 89th Congress passed the Voting Rights Act as Public Law 89–110 in 1965. The Voting Rights Act is actually made up of 19 sections. Each section specifies the regulations that guide voter registration, the creation of new congressional boundaries after the census, and the role of the US attorney general to ensure that there are no violations of the 15th Amendment. Other sections outline the criteria necessary to determine that one's voting rights were violated, various sanctions for violating the 15th Amendment, and a single section, Section 16, that covers men and women serving in the armed forces. Legal and constitutional scholars zero in on Sections 2, 4, and 5 as the backbone of the Voting Rights Act. Section 2 prohibits establishing voter qualification based on race. Section 4 prohibits the use of devices like literacy tests to deny voter enfranchisement. Unlike Sections 2 and 4, Section 5 is a temporary provision that Congress has to reauthorize. Section 5 deals with the issue of preclearance. Preclearance requires any changes to voter quali-fication to be cleared by the attorney general. The history of black disenfranchisement from the end of slavery to the civil rights era helps put the importance of these three sections into perspective.[1]

The US Constitution legally prohibited blacks from the status of citizenship. The Supreme Court ruled in the 1857 *Dred Scott v. Sandford* decision that persons of African descent, including an individual like Dred Scott, who had African and European ancestry, were ineligible for American citizenship. Elite whites did not automatically grant black men the right to vote following the conclusion of the Civil War. The aftermath of the Civil War is known as radical reconstruction because it reassembled the union through new fields of citizenship, racial relations, and geographical sites of power. Elite white men reaffirmed their control over the state and economy, but blacks were granted the status of citizenship, albeit on a very limited basis, because it did not initially include the right to vote. The federal government freed black slaves via the 1863 Emancipation Proclamation but did not formally end slavery until the states ratified the 13th Amendment in 1865. The 13th Amendment did not grant blacks the right to vote. It did make blacks count as one whole person instead of three-fifths of a human being when deciding congressional reapportionment. Counting blacks as a whole person without the right to vote would have inadvertently empowered the southern states over northern states, the agrarians over the industrialists and bankers, and the Democrats over the Republicans. Northern elite whites needed the black vote to solidify their control over the state after they assumed control of the South.

Black men obtained the legal right to vote via the 15th Amendment in 1870. Led by elite whites in the North, Congress passed the Civil Rights Act of 1866, which was immediately vetoed by President Andrew Johnson. The Civil Rights Act of 1866 would have abolished the various black codes and granted blacks equal access to the law. In response, Republicans led the fight for the 14th Amendment. President Andrew Johnson did not support the 14th Amendment, but since the executive branch does not vote on the ratification of constitutional amendments— only Congress and the states vote on constitutional amendments—his efforts to continue black disenfranchisement were left to lobbying other elite whites on the merits of limiting black citizenship rights. The states ratified the 14th Amendment in 1868. It extended citizenship to former slaves but not Native Americans and did not grant black men the right to vote. The federal government did not automatically grant Native Americans citizenship until the 1924 Indian Citizenship Act. Black women would wait another 50 years after the ratification of the 15th Amendment until the 19th Amendment granted all women the right to vote.

The passage of the 15th Amendment was the first significant period of black civic inclusion in American history. Over 2,000 blacks won elections at the local level. There were black tax assessors and black state legislators. Fourteen blacks were elected to the House of Representatives. There were two black senators. The black vote was an immediate threat to the agrarians. On the local level, elite southern whites launched a multifaceted attack on blacks. The Ku Klux Klan used violence. But it was old-fashioned elite white deal making that curtailed black political power. The period of reconstruction ended in 1877 after northern Republicans and southern Democrats struck a deal that gave the presidency to Rutherford B. Hayes. The election between Samuel Tilden and Hayes was a mess for elites. Tilden won the popular vote but did not have the majority of the electoral college votes to claim the office of the executive branch. The deal gave Hayes the election in exchange for withdrawing federal troops from the South. The agrarians resumed their control over the southern states, rewrote state constitutions that instilled Jim Crow segregation laws, and developed a series of devices to drastically curb the black vote.

The devices invented by southern elites were the myriad of ways to get around the 15th Amendment and deny blacks the right to vote. The devices included literacy and understanding tests, poll taxes, residency requirements, property ownership requirements, and grandfather clauses. Grandfather clauses exempted white men from the literacy tests and poll taxes as long as they had a father or grandfather who voted in a previous election, before the states implemented the devices and before blacks were eligible to vote. Southern states empowered the local registrars to deny individual black applicants and remove existing blacks from the voter rolls. The local registrars' power was institutional and administrative, in that it was up to them to exercise power by their application of the devices. The number of registered black voters in Louisiana dropped from 130,000 in 1896 to 1,342 in 1904. In Virginia, the number of registered black voters dropped from 147,000 to 21,000 in the same time period. The devices developed by southern elites became the main subject of Section 2 of the Voting Rights Act.[2]

The black civil rights movement demanded the unfettered right to vote as part of the movement's struggle for overall black civic inclusion. In the aftermath of the Montgomery movement's success in desegregating the buses, the burgeoning civil rights movement formed the Southern Christian Leadership Conference (SCLC). The SCLC's initial focus was on voter registration. They organized voter registration drives in Alabama but with little success. Sensing that the right to vote was only part of

PIECEMEAL BLACK DISENFRANCHISEMENT 57

the equation to achieving racial equality, Ella Baker took a prominent role in setting up SCLC's citizenship schools. SCLC's citizenship schools were modeled directly from the Highlander Folk School. Although the citizenship schools organized their pedagogical instruction around the merits of good black citizenship, they never abandoned their focus on voting rights. Indeed, good black citizenship was the normative image used to debunk racist white stereotypes that blacks were not morally qualified to vote and became the dominant representation of black citizenship associated with the civil rights movement.

SNCC also focused on registering blacks to vote. It's what brought Bernard Lafayette to Selma, Alabama, in 1963. Lafayette met up with Sam and Amelia Boyton, the two mainstays of Selma's local black civil rights movement and organizers of the Dallas County Voters League. Lafayette was introduced to the racial violence of Dallas County Sheriff Jim Clark. When Lafayette left Selma in 1963, he left a small local network of activists who would make up the Selma movement. The Selma movement became known for its focus on voting rights after the passage of the 1964 Civil Rights Act opened the doors for the movement to refocus on the right to vote. Blacks lined up at the door of the courthouse to register to vote only to endure verbal harassment and physical violence from Clark and his deputies. After the murder of Jimmie Lee Jackson in nearby Marion, Alabama, the Selma movement organized a march from Selma to Montgomery to pressure white lawmakers to pass voting rights legislation. Alabama Governor George Wallace ordered state police to intervene in the march. Along with Baker's deputized posses, the state police attacked black marchers. The Selma to Montgomery march became known as Bloody Sunday. *ABC News* interrupted a nightly movie to show the American public the police attacking black protesters. Whites murdered two white civil rights volunteers, Violet Liuzzo, a woman from Michigan who came to Alabama to help drive volunteers, and James Reeb, a white minister murdered while leaving a local diner. A movement designed to pressure lawmakers ended up in white violence, black bloodshed, death, and federal troops arriving in Selma on 20 March 1965.

Lyndon Johnson signed the Voting Rights Act into law on 6 August 1965 after the Senate passed it by a vote of 77–19. Only southern senators voted against the final version bill. The final version of the Voting Rights Act was the result of a series of political negotiations between various elite whites. The representation of racially nonthreatening good black citizens swayed white elites on a national level. Some elites understood the denial of the right to vote as simply un-American. Some were swayed to support the Voting Rights Act because of the violence at Selma. Other elites saw it as a political opportunity. Liberal Democrats looked to build a black-labor coalition while Republicans were happy to welcome racist white senators and congressman, as well as ordinary white racist voters to their party. The racial bifurcation of the two parties, driven by the exodus of middle-class white voters from the Democratic Party to the Republican Party, an exodus that began with Barry Goldwater's 1964 presidential campaign, foreshadowed the subsequent elite white strategies to deregulate the Voting Rights Act in the neoliberal era.

Deregulation

Deregulation is the process of reconfiguring an already existing regulatory field to benefit one set of actors over another set of actors. The Voting Rights Act established a regulatory field. It benefited black voters over racist white elites. A regulatory field is simply a set of rules that govern all entities and actors that fall within the framework of the specific field. The Voting Rights Act is itself a legal field nested in a broader legal field comprised of actors, including lawyers, judges, legislators, and administrators. These field-specific actors exercise power via the decisions they make, as well as the decisions they don't make, over the enforcement and interpretations of regulations.

Fields are organized in such a way that some actors enjoy a strategic position in the field in relation to other actors based on the rules set by the fields and the actors' ability to strategically make gains at the expense of others. Pierre Bourdieu described the latter as having a 'feel for the game'. An actor's feel for a game can come from experience, knowledge of the laws, or having the ability to identify the right political climate in which to take risks to test the limits of the specific fields. Actors make conscious decisions and deliberate choices and develop intentional strategies to secure advantages for one group over another.[3]

There is no one singular field or universal set of rules that govern all markets or all laws. This means that the housing market has its own field defined by a set of rules and corresponding strategies that is different from the field of banking, even though the two are linked and supported by state tax credits. Markets have their own logic of supply and demand that is not identical to the logic of a judicial field organized around legal precedent and ideological interpretations of the Constitution. The legal aspect of the field will have its own logic corresponding to legal discourses and officials responsible for enforcing, or not enforcing, the regulations.

In short, deregulation does not mean removing regulations. Removing regulations would involve eliminating the field itself. Theoretically, the removal of a regulatory field would mean either no single group gets an advantage over others, a proposition that would weaken regional elites relative to national elites. A regulatory field allows the state to ensure a level playing field between elites while also ensuring that the state can be mobilized to protect elite white capital when necessary.

Beginning with the Reagan era, elite whites have worked through Congress and the Supreme Court to slowly change the regulations that guide the enforcement of Sections 2 and 5 of the Voting Rights Act. Elite whites make up the majority of Congress and the Supreme Court, which have historically been linked by some kind of shared ideology. However, they are two distinct branches of government nested within two distinct fields. The Supreme Court works within a field that is defined by legal languages as it corresponds to existing laws, legal precedents, appeals, and the US Constitution. The Voting Rights Act was written in such a way that it couldn't simply be invalidated, deemed unconstitutional, or discarded, in spite of conservative efforts to do so. Legal languages that dictate the law are not easily circumvented by ideology, even though the Supreme Court is just as ideological and political as the rest of government. The duration of the Supreme Court justices gives courts an identifiable liberal or conservative shift. Congress works within a broader political field made up of groups from civil society, the business sector, and think tanks. Congress is more susceptible to immediate political pressures. For our purposes here, we have to understand the sociological logic of how the language of neoliberalism

60 PIECEMEAL BLACK DISENFRANCHISEMENT

acts as a nexus between elite whites in distinct fields. Challenges to the Voting Rights Act from both fields have followed real instances of increased black civic inclusion.

The language of white-private is activated by real instances of racial integration and black civic inclusion. The first elite white response to the Voting Rights Act came from the ever enigmatic Richard Nixon. Nixon wanted to continue the major political realignment that began in the late 1960s. The Voting Rights Act was renewed and expanded in the 1970s. Nixon supported the 1970 renewal for political reasons. May argued that "Nixon saw that the Act had profoundly alienated many white voters from the Democratic Party," and quoted Nixon political strategist Kevin Phillips: "The more Negroes who register as Democrats in the South, the sooner the Negrophobe white will quit the Democrats and become Republican." In the 1970s, black civic inclusion meant black Democrats. It meant black mayors and representatives in black urban areas. The struggle over the future voting rights in the neoliberal era pivoted on party membership and geography.[4]

Mapmaking: Racial Gerrymandering and Deregulating Section 5 of the Voting Rights Act

A map has never been a politically neutral device. A line that divides a community may be arbitrary, but that line creates the boundaries of a political community. Jean Baudrillard noted that the mapmaker always preceded the actual making of the topographical map. Baudrillard was alluding to the political power of maps to inscribe political power by drawing political boundaries over geography. Sixteenth-century Italian mapmakers used circled sirens and horses as official watermarks to note the map's authenticity for their feudal political patrons. Maps were indispensable devices for European colonialists. Today, a host of computer software programs exists not only to make maps but also analyze the population, surface topography, and underground water networks. The electoral college is one racist system that resulted from political mapmaking. It represented the power of slave-owning landowners. The electoral college is not subject to the Voting Rights Act regulations. But congressional redistricting is. And the debates over congressional redistricting offer a glimpse of how the practice of racial gerrymandering changes in relation to changes in the overall regulatory field.[5]

State and local elite whites have historically utilized the practice of racial gerrymandering to either deny or neutralize the black vote. Up until the Voting Rights Act, racial gerrymandering wasn't all that common or, for that matter, necessary. Southern elite whites used literacy tests and poll taxes to simply deny blacks the right to vote. Elite whites used racial gerrymandering in areas where blacks were able to muster up enough registered voters to influence the outcome of an election. Racial gerrymandering diluted the black vote by splicing up a black neighborhood or concentration of blacks into multiple districts dominated by white voters. Racial gerrymandering literally involved drawing new political districts that could extend across county lines. These new districts took the shape of snakes, neckties, and crescents.

Racial gerrymandering is different than political gerrymandering. Elites have used political gerrymandering to dilute the political power of urban areas and protect regional elite interests. It was referred to as the county unit system in Georgia and simply political apportionment in states like Alabama. In Georgia, Atlanta's elite white business class worked with black elites to gather enough votes to eliminate the county unit system. The county unit system gave rural areas a disproportionate amount of political control over the state. In other cases, state elites vetoed proposed forms of racial gerrymandering when they were entangled in broader struggles of political apportionment. Such was the case surrounding a proposed redistricting of Tuskegee, Alabama, in 1958. Sam Engelhardt, the self-described "farmer businessman," executive secretary of the Citizens' Council, and state senator introduced the political world to extreme gerrymandering when he proposed a 28-sided congressional district that was described as "dragon shaped" to keep blacks in Tuskegee, where they grossly outnumbered whites, from gaining political control over the city. Alabama's growing white liberal business class nixed this plan on the state level as they were simultaneously trying to limit statewide agrarian political power. The tensions between racial and political gerrymandering are underscored by the ways blacks were systemically excluded from having a say in who represented black citizens.

Elite whites found little success in trying to declare the Voting Rights Act as unconstitutional through a series of lawsuits in the early 1970s. They switched their strategy from removing the Voting Rights Act to deregulating Section 5, reflecting their overall strategy of establishing a regulatory field ideally suited to reproduce elite white power while giving the impression that they were for racial equality. The last attempt to invalidate the Voting Rights Act came via the Supreme Court's 1980 *City of Mobile v. Bolden* decision. John Roberts, a former US Justice Department attorney, who is currently the chief justice of the US Supreme Court, successfully argued against the constitutional legality of the Voting Rights Act. The *Bolden* decision stipulated that in order for an actor to violate Section 2 of the Voting Rights Act the plaintiff must show that an actor's decision to dilute the number of minority voters in a district or place polling stations in an inaccessible location was intentional. In a surprising move, Congress responded by overturning the *Bolden* decision by deregulating the Voting Rights Act in 1982.

The intended outcome of the 1982 Voting Rights Act deregulations was to protect the minority vote. The 1982 Voting Rights Act deregulations stated that it was not necessary to prove discriminatory intent and that it would be up to the courts to decide if there was a violation of the Voting Rights Act. Congress stipulated that courts would have to use actual voting data, a practice about which legal scholar Richard Pildes stated, "Law and social science are perhaps nowhere more mutually dependent than in the voting rights field." Although the reason for the 1982 Voting Rights Act deregulation pivoted around a violation of Section 2, the deregulatory field was set around Section 5 and congressional redistricting. Congressional redistricting became the focus of the 1982 Voting Rights Act deregulations because blacks were only able to elect black candidates if the districts were at least 55% black. These new regulations included a results test that stipulated that the court had to decide if a group's right to vote was violated based on voting outcomes. Courts had to rely on district-level data on voting rather than racial composition of the district or political party membership. In some districts, because of a combination of age and lower black voter turnout relative to whites, districts had to be as much as 65% black to give blacks a meaningful say in the outcome of the election. The result was a congressional act that focused on creating majority-minority districts.[6]

The unintended consequence of the 1982 Voting Rights Act and majority-minority districts was that they inadvertently undermined the political influence of black and Latino voters over broader political policy. Majority-minority districts were considered safe districts, in that there was a very high probability that blacks could elect their candidate of choice. The preferred black candidate was usually black. Whites didn't vote for black candidates in races that pitted a black candidate against a white candidate in the 1980s. In Georgia, 86% of whites voted for the white candidate. In South Carolina, between 1972 and 1985, whites voted for the white candidate 90% of the time. Nationwide the black candidate stood a 1% chance of beating the white candidate, regardless of the districts' income and educational levels, region, or number of urban voters. No blacks were elected in Alabama, Florida, North Carolina, South Carolina, and Virginia until 1992, after the creation of majority-minority districts. In short, black candidates basically had no chance of winning an election outside of a majority-minority district. Republican-controlled legislatures figured out that they could create a single gerrymandered majority-minority black district in relation to multiple safe white districts. This would ensure elite white political power while remaining compliant with the Voting Rights Act.[7]

The failure of the 1982 Voting Rights Act deregulations to ensure that blacks and Latinos had a fair chance of electing a political candidate of their choice highlights the relationship between deregulation and systemic racism. Even the establishment of a well-intended regulatory field to even the political playing field still created a white-private regulatory system of redistricting that benefited elite whites at the expense of minority communities.

The white response to increased black civic inclusion via the 1992 election was to usher in a second and arguably more destructive wave of American neoliberalism in 1994. The 1994 elections were highlighted by Newt Gingrich's "Contract for America" and gave neoliberal Republicans control of the House and Senate. The first US elections based on the 1982 VRA regulations that stipulated the creation of majority-minority districts was in 1992. There were 110 new members of the

House of Representatives elected in 1992. The number of Hispanics elected to the House increased from 10 to 17, while the number of black members increased to 38 from 25. Bill Clinton defeated incumbent George Bush in 1992. Lublin's analysis of the 1994 election data indicated that the creation of majority-minority districts not only "assured that the Republicans won solid control over the House in 1994", it also assured that the house was "less likely to adopt legislation favored by blacks." In other words, neoliberal Republicans used the 1982 Voting Rights Act deregulations to limit substantive black political power through racial gerrymandering in the 1990s.[8]

Elite white Republicans continued to question the validity of the Voting Rights Act during the 1990s. North Carolina used the 1982 Voting Rights Act regulations to draw a single majority-minority district in the state. This led to the election of Melvin Watt, who became the first black man to represent the state of North Carolina in the House of Representatives since 1898. The US Justice Department rightly felt that there could have been more than a single majority-minority district. North Carolina officials responded by drawing a second majority-minority district, a 160-mile snakelike district that connected black neighborhoods across multiple counties. The case was actually brought to the court by white constituents who apparently could not stomach a second black representative in North Carolina. In *Shaw v. Reno* (1993), the Supreme Court found that making bizarre-shaped districts was basically a form of political segregation. The *Reno* decision was upheld in later challenges to Section 5 of the Voting Rights Act, notably *Miller v. Johnson*, which involved a similar scenario in Georgia. Georgia and multiple counties in North Carolina were on the Voting Rights Act preclearance list.

The 1990 congressional reapportionment was central in creating the representation that America was finally over its racist history. The increase of black civic inclusion exemplified by an increase in the number of blacks elected to office in the 1990s masked the extreme racial marginalization exemplified in poverty and imprisonment rates and helped set the groundwork for the debate over whether or not America had entered a color-blind or some kind of postracial era. The debates over whether or not America become postracial were fed by voting data that indicated that about 33% of whites would regularly vote for a black candidate over a white candidate. In other words, America became a postracial country because only 67% of whites were reliable racists. This prompted Pildes to suggest that coalition districts should replace strict majority-minority districts. Whereas majority-minority districts reflected the need to have a minimum percentage of voting-age blacks to comply with Section 5 of the Voting Rights Act, Pildes argued that coalition districts complied with Section 5 of the Voting Rights Act because they still gave blacks and Latinos a meaningful say over electing the candidate of their choice. Coalition districts reflect the civil rights era goal of creating interracial alliances. Coalition districts would allow for the geographical deconcentration of the black vote and for blacks to exercise substantive citizenship through minority influence over social policy.[9]

Georgia was the most significant state to use the principle of coalition districts. It was an ideal location for coalition districting. America's largest black middle class can be found in Atlanta. As civil rights activist and longtime Georgia Congressman John Lewis noted,

> More and more, black and white voters, especially in the South, see that they're in the same boat. A lot of issues, like protecting the environment, creating jobs, protecting neighborhoods, cleaning up a toxic site, or trying to do something about Iraq, have very little to do with race.[10]

However, Georgia was one of the states required to file preclearance with the US attorney general before they can redistrict. At the time, US attorney general John Ashcroft, a staunch neoliberal Republican who vetoed attempts to address racial inequalities in voting, denied Georgia's request to create coalition districts. Ashcroft argued that any attempt to form coalition districts violated Section 5 of the Voting Rights Act because they lowered the amount of voting-age minorities in a district. He understood that coalition districts posed a regional threat to elite white power and perhaps a long-term threat to Republican control over the House of Representatives. The Supreme Court did not agree with Ashcroft. The 2003 Supreme Court decision *Georgia v. Ashcroft* allowed for congressional redistricting that did reduce the number of voting-age blacks in a district so long as it did not diminish the influence of minority voters.

PIECEMEAL BLACK DISENFRANCHISEMENT

It turned out that the possibility of interracial political coalitions were short-lived victories in the long struggle for minority rights and racial equality. The increase of black civic inclusion prompted the predictable white backlash that characterizes the neoliberal era. The initial backlash was found when Congress once again deregulated the Voting Rights Act via the 2006 Voting Rights Act amendments. Despite the political theater where senators and congresspersons publicly supported the Voting Rights Act and racial equality, the actors within the juridical field continued its piecemeal deregulation strategy. Whereas other amendments responded to changes in the formula to draw congressional districts, the 2006 Voting Rights Act amendments simply overturned *Georgia v. Ashcroft* and *Reno v. Bossier Parish School Board* (2000) by narrowing the requirements for judicial review of redistricting plans.

The second white backlash to the Voting Rights Act once again came on the heels of a significant moment in the history of black civic inclusion: the election Barack Obama as the 44th president of the United States. Although Obama continued the main principles of the neoliberal project, with a few exceptions that I will address in subsequent chapters, his election immediately renewed calls that America was *once again* postracial. Immediately after Obama's election, Thernstrom and Thernstrom eloquently wrote in a *Wall Street Journal* op-ed, "The myth of racist white voters was destroyed by this year's presidential election." Their proof was that 43% of the white vote was cast for Obama, compared with 55% of the white vote that went to John McCain. The most significant deregulation of the Voting Rights Act since Congress passed the Voting Rights Act in 1965 was the 2013 Supreme Court Decision *Shelby v. Holder.*

Shelby County is in Alabama, about an hour and a half north of Selma. It's an unassuming part of Alabama. About 200,000 people live in Shelby County. You would drive through Shelby on your way from Montgomery to Birmingham if you took I-65. Perhaps you would stop and visit an abandoned coal mine in the town of Montevallo on your trip. Sometimes extraordinary things happen in ordinary places. The black population in the city of Calera increased from 13% in 2000 to 16% 2010. Local Shelby officials responded by eliminating the only majority-minority district by diluting the black vote into three separate white districts represented by Republicans. The US Justice Department negated the election because Shelby County violated Section 5 of the Voting Rights Act. Blum, a local conservative who founded an organization called Project on Fair Representation in 2005 to oppose the renewal of the Voting Rights Act, sued. The Roberts court, the most conservative court since the 1930s, had already opened the possibility for eliminating the Voting Rights Act via its 2009 decision on *Northwest Austin Utility District Number One v. Holder*. Blum simply took them up on their offer. The *Shelby* decision targeted Section 4b of the Voting Rights Act rather than Section 5. Section 4b of the Voting Rights Act mandates that the nine southern states receive preclearance before congressional redistricting. The elimination of the preclearance statute also eliminated the formula used to decide if an actor was in violation of Section 5. Without Section 5, there is essentially no Voting Rights Act.[11]

The future of the Voting Rights Act is in doubt. The Supreme Court's existing guidelines stipulate that states have to figure in race while redrawing congressional districts but that race cannot be the predominant issue in establishing district boundaries. It is impossible to both figure in race and not figure in race. Racism is the predominant variable in the two most meaningful factors tied to making districts: where we live and whom we vote for. Neighborhoods and political parties are racially segregated. Elite whites' white-private deregulation strategy to chip away at Sections 2 and 5 has established a regulatory field where elite whites are now claiming that congressional redistricting that ensures minorities have a chance at electing their preferred candidates actually hurts white voters and white candidates. In *Wittman v. Personhuballah* (2016) The Supreme Court surprisingly denied the state of Virginia's appeal that Virginia's redistricting plan that packed black voters into a single district represented by Robert Scott, a black Democrat, in order to help the Republican incumbent win reelection. The *Wittman* case dealt more with making districts favorable to incumbents than making districts fair to minority voters. During the oral arguments of the *Wittman* hearing, Elena Kagan summed up the mind-set of what she characterized as a hypothetical "racist map drawer":

> We don't like African American voters, and we're just going to keep them all in one district. But we also have a second aim . . . it turns out that African Americans vote in a particular way. And

68   PIECEMEAL BLACK DISENFRANCHISEMENT

so our aim is that we are going to achieve some kind of partisan advantage as a result of this segregation.[12]

From the Motor Voter Law to Voter ID Laws

The 1992 elections ushered in a majority of congressional legislatures who were members of the Democratic Party. It was also the first time since the late 1970s the Democrats controlled the House, Senate, and executive branch. The Democratic Party of the early 1990s was much different than that of the 1970s. Whereas the Democratic Party of the 1970s struggled with internal regional differences over issues like continued segregation, they still championed the Keynesian ideals of full employment embedded in Johnson's Great Society programs. As I will show in the next chapter, the Democrats adopted their own brand of neoliberalism, eschewing special interest groups in favor of the white-private market. The common thread between the old and new Democrats was that elite whites in the Democratic Party relied on minority votes to put them in office. The result was the 1993 National Voter Registration Act, more commonly known as the Motor Voter Law.

The point of the Motor Voter Law was to make it easier for Americans to register to vote, an innocuous goal for a country that proclaims to be the greatest democracy on earth. Elite whites in the Republican Party did not see it that way. George H. W. Bush vetoed a similar bill in 1992. The segregation of political parties on a national level replaced regional differences. Republicans viewed the Motor Voter Act as an explicit Democratic strategy to register more black voters. The potential of more black civic inclusion actually brought out more white voters in the 1994 elections and implementation of an elite white strategy of white-private deregulation.

The Republicans' initial strategy to repeal the Motor Voter Act was to challenge it on the grounds that it was unconstitutional. In 1995, nine states—California, Illinois, Michigan, Mississippi, Pennsylvania, New York, South Carolina, Vermont, and Virginia—all with Republican governors with the exception of Vermont, led the initial challenge. Challenging social policy that encourages civic inclusion or redistributing pubic resources to the poor on constitutional grounds is an old elite white strategy. It's also a strategy that has consistently failed. It failed to stop the passage of the Social Security Act, the 1964 Civil Rights Act, and the 1965 Voting Rights Act. The Republicans seized on their opportunity after the contested 2000 election. Although they directed most of their efforts at legal challenges, they managed to find the time to deregulate the Motor Voter Law. The Federal Election Commission (FEC) initially provided the states with guidance on how to develop a national voter registration application form. In 2002, Congress passed the Help America Vote Act, which ended the use of punch cards and lever-pull machines in US elections and established a single statewide system of tallying votes. Although the Election Assistance Commission (EAC) was originally intended to be an independent agency, it became a partisan political actor. Republicans used the EAC to champion unfounded claims of minority voter fraud and refused to address issues of white intimidation of minority voters.

A second elite white strategy targeting the Motor Voter Act focused on creating the impression of black voter fraud. Elite whites used the language of white-private/black-public to drum up political support against the Motor Voter Act. On 14 March 2001, John Samples, the acting director for the Center of Representative Government at the Cato Institute, a leading neoliberal think tank dedicated, in their own words, to "individual liberty, limited government, and free markets", testified to a US Senate committee on election reform. Samples spoke against the Motor Voter Act on the grounds that it created the conditions for voter fraud. Since Samples had no evidence of actual voter fraud and actually admitted toward the end of his testimony that "looked at technically, registration fraud is not the same as vote fraud," he used the language of neoliberalism to create the impression that black voter fraud existed by tying the black vote with wasteful government spending, corruption, and fraud.[13]

Samples began assembling black-public by highlighting the potential financial costs and burden the Motor Voter Act placed on states. Samples argued that the Motor Voter Act "complicated the states' task of keeping the registration rolls clean." He zeroed in on Indiana, which he claimed,

> would have a price tag of about \$2 million or about twice the Election Division's entire annual budget. Given this price tag

70 PIECEMEAL BLACK DISENFRANCHISEMENT

and the limited resources of most local election boards, we should not be surprised that the registration rolls throughout the nation are enormously inaccurate . . . . Such costs are not trivial, especially since the state gets nothing in return for such spending. Such costs for the nation as a whole must be large.

On its own, Samples's abstract claims that the Motor Voter Act is a financial burden and an example of big government is not enough to create the impression of rampant black voter fraud. Samples needed a black villain to couple with his neoliberal rhetoric and found it in the Democratic Party's strategy to register more black voters in the aftermath of the controversial 2000 Bush versus Gore presidential election. He found his black villain in St. Louis. Samples singled out an Operation Big Vote campaign in that city. Operation Big Vote is a campaign that seeks to register black voters and has been going on since the 1970s. Samples indicated that the national voter sign-ups have been characterized by willful fraud, specifically including

an attempt to register prominent businessmen using their childhood addresses, a former deputy mayor using an old address for an alderman, and a former alderman who has been dead for years. They also found cards for convicted felons and for residents who did not seek to register themselves in the primary. The woman at the center of this vote fraud investigation 'doesn't deny' that some of her canvassers may have turned in bogus voter registration cards.[14]

A third elite white strategy came in the aftermath of the 2008 election. Elite whites steadfastly held on to their white-private economy in spite of the Great Recession it created. It was the image of Obama sitting in a Concorde chair behind the Resolute Desk in the Oval Office that prompted a new Republican strategy of voter ID laws. Individual states, rather than the federal government, looked to restrict the number of minority and poor white voters. Their solution was to require registered voters to show a valid government ID, a list that included a driver's license, passport, military ID, an official government ID, or a dated student ID. The idea was that if Republicans could not legally stop minorities from registering to vote, then they would stop minorities from voting. Roughly 11% of all registered voters lack an official government ID. Data from Indiana shows that 81% of eligible white voters had a qualifying ID while only 55.2% of black voters possessed a qualifying ID. By 2016, 32 states had some version of a voter ID law on the books. Seven states require a photo ID. Ohio and Arizona require two forms of ID.[15]

Are voter ID laws motivated by white opposition to racial inclusion or real cases of voter fraud? The influx of voter ID laws is unrelated to voter fraud. Voter fraud is a myth. The *Washington Post* found a total of 2,068 alleged cases of voter fraud were reported from 2000 to 2012. Hunter noted that since 2000, only 10 cases out of 146 million voters were actual instances of voter fraud. In the extremely rare cases of voter fraud, the problem is found in the use of absentee ballots. America's decentralized system of government across geographical areas makes any purposeful and systemic attempt at voter fraud impossible. Voter ID laws are associated with a state's proportion of black voters. Bentele and O'Brien's excellent study on the restrictive voter practices found that a state with a combination of a high proportion of black and minority voters and a Republican governor were more likely to propose and pass voter restriction laws. Although opponents to voter ID laws point out that the elderly also disproportionately lack official IDs, voter ID laws are not targeted at someone's white grandma or papa.[16]

The racial segregation of America's two political parties has splintered political elites. Republicans have actively sought voter suppression strategies because of the increasing racial diversity of the Democratic Party and their inability to eliminate the Voting Rights Act. Republicans have skirted federal voting rights laws by developing an individualized strategy that emphasized fraudulent black voters instead of focusing on the racial composition of voting districts. Republicans have been successful at creating the impression of the fraudulent black voter because it fuses the neoliberal emphasis on personal responsibility with bad black citizenship. Republican governors and Republican-controlled state legislatures created the opportunity for the passage of black and minority voter suppression policy.

Indirect Voter Suppression: Campaign Finance Reform

There are indirect means to suppress minority voters that exist alongside voter ID laws and racist congressional district maps. One is mass incarceration. America's incarceration rates rose dramatically in the neoliberal era. Only Maine and Vermont, two states with no significant proportion of minority residents, allow felons to vote. Every other state restricts an inmate's right to vote. Twenty-nine states restrict voting even when on probation or parole. Nine states require either a court order or the governor to restore a convicted felon's voting rights, even if he or she served out his or her sentence and is legally free of all direct surveillance from the criminal justice system. Other indirect ways of suppressing the minority vote are deregulating the voting hours to limit the amount of time the voting booths are open. Another example is when the board of elections supplies only one or two voting machines at a polling station, creating long lines, which, because of lack of time or simple frustration, provide a cue to go home.

The second indirect means to repress minority voting is how and who finances political campaigns. Despite America's decentralized system of governance, which distributes power between three branches of government and 50 states, there are only two political parties. The only historical exception was in the South from the end of reconstruction to the civil rights era, when a single political party, the Democrats, represented the entire region. White-private money funded the two-party system. Elite whites of all political stripes use white-private money to influence the policy proposal stream, ensuring favorable legislative outcomes, keeping unfavorable legislation off the broader public agenda, or at the very least, providing loopholes and exclusions in major legislative defeats. In the neoliberal era dominated by digital media of communication, white-private ensures that candidates can hire extensive campaign staffs, including public relations officials and social media experts, to dominate 24-hour news cycles. It takes millions of dollars to run for a major political seat. If there were ever an example that highlights the long-term stability of America's racial and wealth hierarchy, this is it.

The United States deregulated campaign finance shortly after turn of the 21st century. Campaign finance deregulations established a field that benefited the top 1% by extending the definitions of who, how, how much, and which entities can contribute money to political campaigns. Campaign finance deregulation was a bipartisan attempt to clean up elections after the 2000 presidential race. The Campaign Finance Reform Act of 2002, also known as McCain-Feingold, banned soft money from elections. Soft money is money donated to a political party for everyday political uses, like advertisements or getting-out-the-vote campaigns. It also capped hard-money donations: individual contribution levels were set at $2,000 and party donations were capped at $25,000. Finally, it restricted the amount of money corporations and unions could spend on elections and restricted for-profit and nonprofit entities from funding smear ads right before an election. McCain-Feingold deregulations fell well short of leveling the playing field. While they limited the extent that any single elite or small group of elites could funnel white-private money into political campaigns, it did not address the structural economic inequalities where only elites have the excess income to finance political campaigns. In 2004, households that earned more than $100,000 a year gave 85.7% of contributions over $200 to the George Bush and John Kerry presidential campaigns.[17]

In *Citizens United v. FEC*, in 2010, the conservative majority of the Roberts court, which had long established itself to be anti–minority voting rights, extended their contempt for black equal political participation to all ordinary citizens and ruled that nonprofit corporations enjoyed the same First Amendment constitutional rights as US citizens. The Roberts court created an idealized, indeed almost perfect, regulatory field for elite whites via the *Citizens United* ruling. Dark money replaced soft money in the new regulatory field of campaign finance. Dark money refers to monetary contributions from nonprofits who do not disclose the origins of the money. The Super PAC replaced Political Action Committees (PACS) that were still bound to the individual limits set by the McCain-Feingold Act. Super PACs are nonprofit organizations that can raise an unlimited amount of money to be spent on political campaigns. Individual billionaires fund their own personal Super PACs to influence national and local elections and by donating to other Super PACs. Individual billionaires and their Super PACs of note include Charles and David Koch's Americans for Prosperity and Michael

Bloomberg's Independence USA. Billionaire Sheldon Adelson donated about $100 million to candidates Super PACs just in 2012. Super PAC money directed just at the US Senate races accounted for $486 million in 2014, up from $220 million in 2010. The amount of dark money targeted at US Senate races increased from $105 million in 2010 to $167 million in 2012, to $226 million in 2014.[18]

Are the white-private deregulations of campaign finance reform inherently racist? Absolutely. Combined with the deregulation of Section 5 of the Voting Rights Act, the Roberts court has ensured the continuation of systemic racism and the suppression of minority voices in politics for the foreseeable future. In spite of their misgivings on the power of the vote in a "weak party system penetrated by moneyed interest groups and a strong laissez-faire culture," Richard Cloward and Francis Fox Piven noted that increased voting from marginalized groups could "at least moderate the distinctly harsh features of American capitalist development in the twentieth century." I would add that racist voter suppression emerged as the key elite white political strategy after the civil rights era. A regulatory field that allows elite whites to spend freely on national, state level, and local elections is a reflection of the overall assemblage of a society characterized by systemic racism.[19]

The Republican-led strategy of minority voter suppression represents the case where a fissure exists between elite whites. Republicans want fewer black and minority voters because they vote Democrat. Democrats want more black and minority voters because they vote Democrat. This ideological split is meaningful when it comes to women's rights, especially women's right to have an abortion, have insurance pay for birth control, and receive equal pay in the workforce. The split between Republican and Democrats is not as meaningful when it comes to race. Black loyalty to the Democratic Party has not corresponded to party platforms that reflect black interests or black needs. Paul Frymer argued that America's two-party system was designed to keep black interests off the national political agenda. In the neoliberal era, the split between Republicans and Democrats matters in the degree and intensity that privatization, deregulation, and austerity policies become law. As I show in the next chapter, a considerable degree of elite white cohesion remained over the economy.[20]

The failure of congressional reapportionment in the 1990s also high-lights one of the central paradoxes of this book: how an increase in black civic inclusion triggers a subsequent and more intense wave of neolib-eralism. The history of voter suppression is one of limited black gains followed by white backlash aimed at eliminating or privatizing public institutions. The 1982 Voting Rights Act deregulations prevented states from diluting the black vote by mandating majority-minority congres-sional districts. It was a key reason for the election of Bill Clinton and a Democratic Congress in 1992 and the passage of the Motor Voter Act designed to increase voter registration. One unintended consequence of majority-minority districts was to create a single black district via multiple white districts, effectively neutering black influence over broader social policy. Another unintended consequence was the 1994 elections that ushered in a neoliberal Republican Congress and a neoliberal Demo-cratic president. The latter half of the 1990s featured significant deregu-lation and privatization of finance, health care, and social welfare policy.

The implementation of voter ID laws and the various deregulations to make it harder for minorities to vote created the conditions to mini-mize the black vote as opposed to outright banning the black vote. It's important to make the distinction between outright denying or elimi-nating something and minimizing it. Minimizing the black vote keeps the door open for good black citizens to vote and reinforces Republicans' self-impression that their policies are not driven by racist motives. Deny-ing blacks and other racial minorities the right to vote is a naked and overt racist strategy that opens Republicans up to public criticism. Denying a social group the right to vote is a blatant violation of the Voting Rights Act. Creating universal criteria that target irresponsible individuals, even though it's directed at racial minorities, is not. It's debatable whether elite white efforts even needed the mythology of the bad black fraudulent voter to pass voter suppression laws. The threat of real black voters was enough. Mythology and narratives are powerful, and the assemblage of a mythology can have a long-lasting impact on real behavior. The *Washington Post* and *ABC News* conducted a survey 2 months before the 2016 presidential election and found that 46% of registered voters believed that voter fraud was common.[21]

Notes

1. The complete Voting Rights Act is available at http://library.clerk.house.gov/reference-files/PPL_VotingRightsAct_1965.pdf
2. Gary May, *Bending toward Freedom: The Voting Rights Act and the Transformation of American Democracy* (New York: Basic Books, 2013), xii.
3. Pierre Bourdieu and Loic Wacquant, *An Invitation to Reflexive Sociology* (Chicago: University of Chicago Press, 1992).
4. May, *Bending toward Freedom*, p. 204.
5. Jean Baudrillard, *Selected Writings* (Stanford: Stanford University Press, 2001), 169; David Woodward, 1987, "The Analysis of Paper and Ink in Early Maps" *Library Trends* (Summer): pp. 85–107.
6. Richard H. Pildes, "Is Voting Rights Law Now at War with Itself? Safe Election Districts Versus Coalition Districts in the 2000s" *University of North Carolina Law Review* 80 (5): Article 2, pp. 1517–1573.
7. David Lublin, *The Paradox of Representation: Racial Gerrymandering and Minority Interests in Congress* (Princeton, NJ: Princeton University Press, 1997); Pildes, "Is Voting Rights Law Now at War with Itself," p. 1518.
8. Lublin, *The Paradox of Representation*, p. 4.
9. Pildes, "Is Voting Rights Law Now at War with Itself."
10. Henry Louis Gates Jr., "When Candidates Pick Voters" *New York Times*, 23 September 2004, located at www.nytimes.com/2004/09/23/opinion/when-candidates-pick-voters.html?_r=0
11. Quote located at Abigail Thernstrom and Stephan Thernstrom, "Racial Gerrymandering is Unnecessary" *Wall Street Journal*, 11 November 2008, located at www.wsj.com/articles/SB122637373937516543
12. Elena Kagan quote found in the transcript to the oral arguments in *Wittman v Personhuballah (2016)*, p. 24, located at www.supremecourt.gov/oral_arguments/argument_transcripts/14-1504_5he6.pdf
13. John Samples testimony located at www.cato.org/publications/congressional-testimony/motor-voter-act-voter-fraud
14. Ibid.
15. Marcus Anthony Hunter, "How the New Voter ID Laws Impede Disadvantaged Children" *The Society Pages*, 2012, located at https://thesocietypages.org/ssn/2012/10/16/how-the-new-voter-id-laws-impede-disadvantaged-citizens/
16. Phillip Bump, "Here's How Rare In-Person Voter Fraud Is", located at www.washington post.com/news/the-fix/wp/2016/08/03/heres-how-rare-in-person-voter-fraud-is/?utm_term=.e29dd86401c0; Lorraine Minnite, *The Myth of Voter Fraud* (Ithaca, NY: Cornell University Press, 2010); Keith Bentele and Erin O'Brien, 2013, "Jim Crow 2.0? Why States Consider and Adopt Restrictive Voter Access Policies" *Perspectives on Politics* 11 (4): pp. 1088–1116.
17. McCain-Feingold cite www.fec.gov/press/bkgnd/bcra_overview.shtml; Spencer A. Overton, 2004, "The Donor Class: Campaign Finance, Democracy, and Participation" *University of Pennsylvania Law Review* 152: pp. 73–118.
18. Ian Vandewalker, "Election Spending 2014: Outside Spending in Senate Races Since Citizens United" Brennan Center for Justice Analysis, New York University School of Law, 2015.

PIECEMEAL BLACK DISENFRANCHISEMENT

19. Frances Fox Piven and Richard Cloward, *Why American's Still Don't Vote: And Why Politicians Want It That Way* (Boston: Beacon Press, 2000).
20. Paul Frymer, *Uneasy Alliances: Race and Party Competition in America* (Princeton, NJ: Princeton University Press, 2010).
21. Emily Guskin and Scott Clement, "Poll: Nearly Half of Americans ay Voter Fraud Occurs Often" *Washington Post*, 15 September 2016, located at www.washingtonpost.com/news/the-fix/wp/2016/09/15/poll-nearly-half-of-americans-say-voter-fraud-occurs-often/?utm_term=.38272526c7fe

3

PRESERVING THE WHITE ECONOMY AT ANY COST

After Americans elected Ronald Reagan president of the United States, elite white men of different political stripes gathered in conference rooms to discuss the future direction of the United States.

Ronald Reagan created the Private Sector Survey on Cost Control in 1982. It became known as the Grace Commission after its chairman Peter Grace, president of the chemical company W. R. Grace and Company. This wasn't the first time Reagan commissioned such a study. He created a similar group while serving as governor of California. Reagan's interest in privatization dated back to the early 1960s, notably in his infamous opposition to 'socialized medicine' and his support for the existing system of privatized medicine sponsored by the American Medical Association and distributed via a spoken work LP vinyl record. Reagan's commitment to privatization ran so deep that he supported the creation of a nonprofit entity titled the Foundation for the President's Private Sector Survey to solicit tax-deductible donations from businesses to pay for the Grace Commission. The nonprofit raised $3.3 million to pay for rented office space and salaries for 50 employees, who designed work plans and project management systems and wrote reports. One hundred and fifty-four of the 161 members of the Grace Commission were either CEOs or sat on business executive committees. They conducted thousands of interviews with government officials and, with the

PRESERVING THE WHITE ECONOMY AT ANY COST   79

help of rank and file bureaucrats, analyzed budgets and everyday life as public sector employees. The result was over 2,500 suggestions found in 47 separate reports spread out over 38 volumes.

The essence of the Grace Commission was an unapologetic championing of privatizing various government agencies where a potential profit could be made *and* deregulating various fields to help businesses and hurt citizens. The Grace Commission suggestions read like a Christmas wish list for businesses. As Charles Goodsell explained, "The privatization proposals . . . are not limited to such relatively mundane operations." The list of potential public entities that could be privatized included cafeterias on military bases, hydroelectric power plants, space exploration, minting coins and printing money, Coast Guard search and rescue, municipal wastewater treatment, Social Security Automatic Data Processing (ADP) operations, and user fees, ranging from the use of public campgrounds to Freedom of Information (FOI) requests. Deregulations emphasized letting businesses like nuclear power plants and the poultry industry conduct their own inspections and removing environmental protections rules when constructing roads. The rationale for deregulation was that companies had market incentives not to supply food containing high levels of salmonella or cause a nuclear meltdown. The Grace Commission indicated that their recommendations would save over $400 billion in 3 years. Congress did not believe it, and the commission's recommendations were not put into law. Many of the Grace Commission's privatization recommendations happened anyway.

The Grace Commission immediately linked with the language of white-private/black-public to gather support from ordinary whites. Typically, we can identify the relationship between white-private and racism indirectly via the association between austerity and privatization. Indeed, Peter Grace gave us our link when he characterized food stamps "as basically a Puerto Rican Program." In an attempt to apologize for the overt racist statement, he clarified his position:

> What I'm trying to do is not designed to hurt anyone or reduce benefits, but an attempt to help the Federal Government in a business like manner to provide the same level of help and services, whatever that level might be, but a lower cost to the taxpayer.

Grace understood that he needed to deploy the language of white-private austerity to activate broader white support for privatization.[1]

The Grace Commission is important because it nationalized privatization and deregulation strategies. It provided a material basis to guide and rationalize privatization and deregulation as a political project in of itself. It did not invent privatization. Southern states privatized schools rather than integrate them during the civil rights era. What the Grace Commission did was unite a series of otherwise heterogeneous audiences into a single audience. The creation of a single audience not only allowed for generalization of an ideology of privatization; it unlocked the potential for everything to be privatized.

A second gathering of elite white men happened in Reston, Virginia, from 21 to 23 October 1983, about year after the formation of the Grace Commission. Charles Peters, the editor of the *Washington Monthly*, a left-leaning beltway magazine, gathered a few senators, lawyers, journalists, and university professors to Reston to discuss neoliberalism. Peters claimed to coin the term 'neoliberalism'. The term 'neoliberal' has appeared in the past. Dividing the world of American politics into liberals and conservatives only began in the Eisenhower era. Prior to that, everyone was a liberal of sorts. In the early 1950s, Raymond Moley characterized FDR's New Deal as neoliberal because he saw it as a mixture of socialism and democracy that used the power of the federal government to restrict individual freedom. For Moley, a real liberalism still reflected its British origins of protecting individual rights. But to be neoliberal in 1983 was something entirely new. And it was the first time Democrats were self-consciously describing themselves as neoliberals.[2]

The Conference on Neoliberalism was an explicit rejection of the New Deal and War on Poverty policies that defined postwar liberalism. As Peters explained to the *New York Times*,

> We took a hard look at the old liberalism. We are still concerned about helping the down and out, and about fair play. But a lot of programs to do this didn't work. And we were prounion and anti-big business; antimilitary and pro-big-Government. We're not automatically pro or con any more.

PRESERVING THE WHITE ECONOMY AT ANY COST   81

The rise of neoliberal Democrats in the 1980s, such as Gary Hart, Bill Clinton, and Paul Tsongas, challenged the old guard of Walter Mondale, Ted Kennedy, and Michael Dukakis. The neoliberals pointed to the Democrats' bad showings in recent national elections as proof that they lost the support of the white middle class.[3]

The Conference on Neoliberalism was remarkable in that it outlined a political agenda that would define Democratic neoliberalism for the next four decades. Much of the policy proposals mirrored Republican neoliberalism. The conference presenters discussed the need to get rid of bad teachers protected by unions but rejected school vouchers favored by their Republican counterparts. They discussed the need for market solutions to break up lawyer monopolies over licensing and how liberals rely too much on the courts "to accomplish their ends." The most significant difference between Republican neoliberalism and Democratic neoliberalism was over the topic of health care, where Keisling stated neoliberals were "radical on health care" because they still favored eliminating the fee-for-service model, establishing national health care, and free medical schools. The point of where Democratic neoliberalism converged with Republicans was over the economy, with both supporting business over social welfare programs by the mantra "celebration of economic growth itself" and specific policy condemnations, such as the payroll tax as "basically a tax on the act of employment."[4]

The conference was also an implicit rejection of the civil rights era that helped drive the expansion of the American welfare state via black civic inclusion. The implicit rejection of the civil rights era seems absurd at first glance. But that a room full of self-described liberals, led by a man who was a former Peace Corps official, would implicitly turn their backs on blacks doesn't seem that absurd given that they were simultaneously turning their backs on working-class whites. Peters himself continuously conjured up the bad black guy to make his point on why Democrats needed to embrace neoliberalism. In his opening remarks, Peters said liberals were always antipolice, antibusiness, and antireligion "unless, of course, they happened to be black." Recounting his time as a lawyer, he said that liberals think everyone is innocent, especially poor black criminals, despite the fact that "the people they [the police] did arrest had usually been apprehended as they were passing color television

82   PRESERVING THE WHITE ECONOMY AT ANY COST

sets out store windows." It was an implicit reference to the urban race riots of the late 1960s. During the discussion over entitlements, a panelist equated the increase in welfare spending in the 1970s with broken black families: "When social spending was much less, 15% of all black children in this country were born out of wedlock. By 1979 55% were born out of wedlock."[5]

Audience members questioned neoliberal strategies that emphasized market solutions to social justice. For example, Michael Kinsley, then an editor at *Harper's* magazine, who formerly wrote for the *New Republic* and would represent the liberal perspective across from noted neoconservative Patrick Buchanan in CNN's political show *Crossfire* in the 1990s, noted that "social justice is achieved through substantive measures, job creation, the kinds of things that are going to be discussed in other panels." This was his answer to a point raised by an unnamed audience member, who stated, "I don't see any black faces in this room. I don't know how many Hispanic faces there are in this room. I don't know what the socioeconomic background of the people in this room is." Other audience members raised the question of the diversity of the panelists. Peters's closing remarks addressed the number of comments and ongoing discussion over his assemblage of panels made up of all white males, with the exception of a single female panelist, a school principal who spoke on the need to fire bad teachers. Peters indicated that Betty Friedan canceled at the last moment and that Lee Brown couldn't fit the conference into his schedule. He promised more future diversity in the neoliberal movement. No one asked any questions about the absence of blacks and other minorities on the Grace Commission.[6]

The Grace Commission and the Conference on Neoliberalism illustrate how in the face of political differences elite whites can still come together over issues of what's best for the white economy. Elite white self-awareness of their economic power is typical of how elite whites operate. Historically, they've formed trade associations to protect their economic interests from trade unions and established exclusive and homogenous social networks around schooling and social clubs. It's no coincidence that a seismic shift in American liberalism came on the heels of the civil rights era through the new notion of good white-private citizenship. The first time there was a real threat to the white economy came courtesy of the

1964 Civil Rights Act and affirmative action regulations. The elite white response was to pit the black-public teachers, unions, and special interest groups against the white-private businesses.

In spite of their political ideological differences over managing the economy, elite white men are generally united in preserving the white economy at any cost. This was never so apparent than in the mid- to late 1990s, as Bill Clinton teamed up with the Republican-led Congress to initiate a series of deregulations over everything ranging from health care to banking. Bill Clinton signed the Financial Services Moderation Act, also known as Gramm-Leach-Bliley, into law in 1999. It was the final act of white-private banking deregulations that began in 1980. The Financial Services Moderation Act allowed for commercial banks, investment banks, and insurance companies to merge. This placed investment banks in a favorable position relative to commercial banks and consumers. They had the capital to buy smaller regional banks. Nine years later, the American economy entered its most devastating recession since 1929. At the heart of the recession was a liquidity crisis—the limited supply of available money to be lent—due to American banks holding so many risky securities. The riskiest securities were mortgage-backed derivatives, or a bundle of housing portfolios made up of subprime loans, high-risk loans that carry very high interest rates and acquire the first lien on the mortgage. The 1929 depression was also the result of a liquidity crisis. The American government bailed out the banks by providing them access to interest-free loans in a program known as the Troubled Asset Relief Program (TARP). TARP totaled $425 billion. The Federal Reserve actually made $15.3 billion in profit after selling their assets in Citibank, Bank of America, General Motors, Chrysler, AIG insurance, and Ally Financial, among other holdings. Ordinary American homeowners were not so lucky. The Federal Reserve did not bail them out. How we arrived at the 2008 Great Recession and its aftermath is part of a longer history of elite whites preserving their economy at any cost.

Taxes and a Brief History of White-Private Revenue

Taxes are a political issue that addresses broader questions of social power. In part, taxes are a political topic simply because everyone pays them—including citizens, noncitizens, tourists, and businesses. However,

84   PRESERVING THE WHITE ECONOMY AT ANY COST

taxes are not just objective transactions. Citizens interpret taxation in terms of fairness, being a burden, and, most important for our purposes here, which social groups benefit from the distribution of tax dollars. When we analyze taxes, we are really asking two questions: who gets taxed, and which social groups benefit from tax revenue? Governments rely on tax revenue to fund various public services. Public services range from building and maintaining public highway networks to funding institutions like schools, police forces, and public parks and beaches. Taxation varies by the state and federal level and the region—North and South, coastal and inland—so it's impossible to make a sweeping generalization that captures every point of taxation. My goal here is to highlight how the relationship between racism and elite white power shapes how whites understand taxes. Specifically, this means analyzing how race shapes whites' perceptions of who pays taxes, who doesn't pay taxes, who benefits from the distribution of public resources, and how a generic opposition to all forms of taxation emerged as taxes became black-public.[7]

The origins of America's modern tax structure took shape under the white-public cultural framework. Americans paid no tax on their incomes until 1913, when the states ratified the 16th Amendment authorizing the federal government to collect taxes on personal income. Prior to that, public tax revenue came from tariffs, property taxes, and excise taxes. Socialists, populists, and eventually the Democratic Party pushed for a progressive tax on income in the late 1800s. A progressive tax means that the more you make the greater the percentage of your income you owe the government. A white-public political coalition was possible because ordinary whites theoretically stood to benefit from increases in public revenue. The first income tax only targeted the very wealthy. The white-public movements were responding to the rapid growth in economic inequality and concentration of political power triggered by industrialization. The expansion of white-public taxation funded the expansion of the segregated welfare state: the state that distributed benefits almost exclusively to whites. The development of a segregated neoliberal state coincides with the transition to white-private taxation that essentially flattened the progressive income tax bracket and tax credits for businesses.[8]

There is a history of elite whites viewing tax revenue as white tax dollars. Elite whites were the only groups to own property and control the commodity networks that were subjected to taxation. Agrarian elites went to great lengths to limit public spending to prevent increases in their property taxes. These included a practice of underassessing the value of land for tax purposes, levying minimal tax rates on property, and, most important, shifting the burden of taxation away from the wealthy and onto the poor. States began to impose transactional taxes, more commonly known as the sales tax, to raise additional revenue in the 1930s. Transactional taxes are different from excise taxes because revenue goes into a general fund. They are also different from progressive taxes because everyone pays the same rate. A legacy of underassessed property created revenue shortfalls in southern and Midwestern states. In 1930, the Mississippi legislature imposed the first sales tax because agrarian elites blocked attempts at market-rate assessment of their land. The implementation of the sales tax was largely driven by white perception that blacks did not pay any taxes. Thus, even within a white-public culture, elites still found a way around paying their fair share of taxes. Regressive taxation created a link between elite whites and other whites regarding where the tax revenue was spent. If ordinary whites wanted more, it would cost them. Racism amplified the perceptions of fairness, who paid taxes, and who didn't pay taxes.[9]

Another reason whites turned away from a white-public welfare state was that they could not redistribute or earmark public money only to whites. The 16th Amendment also gave Congress the authority to spend tax revenue as they saw fit. The creation of an account for income taxes helped provide the link for a general opposition to taxes. For example, upper-middle-class whites move into neighborhoods with high property taxes because the property tax revenue pays for their schools and prevents all poor and working-class families from moving into wealthy suburbs. Yet, these same upper-middle-class whites balk over income taxes that redistribute tax money to other social groups. Taxes spent on other social groups, especially minority groups, whom whites define as unworthy of receiving tax dollars, prompts a general opposition to taxation.

The growing perception of white-private tax dollars was aided by building in tax credits and tax deductions into the tax structure that benefit the white middle class. The federal tax code provides structural advantages that benefit some groups but not others. The tax code allows homeowners to deduct the interest they pay on their home mortgages from their income taxes. The tax deductions that surround housing have macroeconomic functions: new housing indirectly employs other job sectors, such as the skilled trades, retail sales of appliances and furniture, and financial services that manage mortgage payments. It's a Keynesian approach to stimulating economic demand. It also benefits the wealthy and members of the upper middle class, who can afford more expensive housing and thus have more to deduct. They are also the only social groups who can have access to credit in times of a tight credit market. It does not benefit those who can't afford to purchase a home. The combination of regressive taxation and structural tax advantages inadvertently tied elite whites with middle-class and other ordinary whites into the framework that only whites pay taxes. In both cases, elites used the perception that tax revenue was white to rebuild the progressive tax code into a more regressive tax code.

The link between whites and taxes within a white-public culture expanded the segregated welfare state but did not include the widespread practice of redistributing public money to businesses until the tax reform acts in the 1980s. The practice of redirecting public dollars to private industry began in the Depression-era South. Southern states introduced the systemic use of tax credits and tax subsidies to spur economic development by exempting companies from paying local property and sales taxes. Southern states formed public-private organizations that gave businesses money in exchange for creating new jobs. Mississippi was the first state to adopt this practice, making a change in their state constitution to allow their Balance Agriculture with Industry (BAWI) program to subsidize textile factories to relocate from Massachusetts to Mississippi. Alabama soon followed suit, changing their laws to create industrial development agencies that exempted companies from local sales and property taxes.

Elite whites could not round up broad white support against taxation until the civil rights era. Congressman Ralph Gwinn originally proposed the Liberty Amendment in 1952 to repeal the 16th Amendment but found little public support among whites for a pro-elite tax policy. The

1964 Civil Rights Act quickly changed how whites understood regulations. The Progressive Era ideal of regulations protecting the white consumer was gone. Regulations suddenly became a hindrance on elite whites to create jobs and run their business. Why? Because the 1964 Civil Rights Act contained provisions that would ensure that the private and public sector hired qualified black applicants. Affirmative action is a federal policy that states a number of positions must be set aside for members of minority group of greater than or equal qualifications to whites. The idea behind affirmative action is giving minority groups opportunities they would not have otherwise received because of institutional policies like 'last hired first fired,' patronage hiring, and outright racism. Although affirmative action predated the 1964 Civil Rights Act by 3 years, the 1964 Civil Rights Act gave the federal government a mandate to enforce affirmative action rules.

Welfare state policies designed to give members of a minority group a fair chance at gaining meaningful employment haven't always worked as advertised. But they provide a point for elite whites to round up broader white support for the white-private economy.

The primary reason affirmative action hasn't had a larger impact is that the white businesses class seized on whites' overall opposition to link affirmative action policies with black-public regulations in order to shore up elite white control over the economy. The white business class argued that black-public regulations hurt the economy because they forced white-owned businesses to hire unqualified blacks over qualified whites. Mississippi senator John Bell proclaimed, "No businessman will be free to hire anyone or fire anyone without first consulting the government." As elite whites linked regulations with black-public, they simultaneously drew from white-private to make claims that private businesses have the right to discriminate and that affirmative action is reverse racism. Strom Thurmond thought that "when you have to tell a man that he has to service someone on his own property or that he has to serve someone on his own private property if he doesn't want to, then that's an invasion of his private rights."[10]

The second reason that affirmative action policies have not worked is that they do not make distinctions that actually favor blacks. Studies have consistently shown that middle-class and elite white women are

88   PRESERVING THE WHITE ECONOMY AT ANY COST

the biggest beneficiaries of affirmative action. Although women of all social classes face gender discrimination and sexual harassment at the workplace and a wage gap still exists between men and women, women from upper-middle-class backgrounds possess types of cultural capital and are embedded in social networks that give them the capacity to take advantage of affirmative action opportunities. In order for affirmative action policies to benefit blacks and other racial minorities, there would have to be a class component to address the long-term effects of systemic racism. The only policies shown to decrease the racial wage gap are enforcing antidiscrimination laws and increasing educational opportunities for racial minorities. This is an issue of enforcing existing regulations, and the federal government has been unwilling to enforce laws to fight racism in the neoliberal era.[11]

The debates around affirmative action that pit white women against racial minorities are tabloid fodder and entirely overlook the logic and history of systemic racism.

Finally, an unintended consequence of the rise of good black citizenship is that being a good black citizen was a symbolic qualification for entrance into the labor force. King linked good black citizenship with affirmative action:

> The struggle for rights is, at bottom, a struggle for opportunities. In asking for something special, the Negro is not seeking charity. He does not want to languish on welfare rolls any more than the next man. He does not want to be given a job he cannot handle.

Good black citizenship made it easier for some blacks to attain employment because it diversified the workplace in a nonthreatening manner. The increased employment opportunities for blacks moved blacks out of poverty and subsequently enhanced their status as good black citizens. Affirmative action should have accelerated the process of racial inclusion into the labor force. Instead, the white backlash against affirmative action delegitimized black success. Although affirmative action has had no effect on how blacks rate their own job performance, white-private opposition to affirmative action undermined the power of good black citizenship by changing the basis of economic inclusion from debates over worthiness to a debate over qualifications. A distinction between qualified and unqualified replaced traditional white readings that a black person is worthy or unworthy of a job. Whites shored up their white racial framing of success by denouncing black professionals as tokens, unqualified for the position but propped up as proof of white racial tolerance.[12]

The link between white-private and white opposition to affirmative action has basically remained consistent over the past few decades. A 2013 Gallup poll indicated that 75% of whites believed that colleges shouldn't include race in admission decisions, compared with 44% of blacks and 59% of Hispanics. The pollsters noted that support for affirmative action remained virtually unchanged since a similar 2003 poll on racial group support for affirmative action policies.[13]

The emergence of black-public spending at the expense of the white-private economy assembled a general white backlash against taxation that did not exist in the white-public era. Although affirmative action helped trigger the initial white backlash, the emergence of white-private/black-public in the 1970s was helped by a combination of the expansion of means-tested programs in the mid-1960s, new school desegregation regulations that inadvertently encouraged white flight and suburbanization, growing inflation, and standardized assessment practices that eliminated tax breaks for wealthy homeowners. I discuss how the racial integration of the welfare state prompted a white-private austerity strategy to limit public spending on the poor in the next chapter. For now, let's look at how the white-private tax revolts of the 1970s brought all these issues together and spearheaded the neoliberal tax cuts.

Tax revolts are the politics of antitaxation. There are two general types of tax revolt. Supply-side tax revolts include tax exemptions on property, reductions of income taxes, and installation of tax and expenditure limitations (TELs) that tie state revenues to an outside indicator, like a state's gross domestic product (GDP) or growth of personal income. Supply-side tax revolts also include corporate tax inversion, when a corporation moves their headquarters to an offshore tax haven to avoid paying taxes. The most widespread supply-side tax revolt is tax avoidance, the use of state deductions, tax shelters, exemptions, and loopholes in existing tax policy. The other general type of tax revolt is tax revolt of the marginalized. Tax revolts of the marginalized include working off the books or hiring undocumented workers to avoid the payroll tax, the black market, and not filing income taxes. Social groups that do not have the power to change policy practice marginalized tax revolts.

The tax revolts appeared in states with low taxes and high taxes, in liberal states and conservative states, and in western states and northeastern states. In Kansas, voters installed TELs to limit local government's legal authority to raise taxes. Twenty-three states enacted TELs between 1976 and 1980. There was no tax revolt in the South. Agrarian elites blocked attempts to modernize property-tax assessment. In turn, southern states were unable to provide adequate funding for public schools or take full advantage of the interstate highway system. The few southern tax revolts were urban and over the issue of property taxes. In Atlanta, ordinary whites led a tax revolt when they felt they were no longer the main beneficiaries of their taxes. Working-class whites claimed that their rights as property owners gave them a say on how the city spent their tax dollars. As Kevin Kruse argued, "Whites [in Atlanta] think they paid the vast majority—or in some interpretations, all—of the taxes collected by the city." Working-class opposition to taxation was part class and part race; they resented blacks for moving into white neighborhoods and middle-class whites for moving away. The tax revolts coincided with black migration patterns into urban areas.[14]

The most famous and successful tax revolt was the short-lived tax revolt in California. The story of how California arrived at Proposition 13 follows a simple narrative. A corrupt tax assessor from San Francisco took money from businesses in exchange for lower tax assessments. Led by Howard Jarvis, the charismatic but enigmatic businessman, California citizens petitioned to get Proposition 13 on the ballot. California voters approved Proposition 13 in 1978. Proposition 13 capped the maximum property tax increase at 1% a year, rolled backed the assessed values of housing to their assessed value in 1975–76, capped increases in the assessed price of a house at 2%, and required a two-thirds voting majority in the state legislature to pass new tax legislation. Building off the success of Proposition 13, Jarvis mobilized California voters to pass Proposition 4 in 1979. Proposition 4 limited the amount of tax increases to a percent of the increase in cost of living and mandated that extra revenue be returned to the taxpayers. The tax revolt in California ended in 1980 after voters failed to approve Proposition 9. Proposition 9 would have reduced income taxes.[15]

The success of California's tax revolt illustrated the transition from white-public to white-private. The cultural change was triggered by the combination of the civil rights movement, the Watts race riot, the increase in the number of black women receiving AFDC associated with the welfare rights movement, and the issue of school busing to achieve racial integration. The first attempt at a tax revolt in California was in 1968. Philip Watson, the tax assessor for Los Angeles, introduced legislation to reduce property taxes but found little support. He also led a failed tax revolt in 1972. Why? In 1968, only 41% of whites in California believed that government wastes a lot of money compared to 51% of blacks. These numbers flipped to 66% of whites and 18% of blacks the year Proposition 13 was passed in 1978 and 70% of whites and 58% of blacks the year Proposition 4 was passed in 1979. California homeowners were disproportionately white. Of California homeowners, 81% who were employed in the private sector supported Proposition 13. According to public opinion surveys at the time, the only public program that a majority of whites wanted to cut was welfare. Welfare included public housing, food stamps, and unemployment benefits. The link between white-private tax dollars spent on black-public welfare programs became a national sentiment after the nationalization of the neoliberal project. Gallup polls taken in the early 1980s indicated that whites resented what they considered "excessive" spending on social services. The changing white perception of tax revenue and who paid taxes illustrates the link between white-private and taxation.[16]

Elites seized the combination of ordinary whites' growing racialized and economic insecurity to implement what was three decades of massive structural changes in the federal tax code and budgetary decisions on the allocation of resources. The language of neoliberalism gave elite whites a way to connect with middle-class whites. The link between white and tax revenue contrasted with the link between black, public spending, and regulations. In turn, the complex political and economic tax code was simplified into a neat black-white binary.

Reagan, his Republican allies, and the growing number of neoliberal Democrats from the South, known as the 'blue dog' Democrats, drew from white-private taxes versus black-public spending to usher in three decades of tax cuts for the rich. The most notable was the Economic Recovery Act of 1981, also known as the Kemp-Roth tax cuts. The 1981 Kemp-Roth tax cuts lowered the tax bracket for the wealthiest Americans from 70% to 50%. It also cut estate taxes and corporate taxes. A second major tax cut for the wealthy quickly followed: the 1986 Tax Reform Act. The top tax bracket was lowered again from 50% to 28%. The lowest bracket was raised from 11% to 15%. Americans were no longer allowed to deduct credit card interest from their income taxes. Capital gains were taxed at ordinary income levels. IRA deductions were decreased while the mortgage tax deduction was increased. Taken together, it took 5 years for the highest income bracket to go from 70% to 28%.

The beginning of the 1990s featured a period of increasing taxes on the highest earners, but those increases were balanced out by cuts in capital gains taxes. Tax laws allow employees and owners of some financial firms, notably hedge funds, to pay taxes at the lower capital gains rate instead of the income tax rate. The last major tax cuts were the 2001 Economic Growth and Tax Reconciliation Act and the 2003 Jobs and Growth Tax Reconciliation Act, also known as 'the Bush tax cuts'. The Bush tax cuts slashed taxes across the board. The highest earners' income tax rate was reduced to 35% while the lowest income bracket was reduced to 10%. President Barack Obama extended the Bush tax cuts in 2010 and eventually signed the American Taxpayer Relief Act of 2012, which kept the tax brackets the same. The exception was the tax bracket for the highest income earners. The top tax bracket was raised to 39.6%, still a far cry from the 70% level in 1980.

Banking and Finance: A History of White-Private Deregulations

The story of America's rise from colony to global superpower generally starts at the importance of cotton, then industrialization and companies like US Steel and Standard Oil, and ends at its military strength. Slavery is typically absent from this story. So are banks. Yet, banking was central to providing the capital to move slaves and commodities from one side of the Atlantic Ocean to the other.

America's first real attempt to reign in the excess of capitalism came during the first two decades of the 20th century, what is today known as the Progressive Era. The Progressive Era exemplified how a white-public framework created the conditions for the establishment of a regulatory field to protect the white middle class. Theodore Roosevelt was an ardent crusader against corruption and monopolies. He also believed in the racial superiority of Northern Europeans and maintaining the existing social order of his day. Roosevelt championed and ultimately achieved railroad regulations that gave the federal government the power to set laws, otherwise known as regulations, governing shipping rates. This was the first time the federal government stepped in to break up a monopoly that hurt other white-owned businesses.

Woodrow Wilson continued the spirit of the Progressive Era and established a regulatory field around banking. When the state created banking regulations, they created a regulatory field. The state creates a field in relation to new problems. In this case, the problem was rooted in the existing money supply and availability of credit. There wasn't enough of either. Local white elites, specially local and regional bankers and merchants, demanded banking reforms after the Pujo committee showed how a handful of banks, notably J. P. Morgan, controlled America's money supply. An economic recession triggered the Bankers' Panic of 1907. The stock market fell 50%, and there was little available credit outside of the largest banks. The Democrats, agrarians, and populists pressured Wilson to create a banking system where the state could increase the availability of money and credit during times of an economic crisis. This led to the creation of the Federal Reserve Bank. The Federal Reserve Bank indirectly sets interest rates by changing how much they charge in interest to banks. The establishment of a regulatory field around banking in the Progressive Era did not open the economy to racial minorities. Elite whites did not address past racial injustices or put in motion any mechanism to redistribute resources to the general American public. They did protect American capitalism from itself.

What Does It Mean When the State Deregulates
Banks or the Finance Industry?

There are multiple threads of neoliberal banking and financial deregulation. The common theme behind each of these threads is opening up new markets for the elites. For example, retirement emerged as a market in the 1980s as baby boomers moved into their prime earning years and private firms abandoned private pensions to their workers. Companies formed ESOPs that connected workers to the company and the market. 401(k)s are part of a privatized system of retirement that links private individuals to the market. Public pensions invest into the market to generate high returns in order to pay their beneficiaries. Opening up the retirement market has been quite lucrative for Wall Street. But not all markets are as lucrative as the retirement market. People on the margins need access to credit, but bankers view lending money to poor people as risky. Poor people, especially poor blacks, have historically been at the mercy of a shadow banking system of loan sharks, pawnshops, and payday loan centers for credit. The first major form of neoliberal banking deregulation linked financial firms and commercial banks with the shadowy world of subprime lending.

White-Private Deregulation: Usury Caps and Subprime Lending

The 1980 Depository Institutions Deregulation and Monetary Act eliminated usury caps in America. Usury caps set a maximum limit on what a lending institution can charge in interest. The cultural and legal practice of setting usury caps dates back to antiquity, but the history of usury caps in America starts in the late 19th century. The 1890 southern state constitutions that ended the period of reconstruction and began the era of Jim Crow laws also placed strict usury caps on interest rates. The 1890 state constitutions were populist documents that upheld racial segregation while protecting rural and middle-class whites from predatory lending practices and speculative buyers. Banks were the unintended beneficiaries of the usury caps because the caps prevented them from making risky loans. Recessions triggered by liquidly crises were a semi-regular occurrence in the second half of the 1800s and early 1900s. Yet, the usury caps also limited bank profits because the tightening of the credit market also meant the tightening of the money supply. Wilson

PRESERVING THE WHITE ECONOMY AT ANY COST   95

heeded southern Democrats and northern bankers' demands for breaking up banking monopolies when he set up the Federal Reserve Bank, and the US government was able to put some slack in a tight credit market. Although there was more money to be lent, the usury caps continued to limit the amount of money banks could make on interest.

Usury caps differed by state. A handful of states—Massachusetts, Maine, New Hampshire, and the District of Columbia—did not issue usury caps, but they were the rare exception. The typical state set a usury limit between 6–8% on the first lien and 16% on a second lien, like a second mortgage or home-improvement loan. The usury caps remained relatively stable once they were established. Usury caps made it difficult for banks and other financial institutions to enter riskier credit markets. Thus, banks either sought ways around the usury caps or fought to eliminate competing lending institutions that comprised the shadow-banking system. Shadow-banking systems emerge outside the limits of existing banking regulations. They do not fall under the umbrella of the regulatory banking field; thus, they can extend credit at higher interest rates. This makes shadow banking a free-market banking system. The problem is that without regulatory protection, subprime lenders, mafias, and criminal enterprises are empowered at the expense of citizens and banks.

Alabama was an early example of how elites utilized an early language of white-private to open the subprime market dominated by the shadow banking system to mainstream banks. The 1945 Harris Act made it illegal to charge more than 8% interest in Alabama. Alabama had an elaborate system of shadow banking made up of pawnshops and short-loan companies. Short-loan companies made payday loans. They required individuals to put private property up for collateral. In Alabama, private property was either one's home or one's crop. The usury cap made it difficult for poor families to get access to credit from commercial banks. This left blacks and poor whites at the mercy of an unregulated short-loan system that charged at times 5000% interest, required putting up items and homes that far exceeded the value of the original loan, and had no legal or systematic process of foreclosure or property seizure. There were over 2,000 short-loan companies operating in Alabama in 1954. Alabama led the nation in bankruptcies. Birmingham, Mobile,

96   PRESERVING THE WHITE ECONOMY AT ANY COST

and Montgomery were the 'bankruptcy capitals of the nation' and two-thirds of their residents owed money to loan sharks.[17]

Statewide political and economic elites in Alabama pushed to raise the usury cap. Alabama's subprime market was risky but lucrative. Mafia loan sharks and short-loan companies also dominated the subprime market. James Patterson led a statewide crackdown on the mafia while serving as Alabama's attorney general and led the political move to deregulate the short-loan system while governor. Deregulating the short-loan system meant placing limits on how much interest short-loan companies could charge. Deregulating the short-loan system benefited banks. Patterson criminally prosecuted the Tide Financial Company. He enlisted local black leaders to find a black resident to file a legal suit against Tide. Why would a hardline segregationist help blacks? The answer is that he wasn't. Using a black plaintiff associated Tide Financial and the shadow-banking system with black. On the flip side, it aligned legitimate commercial banking with white. The result was a set of banking deregulations that made lending money above 8% a criminal offense. It basically eliminated payday loan companies operating inside marginalized communities. Alabama's banking deregulations were made to protect banks, businesses, and middle-class white citizens at the expense of short-loan companies and mafia loan sharks.

As the 20th century marched on, local black elites learned to profit in racially segregated markets. Black-owned insurance companies, black-owned real estate companies, and black-owned skin and hair-care companies sprang up in urban areas. Black-owned banks and financial firms supplied the credit for black-owned businesses in the segregated credit market. The segregated credit market was the subprime market, and black-owned banks found a way to remain profitable while supplying credit to the black community.

Black-owned banks were the dominant players in the subprime market up until the 1970s. Reverend William Washington Browne, an escaped slave who enlisted in the Union Army, chartered the first black-owned bank in 1889 in Virginia: the Savings Bank of the Grand Fountain United Order of True Reformers. Until Browne established the Grand Fountain Savings Bank, blacks relied on the Freedmen's Bank established by Congress in 1865 but closed in 1874, leaving a gap in the black credit market. Browne's bank filled this gap, expanding to 24 branches before a series of bad loans and embezzlement forced his bank out of business in 1910. The need for black-owned banks arose in relation to two problems stemming from systemic racism. The first was the need to keep black money away from the eyes of whites. This was an old problem. Before emancipation, a small minority of slaves pooled their money and lent it to other slaves or freedmen to fund small business startups. Whites were especially suspicious of black families who acquired even modest savings, let alone wealth. The second problem was that the white banks would not loan money to blacks on the account that they were not creditworthy. This forced black farmers to borrow money on the credit lien system from larger landowners or agrarian-controlled banks on the condition that blacks used their expected crop yield as collateral. Agrarians used the same practice on white sharecroppers. It was how they used banking and finance to reproduce elite white power in the reconstruction and Jim Crow eras.[18]

Black-owned banks allowed black businesses to carve out a niche within segregated economies by supplying blacks with capital to open retail stores, printing shops, newspapers, and nursing homes for the elderly. By 1969, there were 22 black-owned banks in the United States holding less than 1% of all assets and total bank deposits. This was down from the 57 black-owned banks in 1929. Twenty percent of all black-owned bank loans were real estate loans, indicating that they were the main supplier of credit to black homebuyers and, subsequently, the subprime market.[19]

Black-owned banks were successful in the subprime market by adapting their lending practices to the realities of their customers. For one, they hedged their loans against government bonds and employed a larger staff to vet prospective borrowers. Black-owned banks actually had higher operating costs because of the larger staffs, even though they paid less interest on certificates of deposits (CDs). The larger staffs were necessary because they needed to thoroughly vet prospective borrowers to assess the probability that they could pay the loan back. They made money through higher fees. Overall, black-owned banks were only 25% to 33% as profitable as white banks. Black-owned banks were able to survive the 1970s by increasing their investments in US bonds.

98   PRESERVING THE WHITE ECONOMY AT ANY COST

This tethered black-owned banks to the Small Business Administration (SBA). Once Reagan deregulated SBA policy to eliminate race as a criteria for SBA support, black-owned banks either merged with other banks or reinvented themselves as loan centers and real estate loan associations within the subprime market. The entry of white banks into the black credit market syphoned off middle-class black borrowers and left black banks with only the subprime market. White-owned banks moved into the subprime market after the federal government eliminated usury caps.[20]

A general elite-led movement to deregulate usury caps swept through southern and western states in the mid-1970s. The growing elite opposition to usury caps paralleled the entry of white banks into the black credit market. The rate of inflation surpassed the usury caps in the mid-1970s. This meant that banks would actually lose money by making loans. Elites seized on the rates of high inflation to pressure states to deregulate the usury caps. The same states that were at the epicenter of other neoliberal reforms were the states pressing hardest for usury cap deregulation. In 1977, the Tennessee Supreme Court overturned a lower court ruling that authorized banks to issue loans above the 10% usury cap. Tennessee was also the first state to privatize their prisons. California and Arkansas were the last states to have hard usury caps. Most states made exceptions for large mortgages, a.k.a. jumbo mortgages, acquired by white wealthy and upper-middle-class borrowers. California elites attempted to pass laws to amend California's usury cap in 1970 and 1976 to no avail. In 1977, the California Supreme Court struck down a lower court ruling that usury caps were unconstitutional. California was the political base of Ronald Reagan and the antitax movement that ran concurrent with usury tax deregulation. California's voters approved Prop 2 to allow banks to lend at 5% above the Fed's discount rate for business loans in 1979. Alabama and Florida deregulated their usury caps in 1979. Arkansas had a hard usury rate of 10%. In 1979, the congressional Arkansas delegation introduced a national federal bill that allowed banks to loan money to farmers, businesses, and agribusiness only in Arkansas.[21]

The Arkansas bill was the precursor for the first national neoliberal banking deregulation bill: the 1980 Depository Institutions Deregulatory and Monetary Control (DIDMC) Act. The DIDMC Act preempted all state usury caps for interest on residential, business, and agricultural loans issued by any lending institution whose loans are federally insured. For all intents and purposes usury caps became meaningless. The DIDMC act uncapped interest rates to increase profits in the financial sector. Federal Reserve chairman Paul Volcker raised interest rates from 11.2% to 20%, the highest permissible levels to fight inflation. The DIDMC Act made it legal for banks to charge prime interest rates of 21.5%. Bond yields soared. Taxes on the rich were cut, and they predictably rolled their money into the bond market. The famous 'double dip' recession of 1981–82 ensued.

Elite white bankers argued that usury caps restricted lending and thus, hurt businesses and the consumer. That is, bankers deployed the language of white-private to deregulate usury caps on the grounds that they hurt white-private businesses, white-private consumers, and by extension, the white economy. A 1981 study on comparative lending practices in Arkansas, Illinois, Wisconsin, and Louisiana indicated the usury caps did not restrict lending practices in states with a hard usury cap. Arkansas consumers simply used retail store credit and racked up just as much debt as residents of states with flexible usury caps. In Tennessee, banks added fees to loans and continued to offer credit to existing customers. The real losers of usury caps were blacks and other marginalized groups. Loan officers used a practice of 'face screening' to reject applicants who did not look creditworthy. The inclusion of blacks into the mainstream world of banking happened via the expansion of commercial banking into the subprime market.[22]

White-Private Deregulation: Derivatives and Predatory Lending

The subprime credit market is comprised of individuals and businesses with high debt-to-income ratios and poor, little, or no credit history. Unsurprisingly, borrowers from minority groups make up the majority of the subprime credit market. By 1998, 51% of the total dollar amount of lending in predominantly black census tracts was subprime lending. Subprime lending constituted 58% of all refinanced loans made in predominately black neighborhoods, compared to just 10% of refinanced loans in predominately white neighborhoods. The long history of

100   PRESERVING THE WHITE ECONOMY AT ANY COST

excluding blacks and other minority groups from the core of the economy and racial discrimination in wages disproportionately excludes these same groups from the mainstream or prime credit markets.

Why would bankers target the risky subprime housing market as a lucrative growth market? The answer is not as simple as subprime credit carries higher interest rates. The absence of usury caps theoretically meant that banks could charge whatever interest rate they wanted to whomever they wanted. The answer is found in another set of deregulatory acts. The first was the 1999 Financial Modernization Act, also known as the Gramm-Leach-Bliley Act. The 1999 Financial Modernization Act deregulated the banking field by removing the legal boundaries that kept commercial banking separate from other financial services, specifically investment banking and insurance. The second was the 2000 Commodities Futures Modernization Act (CFMA), which placed limits on the regulatory field to exclude derivative trading from the stricter Commodity Exchange regulations on the basis that derivatives were not future contracts. This allowed a shadow investment banking system to form around derivative trading and credit default swaps (when the seller of the loan compensates the buyer of a loan in the event of a default on the loan). Phil Gramm was the primary backer of both.[23]

Phil Gramm was a longtime congressman and then senator from Texas with a PhD in economics. He would become the biggest proponent of pro-banking deregulations and transitioned to a lobbyist for the global financial firm USB after he left the Senate. His name graces the moniker of the Financial Modernization Act of 1999. In a 2001 Senate debate, he told the story of how subprime lending allowed his mother, who supported her children and disabled husband on her nursing salary, to buy her first house:

> Some people look at subprime lending and see evil. I look at subprime lending as I see the American Dream in action. My mother lived it as result of a finance company making a mortgage that a bank would not make.

Gramm spun the subprime market as containing a bunch of good white citizens who just needed a chance. He made no mention of the predatory lending practices that defined the subprime market of his youth and would once again define the subprime market of the 2000s. The difference was that the consolidation of financial firms made subprime risk national and systemic as opposed to a local problem.[24]

Deregulating the field allowed for various aspects of banking, finance, and insurance to be fused into a single financial firm. White-private banking deregulation removed the boundaries separating commercial and investment banking, and it opened up the subprime market for banks. The new banking field granted investment banks a strategic advantage over commercial banks, large regional banks had an advantage over local banks, and banks over borrowers. There was a massive consolidation of banks after the Financial Modernization Act. From 2000 to 2014, small banks, banks with less than $10 billion in assets, declined by 27%. Large banks increased 32% during this same time frame. Banks entered the subprime market by underwriting the subprime lending firms who were aggressively making new loans and refinancing others. The white-private financial field linked the subprime market to the white-private economy. At the nexus of the subprime market and the white-private finance was predatory lending.[25]

Predatory lending is practically synonymous with subprime lending after the Financial Modernization Act. There are two main components that define predatory lending. One is making a loan irrespective of the applicant's ability to pay. The second is refinancing a home and consumer debt into a single loan where the value of the home is used as collateral. As Norton described the process, the "borrower pays more, subprime lender secures a first lien position, thus, increasing the likelihood of the borrower losing the home to foreclosure in the event of a default." Seventy-five percent of all subprime loans were first-lien loans. Seventy-six percent of home equity loans were subprime. As the Internet matured in the early 2000s, banks increasingly went online to reach new customers. The consolidation of banks left fewer brick-and-mortar banks. Banks left the minimum number of banks in poor and black neighborhoods needed to avoid charges of redlining. Subprime lenders never left the neighborhoods or the market. Subprime lenders also took advantage of middle- and upper-class whites buying homes they couldn't afford. Subprime lenders targeted the poor with a slew of fees packed into the loans to stay profitable. These fees included loan packing (adding unnecessary charges like credit insurance to the value of the loan) and loan flipping (having the borrowers refinance multiple times to make a profit on closing costs and other fees).[26]

Free of usury caps and restrictions on investment allocations, banks' profits soared. Subprime lending grew at an extraordinary rate, from $35 billion in 1995 to $140 billion in 2000. All boundaries in place to protect banks from themselves, meaning, boundaries that kept them out of the profitable but risky housing markets, were now gone. National and large regional banks, such as Chase and Bank of America, increased their ties to subprime lenders like Countrywide Financial and Centex by acting as a trustee to the subprime lending firms. Banks were free to buy the subprime loans, called mortgage-backed derivatives, which were extremely valuable on paper and drove up stock prices. Derivative trading drove up the value of banking stocks and by extension executive compensation and bonuses, because they indicated a rise in future earnings. Because they were backed by the lien of the house, the loans had recoverable assets. These assets became worthless when the housing market bubble popped, led by a real estate speculation driven by white-private jumbo-loan borrowers, and triggered the start of the Great Recession.[27]

It didn't take long for elite whites to blame blacks and poor whites for the collapse of the financial and housing markets. Rather than address the housing market, elite whites attacked national health care. Blaming blacks and others on the margins is significant to the extent that the white-private economy always needs a fall guy, a bad black guy, to rationalize its systemic failures. By 2009, white liberals were ready for the expected backlash. In a *New York Times* op-ed, Barbara Ehrenreich immediately countered the elite deployment of the language of neoliberalism: "An article on the *Fox News* website has put forth the theory that health reform is a stealth version of reparations for slavery: whites will foot the bill and, by some undisclosed mechanism, blacks will get all the care." *Fox News* and the conservative neoliberal echo chamber repeatedly linked Obama to reparations for slavery. *Fox News* seized on the racialized economic insecurity of middle-class whites. After America elected Obama, elite whites had their bad black guy to pin the economic failures of neoliberalism on as they regrouped to preserve the white-private economy.[28]

PRESERVING THE WHITE ECONOMY AT ANY COST 103

White-private banking deregulation amplified inequality between whites, blacks, and Hispanics. Williams et al. argued that "a new inequality" emerged in the 1990s around predatory lending and the disparities in the terms of loans. Black employment and black personal incomes fell between 2000 and 2007. The post-2008 recession amplified the effects of existing residential segregation. Whites' median net worth has actually increased since 2007. In 2014, whites' median net worth was $141,900, 13 times greater than blacks' median net worth, which was a paltry $11,000, and 10 times greater than Hispanics' net worth, which was $13,700. The racial wealth gap is three times larger than the income gap. The racial disparities in wealth are driven by the elites: the top 20% saw their net worth increase by 120%, while the bottom 20% actually fell below zero. Housing is the primarily means that ordinary Americans can build wealth; therefore, any gains in black and Hispanic net worth wealth were wiped out by the financial crash because of the overall decline in the housing market, which sent mortgages underwater. Poor neighborhoods became dotted with zombie houses. Suburban housing developments went unfinished. Elite whites still made money. The connection between racism and elite white wealth confirms the basic theoretical proposition of systemic racism.[29]

White-private deregulations changed the field of banking and finance and were a major part of the causal chain of events that led to the Great Recession. I left out another notable housing crisis and elite white bailouts, the 1987 Savings and Loan Crisis. An ongoing pattern in the neoliberal era is the return of economic downturns reminiscent of the late 19th and early 20th centuries. Elite whites of the white-public Progressive Era established a regulatory field to save the white-public economy and, by extension, capitalism from itself. This all changed, as the economy was no longer the exclusive province of elite whites.

A central piece of the neoliberal project was mending the divisions between elite whites in the 1980s. The impetus for this mending was the crisis of the white economy that featured economic gains redistributed to blacks, poor whites, and other minorities in the 1960s and 1970s. The crisis of the white economy was not stagflation. Stagflation was a scapegoat. The real crisis was the increased black civic inclusion that led to the expansion of the welfare state and the affirmative action policy that loosened elite whites' grip on the economy. Elite white Democrats turned their backs on special interest groups and the identity politics that helped usher in the civil rights era. The new ideal of good white-private citizenship bound neoliberal Republicans and neoliberal Democrats together. Although they differ on some social issues, notably gender equality and racism, controlling the economy brought them together. Elite white group cohesion is not a constant and should be understood via its performative aspects, as something that must constantly be renewed.

Elite white cohesion around the economy fused elite whites with the white middle class around generic values of personal responsibility and hard work. This created broad white support for tax cuts and made the logic of upward redistribution of resources seem like the white-private or 'smart' thing to do. Not only did elites deploy the language of neoliberalism to define the state as black and the economy as white; they divided up tax revenue as white-private and public spending was black-public. The relationship between race and taxes illustrates how black-public is embedded in the perception of where tax dollars are spent, which group benefits from public spending, and how the public values and fiscally supports an integrated public. Coupled with the use of tax credits and other indirect public subsidies to businesses, federal money and surplus capital were continually funneled back to the privileged white classes at the expense of blacks and ordinary whites, who saw the quality of their public schools decline and public health suffer.

American financial institutions continue to be a very complex assemblage of banking and investment firms that deal in commercial and subprime lending, insurance services, supercomputers and communication technologies, a series of agencies specializing in calculating credit scores, and the state, which is willing to protect the white economy at any cost. Through the power of the Federal Reserve Bank, the state slashed interest rates and began buying US bonds in a policy called quantitative easing to put money back into the credit markets. The Dodd-Frank Act partially reset the regulatory field of banking by increasing how much reserve capital banks must have to avoid another liquidity crisis. Neither the state nor the Federal Reserve bailed out families who lost their homes. The elites' white-private market shifted the blame for subprime lending, predatory lending, and banking foreclosure to blacks and the poor for borrowing more than they could afford and being financially irresponsible.

Notes

1. Joseph B. Treaster, "Head of Reagan Panel Apologizes to Puerto Ricans" *New York Times*, 29 May 1982, located at www.nytimes.com/1982/05/29/us/head-of-reagan-panel-apologizes-to-puerto-ricans.html?rref=collection%2Fbyline%2Fjoseph-b.-treaster&action=click&contentCollection=undefined&region=stream&module=stream_unit&version=search&contentPlacement=1&pgtype=collection
2. William E. Farrel, "Neoliberals in Need of Constituents" *New York Times*, 24 October 1983, located at www.nytimes.com/1983/10/24/us/neoliberals-in-need-of-constituents.html; Lawrence Glickman, "Everyone Was a Liberal" aeon.com, located at https://aeon.co/essays/everyone-was-a-liberal-now-no-one-wants-to-be
3. James R. Clarity and Warren Weaver Jr., "Briefing" 6 October 1983, located at www.nytimes.com/1983/10/06/us/briefing-213122.html
4. A Conference on Neoliberalism, October 21–23, 1983, Reston Virginia, Sponsored by the Washington Monthly (Washington, DC), pp. 98, 121.
5. Ibid., pp. 2, 3, 124.
6. Ibid., p. 32.
7. A growing literature on fiscal sociology has brought issues like taxation and monetary policy to the forefront of contemporary sociology. For a good introduction to fiscal sociology, see Isaac William Martin, Ajay K. Mehrotra, and Monica Prasad, "The Thunder of History: The Origins and Development of the New Fiscal Sociology" pp. 1–27 in *The New Fiscal Sociology: Taxation in Comparative Historical Perspectives*, edited by Isaac William Martin, Ajay K. Mehrotra, and Monica Prasad (New York: Cambridge, 2009).
8. Kimberly Morgan and Monica Prasad, 2009, "The Origins of Tax Systems: A French-American Comparison" *American Journal of Sociology* 114 (5): pp. 1350–1394.
9. I've discussed the white perception that blacks do not pay taxes elsewhere; see Hohle, *Race and the Origins of American Neoliberalism*, Chapters 2 and 3.
10. Jennifer Pierce Skrenty, 2003, "'Racing for Innocence': Whiteness, Corporate Culture, and the Backlash against Affirmative Action" *Qualitative Sociology* 26 (1): pp. 53–70; John Bell quote located in Hohle, *Race and the Origins of Neoliberalism*, 40, Strom Thurmond quote located in ibid., p. 43.
11. There are far fewer social science studies than legal studies on affirmative action. A good starting point on the subject includes A. Silvia Cancio, T. David Evans, and David J. Maume Jr., 1996, "Reconsidering the Declining Significance of Race: Racial Differences in Early Career Wages" *American Sociological Review* 64 (4 August): pp. 541–556; Jennifer L. Hochschild, "Affirmative Action as Culture War" pp. 343–368 in *The Cultural Territories of Race: Black and White Boundaries*, edited by Michele Lamont (Chicago: University of Chicago Press and Russell Sage Foundation, 1999).
12. See Hochschild, "Affirmative Action as Culture War"; Martin Luther King Jr., *Why We Can't Wait* (New York: Harper & Row, Publishers, 1964), p. 149.

106 PRESERVING THE WHITE ECONOMY AT ANY COST

13. Gallup Poll, "In US, Most Reject Considering Race in College Admissions", located at www.gallup.com/poll/163655/reject-considering-race-college-admissions.aspx
14. Kevin Kruse, 2005, "The Politics of Race and Public Space: Desegregation, Privatization, and the Tax Revolt in Atlanta" *Journal of Urban History* 31 (5): pp. 610–633, 611.
15. Isaac William Martin, *The Permanent Tax Revolt: How the Property Tax Transformed American Politics* (Stanford, CA: Stanford University Press, 2008); Isaac Martin, 2006, "Does School Finance Litigation Cause Taxpayer Revolt? Serrano and Proposition 13" *Law and Society Review* 40 (3): pp. 525–557; Clarence Y. H. Lo, *Small Property versus Big Government: Social Origins of the Property Tax Revolt* (Berkeley: University of California Press, 1990), pp. 57–59.
16. Jack Citrin and Frank Levy, "From 13 to 14 and Beyond: The Political Meanings of the Ongoing Tax Revolt in California" p. 10 in *The Property Tax Revolt: The Case of Proposition 13*, edited by George Kaufam and Kenneth Rosen (Cambridge, MA: Ballinger Publishing Company, 1981); Ibid., p. 9; Alvin Rabushka and Paul Ryan, *The Tax Revolt* (Stanford, CA: Hoover Institution, 1982), p. 38; Ibid., p. 49.
17. See Gene Howard, *Patterson for Alabama: The Life and Career of John Patterson* (Tuscaloosa: University of Alabama Press, 2008), pp. 74–78 on the short loans system in Alabama.
18. Lila Ammons, 1996, "The Evolution of Black Owned Banks in the United States between the 1880s and 1990s" *Journal of Black Studies* 26 (4 March): pp. 467–489.
19. Andrew F. Brimmer, 1971, "The Black Banks: An Assessment of Performance and Prospects" *The Journal of Finance* 26 (2 May): pp. 379–405.
20. See Ammons, "The Evolution of Black Owned Banks in the United States between the 1880s and 1990s"; Brimmer, "The Black Banks."
21. Maxine Master Long, 1980, "Trends in Usury Legislation—Current Interest Overdue" *University of Miami Law Review* 34 (2): pp. 325–342; Robert Keleher and B. Franklin King, "Usury: The Recent Tennessee Experience" Federal Reserve Bank of St. Louis, July/August, Economic Review, 1978; Lawrence G. Preble and Thomas K. Herskowitz, 1980, "Recent Changes in California and Federal Usury Laws: New Opportunities for Real Estate and Commercial Loans" *Loy LA Review* 13: pp. 1–83.
22. Richard L. Peterson and Gregory A. Falls, "Impact of a Ten Percent Usury Ceiling: Empirical Evidence" Credit Research Center, Working Paper No. 40, 1981.
23. Anne Balcer Norton, 2005, "Reaching the Glass Usury Ceiling: Why States Ceilings and Federal Preemption Force Low-Income Borrowers into Subprime Mortgage Loans" *University of Baltimore Law Review* 35 (2 Winter): Article 5, pp. 215–238.
24. Phil Gramm quoted in Eric Lipton, Stephen Labaton, "Deregulator Looks Back, Unswayed" *New York Times*, 16 November 2008, located at www.nytimes.com/2008/11/17/business/economy/17gramm.html
25. Hester Pierce and Stephan Mateo Miller, 2015, "Small Banks by the Numbers, 2000–2104" Mercatus Center, George Mason University, located at www.mercatus.org/publication/small-banks-numbers-2000-2014
26. Norton, "Reaching the Glass Usury Ceiling", p. 218.
27. Ibid.
28. Barbara Ehrenreich and Derek Muhammad, "The Recession's Racial Divide" *New York Times*, 12 September 2009, located at www.nytimes.com/2009/09/13/opinion/13ehrenreich.html

29. Richard Williams, Reynold Nesiba, and Eileen Diaz McConnell, 2005, "The Changing Significance of Inequality in Home Mortgage Lending" *Social Problems* 52 (2 May): pp. 181–208; Brian C. Theide and Shannon Monnat, 2016, "The Great Recession and America's Geography of Unemployment" *Demographic Research* 35 (20): 891–928; Signe-Mary McKernan, Caroline Ratcliffe, Eugene Steuerle, and Sisi Zhang, 2013, "Less Than Equal: Racial Disparities in Wealth Accumulation" Urban Institute, located at www.nsu.edu/Assets/websites/CARPP/Race-and-Ethnicity/RaceEthnicitydoc2(Article).pdf; The Pew Research Center, "Post Recession and Inequality" 12 December 2014, located at www.pewresearch.org/fact-tank/2014/12/12/racial-wealth-gaps-great-recession/; Fabian T. Pfeffer, Sheldon Danziger, and Robert Schoeni, 2013, "Wealth Disparities before and after the Great Recession" *Annual American Academy of Political Science Association* 650 (1 November): pp. 98–123.

4

SOCIAL WELFARE AND THE SEGREGATED WELFARE STATE

Elite whites have historically used the state to control the economy and funnel the redistribution of public resources back to elites. They've done so by continually deregulating various rules to benefit businesses at the expense of workers and the environment. They've used the state to dole out generous packages of tax incentives and tax exemptions to firms on the grounds that taxes prevent job creation. These are key components of what I call *the segregated welfare state*: how the distribution of state resources and benefits of citizenship are patterned by systemic racism. As I showed in the last chapter, the neoliberal project used a segregated welfare state to protect the white economy. There is another aspect of the segregated welfare state that allows us to study yet another paradox in the neoliberal era: the simultaneous expansion of the segregated welfare state and the rise of a neoliberal state.

At the heart of today's segregated welfare state sits a battle between white-public and black-public. In part, this tension reflects the ideological differences in Republican and Democratic neoliberalism found in issues such as health care. However this tension is also sustained in how ordinary whites view welfare. While the welfare state has a precise technical and academic meaning to capture how nation-states actively manage global and domestic economies, ordinary Americans of all races understand the welfare state as distributions of public assistance to the poor. They are

THE SEGREGATED WELFARE STATE 109

torn between their support for welfare and their perception of the poor as an economic burden on the state and economy. Black inclusion into the state triggers the language of white-private austerity that uses the associations of black-public to rationalize selective budget cuts. I've consistently found the pattern that black civic inclusion triggers white calls for austerity followed by the privatization of public entities. While privatization is fundamentally about control, the language of white-private assembles the limited social services that exist for the poor today. The privatization of social services in the neoliberal era reflects the expansion of the welfare state down a line referred to as the 'third sector': nonprofits, charitable organizations, and religious organizations who bring their own set of moral criteria to the equation that determines eligibility.

The history of America's welfare state as it pertains to social welfare follows a familiar pattern. Elites consented to the expansion of social insurance programs when the beneficiaries were basically all white. Increased political pressure from the political margins and the black civil rights movement helped expand the proportion of blacks eligible for social insurance. Black women were key political actors driving the expansion of social services for all women. By the mid-1970s, black women became visible in debates surrounding welfare for all the wrong reasons. The elite white response to the expansion of Aid to Families with Dependent Children (AFDC) characterized blacks as an economic burden on whites to justify AFDC budgetary austerity. The start of the neoliberal era began with a drastic reduction in ADFC benefits until the system was completely overhauled in 1996. Whites still wanted to help the poor, but not the poor of all colors.

In order to understand the meta history of elite white power as it pertains to the segregated welfare state and America's social welfare system, we have to return to the era after the Civil War, a political landscape that now included freed blacks, veterans, widows, and the start of political movement known as the Progressive Era.

White-Public and the Expansion of the Welfare State

America's welfare state began in the late 19th century. America never developed the same type of social welfare system that its European counterparts did. Nor did it develop a comparable social welfare system to Australia or Canada, its closest neighbor. Welfare state scholars call this American exceptionalism: how America developed a smaller and different social welfare system than Western Europe. America did assemble a welfare state in the 19th century. It was different from European-style welfare states, which centralized on the national level. America's welfare state was fractured between the states and the federal government and between public and private entities. It was made up of a haphazard arrangement of Aid to Dependent Children (ADC), commonly referred to as mothers' pensions, Civil War pensions, old-age assistance, worker compensation, and private nonprofit charities and churches, offering food, money, and counseling, disbursed along lines of patronage and corruption. Although America's welfare state was different from Europe's, it doesn't necessarily mean it was smaller.[1]

America's welfare state was racially segregated from the outset. If there is anything exceptional about the American welfare state, it's the way it was shaped by white racism. Yet American racism is typically overlooked or at best treated as a by-product of a system organized around the worthy and unworthy poor. Katz argued that people who suffered a hardship due to chance, like an accident or being born with a disability, and those who suffered from old age were more likely to be viewed as deserving help. In contrast, the poor who were addicts or beggars or viewed as lazy were not defined as worthy of help. Whether one was deemed worthy of benefits determined eligibility levels and eligibility itself. The origins of worthy-versus-unworthy debates are part of the legacy of the English Poor Laws. The English Poor Laws, a series of laws passed by the English Crown in the 17th and 18th centuries, stipulated that all able-bodied men should work and that local authorities should be responsible for overseeing the distribution of public assistance. Its modern American origins lay in the 19th-century debates over private and public charity, which were an important component in how 20th-century administrators decided which women received mothers' pensions, ADC, and eventually AFDC benefits and which women were left to use their bodies to survive.[2]

How elite whites defined the poor as either worthy or unworthy has to be understood within the white-public framework. The political battles surrounding social welfare included debates over whether the state or private charities should administer welfare. They included political tensions caused by the corruption over who received pensions. The unions fighting for better pay and life insurance contributed to the notion that hard work was a social value in and of itself. Yet, all the political actors and subjects involved in the 19th-century debate over her worthiness or his personal shortcomings were white. Elite whites decided whether poor whites were worthy or not of public assistance. Blacks were always defined as unworthy of receiving benefits simply because of their skin color. They were excluded from the get-go.[3]

The Civil War pensions functioned like a de facto old-age and disability insurance. They provided a monthly stipend to Civil War veterans who fought on the side of the Union. The Civil War was the first war that sent home hundreds of thousands of disabled veterans. Surgeons had been perfecting the art of amputation since the turn of the 19th century as a remedy to treat infections that threatened a person's life. The cost to continue life was often a limb—a hand, a foot, a leg, or both legs. In order to care for the number of injured soldiers, the US government established the National Asylum for Disabled Volunteer Soldiers, the precursor to the Veterans Health Administration (VA) health-care system. Although amputation saved the lives of many young men, they returned home unable to work. The Civil War pensions were not generous sums of money, especially for rank and file soldiers. The public turned on the Civil War pensions because of corruption. As Skocpol noted, the "extension of civil war benefits came after claims directly due to wartime casualties had peaked and were in decline." There seemed to be more war heroes than actual surviving Civil War veterans. The corruption of the Civil War pensions turned middle-class whites against the white-public welfare state. They demanded austerity rather than increased public spending. Elite whites of the Progressive Era were eager to comply with a call for responsible capitalism. Responsible capitalism meant fighting railroad monopolies with a series of new railroad regulations that protected businesses and consumers from increases in shipping rates. It also meant ending the patronage system known as the Civil War pensions.[4]

Black Civil War veterans did not receive the same pensions as whites. Skocpol noted black veterans did not have the necessary documents to make successful claims for pensions. In my estimation, more black Civil War veterans would have received pensions if the North was half as racially tolerant as it likes to see itself. Blacks who served in the Union Army and could produce the necessary documentation received the minimal pension. The army was segregated, and blacks could not serve as officers. Although veterans of the Confederate Army were excluded from the federal pensions, southern states provided small pensions to former soldiers disabled during the war. The state-level confederate pensions were all white. The racially patterned administration of the Civil War pensions did not produce any outrage in the white middle classes. Former slaves received no compensation.

Mothers' pensions were another early attempt at a white-private social welfare program. Right after Congress ended the Civil War pensions in 1910 over corruption and partisan politics involved in granting elderly white men pensions, states began offering mothers' pensions to widows and poor women with children. Forty states offered mothers' pensions to widows between 1911 and 1920. In theory, ADC was available to all poor women in need of financial assistance because of the death of or abandonment by the child's father. Handler noted that in practice relatively few families ever enrolled in ADC, either because of the stigma of being on the dole or because ADC administrators decided that a woman did not deserve a pension and "recipients were almost all white widows." Black women, either poor or widowed, were basically excluded outright from the program.

Mothers' pensions are notable for two reasons. One was that women secured social rights at a time when they could not vote. Only men had the right to vote until the US Congress ratified the 19th Amendment in 1920. At this time, women formed civic groups to pressure elite white men to pass legislation to protect vulnerable mothers and children. Women's groups stoked elite white men's sense of paternalism: that it was their responsibility as elite white men and the state to protect white women and children.

The second notable thing about mothers' pensions was the debate over who was responsible for administering social welfare. The debate was the public sector versus the private nonprofit sector of elite voluntary associations and civic clubs. Elite whites favored private charity over

THE SEGREGATED WELFARE STATE 113

public assistance. They established New York's Association for Improving the Conditions of the Poor (AICP) in 1843. Other charity groups included the New York Charity Organization Society (COS), which had chapters across New York State. Although New York's COSs opposed the passage of ADC, local COS chapters ended up supervising recipients of mothers' pensions. In spite of the influence of New York's elite socialites, they were not able to stop the passage of mothers' pensions. Elite white women, like Josephine Shaw Lowell, "advocated the teaching of values rather than the allocation of benefits." They blamed personal shortcomings, like drinking and laziness, as the causes of poverty. It's not surprising that we find the notion of personal responsibility in 19th-century language of white-private. White-private emphasizes private responsibilities rather than public obligations. However, the outright exclusion of blacks from ADC worked against elites in rallying middle-class white support against the embryonic white-public welfare state. Nevertheless, the elite white belief that noneconomic factors were the causes of poverty was so strong that it remained throughout the Great Depression.[5]

Although the Civil War and mothers' pensions were two vastly different attempts at welfare state policies, they shared one thing in common: how the language of white-public was capable of disbursing benefits in a systemically racist way. The language of white-public led to the expansion of the early American welfare state because benefits were restricted to whites: whites deemed worthy of help or whites who were politically connected to elites. The notion that relief or welfare should be privatized could not overcome ordinary and middle-class whites' embracement of white-public. The privatization of welfare became a marginal voice in the elite white community. Subsequent calls for the elimination of welfare would eventually fall under the umbrella of austerity. Yet, the legacy of corruption associated with the Civil War pensions combined with southern congressmen fighting off new demands for black civic inclusion racialized what is widely considered the greatest piece of American legislation: the Social Security Act.

Franklin Delano Roosevelt signed the Social Security Act into law in 1935. It was the single most important legislation of the New Deal and perhaps the 20th century. It's responsible for lifting millions of

Americans out of poverty. New Deal policies were hashed out between Atlantic coast industrialists, Manhattan bankers, Midwestern farmers, factory workers in the cities hugging the Great Lakes, and southern Democrats, who arguably had the biggest say over the final outcome of New Deal policy. FDR needed the southern Democrats more than they needed him. The southern Democrats were the white agrarian elite whose source of wealth and power was directly tied to controlling black labor. The combination of political tenure and ideological consistency toward preserving the legacy of slavery that made American agriculture profitable also made the southern Democrats a powerful congressional voting bloc. The political compromise between the New Dealers and the southern Democrats created an administrative apparatus that excluded blacks. Jim Crow cast more than a shadow over the Social Security Act. He also wrote part of it.

The original Social Security Act was comprised of Old Age Insurance (OAI), Unemployment Insurance (UI), and Aid to Dependent Children (ADC). There was no uniform application of racism across all three. Instead, racism operated at different points in the writing up of the Social Security Act and its subsequent administration of benefits. OAI excluded the occupational categories associated with black labor, like sharecroppers, seasonal farm labor, and unskilled factory labor. It also excluded occupations associated with women, such as teachers and domestic work in the case of black women. Poor whites were also excluded. Middle-class whites with union factory jobs and white-collar professional jobs were included. The OAI pensions worked and were popular because they were white-public welfare policy. As many others have pointed out, white workers viewed Social Security as a pension, something that they contributed to, instead of as a tax and an insurance policy against poverty. Many of the workers excluded from the original bill were not included in the OAI until the 1954 Social Security amendments that all workers qualified for OAI.

Americans elected Dwight Eisenhower president and voted in a Republican Congress in 1952. It was the first time that the Republicans had controlled the executive branch and Congress since the Great Depression. This ushered in a new era of white elites. Eisenhower was the first president to use the term 'conservative' in a political context. A

THE SEGREGATED WELFARE STATE
115

Republican-controlled Congress meant new committee chairs, chairs that were held by southern Democrats for over a generation. The inclusion of occupational categories associated with blacks and other poor whites was as much of a move to politically weaken the southern Democrats as it was to bring more workers under the OAI umbrella. It turns out that this was only the first in a series of Eisenhower-sponsored legislation and presidential acts that helped usher in the era of a very prosegregation business class across the South during the 1958 gubernatorial elections. Eisenhower also sent federal troops to Little Rock, Arkansas, to enforce a school desegregation ruling and signed the 1957 Civil Rights Act. These acts were a collective threat to southern elite white power, which was tightening its control over the local political economy by refusing to comply with any desegregation measure. But it wasn't the first time southern elite whites adopted this federalist strategy.

UI and ADC are administered by the states. The southern Democrats wrote this provision into the original Social Security Act, and it is still in place today. There are significant differences in terms of who receives benefits depending on whether the federal government or the state governments oversee the program. As Lieberman pointed out, blacks benefited from the administration of the bureaucratic workings of OAI. Social Security numbers are not tied to any ascribed status at birth. The anonymity of administering bureaucratic policy did not protect blacks from a racist job market. Although excluding blacks and women from OAI helped preserve agrarian economic power, the southern Democrats sought complete control of the distribution of benefits by inserting the federalist notion of state rights into the Social Security Act. White agrarian elites and other segregationists have championed states' rights since the Civil War when they argued that states should have the right to decide if they wanted black slavery or not. The call for states' rights is synonymous with racism.[6]

States administer the two Social Security programs associated with financial need and poverty. UI is more of a demand-side macroeconomic policy designed to prevent an economic recession or a depression than a policy designed to assist those who lost their jobs. It's a demand-side policy because it makes direct payments to the unemployed so that they continue to spend and pay their bills while looking for a new job. If the unemployment rate gets too high, people have no money to spend, and businesses go under because of decreased revenue, which causes further unemployment. Short-term unemployment was common in factories. Some manufacturing was seasonal. Car manufacturers closed the factory every year for one to three months to retool the machines for the following year's automobiles. Window factories closed in the winter as the home construction and home improvements markets slowed down. States were allowed to set their own UI rates and policies. However, one has to prove an employment history before one qualifies for unemployment. The white-private economy creates more black unemployment for longer periods of time relative to whites. The wage discrepancy between whites and blacks works against blacks over UI payments. Provisions within UI allow states to deny workers unemployment for refusing to work or for insubordination. Blacks and whites are denied UI for different reasons. Blacks are more likely to be denied for insubordination. Whereas elites have attacked UI as another incentive not to work, UI has remained popular with white workers.[7]

States had the most control over ADC. Unsurprisingly, it is also where we find the most blatant practices of racial exclusions. Local administrators wrote local welfare policy in relation to the specific representations of the poor. Laws, statutes, and standards determining need are only one-half of the equation to determine ADC benefits. The other half was the subjective evaluation of ADC applicants. Local administrators could divide whites into groups of deserving and undeserving poor in states and counties that were almost exclusively white. Blacks were disproportionately poorer and more likely to live in poverty than whites, especially in southern states. Yet blacks were less likely to receive ADC benefits, and when they did receive them, the checks were for much less than those of their poor white counterparts. In 1940, blacks did receive higher ADC payments in northern states, like Pennsylvania, New York, Michigan, and Ohio—states with cities with large industrial manufacturing bases where ADC helped protect the white industrial labor market and supply votes to the local Democratic political machines. The most important variable that explains the variability

THE SEGREGATED WELFARE STATE 117

of ADC coverage from 1940 to 1960 was the percent of the population that was black.[8]

We can see the dominance of white-public during the expansion of the Social Security Act by looking at the weakness of elite opposition to the Social Security Act. For one, the private charity organizations that championed white-private forms of public assistance were virtually nonexistent. These private charities and religious organizations had, for all intents and purposes, disappeared with the passage of the Social Security Act. The private charities of the 19th century, founded through endowments, remained through the 20th century. They included the YMCA (1851), the Salvation Army (1878), and the United Way (1887). Other private charities administering social services, like the Hull House, did not. The privatization of social services would not return until the 1980s. The second was the weakness of elites to stop the passage of the Social Security Act. The southern Democrats attempted legal action on the grounds that the Social Security Act was unconstitutional. They excluded as many blacks as they could, which ended up strengthening the language of white-public.

The development of the American welfare state resulted in a decentered network of federal, state, local, and private entities designed to regulate the white labor market. The expansion of the white-public welfare state across multiple lines indicates the early limits of privatization and austerity strategies. The debates over the worthiness of the poor, the corruption of patronage politics, outright elite opposition, or elite control over the administration of means-tested benefits could not prohibit the expansion of the white-public welfare state. But the potential of black inclusion into the welfare state did. It was impossible for whites to completely exclude blacks without sacrificing the entire system. So elites erected as many obstacles and roadblocks as possible to exclude blacks, whether it was the legal exclusion of occupational categories or the social worker's subjective decision whether a poor family provided a suitable home or not. In states with a high black population, ADC payments were equivalent to 30% of local wages. ADC payments were 70% of local wages in states with a small proportion of blacks relative to whites. When ADC was renamed Aid to Families with Dependent Children (AFDC) in 1962, it was still an expansion of the welfare state because conservative legislators saw ADC as discouraging marriage. It was expanded again in 1967 to include males with a work history. Mass black inclusion into the welfare state initiated the start of the retraction of the welfare state, which began in the early 1970s and lasted until 1995 when Bill Clinton fulfilled his promise to end welfare as we knew it.[9]

Black-Public and the Privatization of Social Welfare: An AFDC to TANF Case Study

The combination of black civic inclusion and increased black migration from rural areas to the cities changed the composition of who was perceived to benefit from means-tested programs like AFDC. The proportion of black families who received ADC benefits rose from 36% in 1953 to 43% in 1961. White America's growing frustration at white tax dollars supporting blacks was not entirely new in the civil rights era. Historians and sociologists who specialize in southern history have long noted the belief among southern elites that only whites paid taxes. I have no reason to think that northern, western, Midwestern, or southwestern whites thought much differently. As Jill Quadagno noted, "There is a good reason for Americans to understand coded messages about social policy as substitutes for discussions of race, for real linkages between race and policy exist." Things changed a bit in the civil rights era. Whereas racist elite whites wrote the Social Security Act to exclude blacks, women, and other racial minorities, their racist policies created a self-fulfilling prophecy: the exclusion of blacks from the booming postwar economy amplified black poverty and the number of black families seeking help from ADC. What was new in the civil rights era was how discussions of the welfare state switched from a discussion of who was worthy to questioning the merits of the entire system once it was racially integrated.[10]

The visibility of the urban black poor, who would dominate representations of urban poverty and crime starting in the 1980s, originated with AFDC in the mid-1960s. Existing black stereotypes that blacks were lazy, unwilling to work, and sexually irresponsible were synonymous with depictions of the undeserving poor. As Martin Gilens showed, white perceptions of who receives welfare and means-tested programs do not reflect who actually receives welfare: "this problem has been exacerbated by the emergence of a highly visible black urban underclass that has exerted an inordinate influence over popular images of blacks, even though it constitutes a small fraction of African Americans." But, as Wilson has pointedly noted, the majority of long-term welfare recipients tend to be women of color in spite of the fact that whites make up the numerical majority on welfare. In other words, black stereotypes did not die during the civil rights era, and the economic situation of marginalized black women worsened.[11]

Johnson's War on Poverty involved creating new federal agencies to administer and disburse federal money. These agencies included the Office of Economic Opportunity (OEO), which funded a series of local Community Action Agencies (CAAs). CAAs were responsible for job training, drug and alcohol rehabilitation, and running local health-care centers. The creation of the OEO seemed like an innocent expansion of the federal bureaucracy. For the segregationists, liberal business class, and other conservatives, the OEO represented the switch from white-public to black-public. The black-public-welfare link was forged through elite white and middle-class racial anxieties over the possibility of empowering poor black communities. This is the point at which we find the origins of abstract neoliberal phrases like 'small government'. The rhetoric of small government acquired its racist code in relation to the expansion of black-public welfare.

Another important process in the assemblage of black-public welfare was the relation between black stereotypes and working. Congressional changes to AFDC in the 1960s stressed the importance of work and returning poor women to the labor market. Work requirements were added to AFDC as part of Johnson's War on Poverty program in 1967. The work requirements included the 30 1/3 rule, which stated a woman could keep the first 30% of her paycheck instead of paying it back to AFDC. It also included a work incentive program (WIN) that funded day care and job training. Finally, the federal government created two new federal programs, Job Corps and Head Start, which were separate from AFDC but still designed to get women back into the labor market. At first glance, this seems like a gendered contradiction. The conservative male belief that a woman's place is in the home was combined with policy changes that encouraged work. In reality, poor women have always worked, often in the most dangerous workplaces. In the mid-1800s, poor white women in Philadelphia worked in matchbook factories where the phosphorous traveled from the match to their fingers and finally to their lips and tongues as they licked their fingers to help them pack matches into the boxes. The phosphorous poisoning dug holes into their cheeks and exposed their teeth. Poor white women worked in textile factories in the North and textile and hosiery factories in the South for much less pay than men. A poor woman did not have the option to stay home and take care of her children like middle-class women did.

Black women have historically worked in the unskilled service sector we now call care work. Care work refers to the aspects of the paid labor force that involve caring for another human being. This includes jobs such as childcare, working in a day care, nursing, and working as an aide in a nursing home. Women continue to do unpaid care work in the private home, caring for children and elderly parents and in-laws, as well as the home itself. Enslaved black women also picked cotton just like enslaved black men. Black women worked as domestics, taking care of elite white families' household chores of cooking, cleaning, and child-care. Sixty-three percent of black women continued to work in private households in 1960. That number was 42% in 1970. Black women worked in laundry services, farm labor, and chicken processing plants and as unskilled factory labor. At the turn of the 21st century, you'll find black women filling the ranks of nurse's aides, day-care workers, and cashiers. The best available jobs for black women were in the public sector, specifically teaching and social work. Black women stood to gain the most from the expansion of the welfare state.[12]

Black women became the face of welfare in the late 1960s. The incorporation of black women into the public arena was due more to the welfare mothers' movement than the civil rights movement. The civil rights movement inspired leftist groups to demand civic inclusion and provided a template on how to achieve protective rights. In this regard, the civil rights era is important for changing the conditions that made subsequent mobilization possible. The welfare mothers' movement, also known as the welfare rights movement, was a loose collection of local chapters that fought the negative stereotypes attached to poor women on welfare and provisions like the suitable home statute to deny black women aid. The National Welfare Rights Organization (NWRO) was active from 1966 to about 1975. Membership levels varied, as estimates ranged from 20,000 to 100,000 members at its peak. Their membership was mostly composed of black women, but white social workers were involved in many of the autonomous local chapters. The NWRO had two policy goals: to drum up public support for the expansion of welfare benefits and for a national guaranteed income. They secured some legal rights for welfare recipients and were enough of a political force to have influence over the distribution of WIN funds. Nevertheless, the importance of the NWRO was that it served as a political medium for black women to articulate their needs and their wants—needs and wants that were not identical to black men or white women.[13]

The success of the welfare mothers' movement was a double-edged sword for black women. The mobilization of poor white women transformed welfare from a handout to a citizenship right. There was a record number of AFDC recipients in 1975. The population of AFDC was racially balanced. There were fewer Americans living in poverty. By all accounts, AFDC was working to protect the most vulnerable Americans from the effects of the 1973 OPEC oil crisis. The collective efforts gave poor women political agency. However, the collision of race and gender over the issue of welfare cemented the visibility of black women with welfare rather than with gender issues like birth control and sexual liberation. The elite white male backlash toward women splintered. The social conservative and Protestant religious fundamentalist movements rose from the ashes of the Catholic-led movement against birth control and abortion. They could not stop women from legally having reproductive rights, but they could stop the federal government from funding social programs that benefit women. Black women were vulnerable to cuts in state spending because they disproportionately depended on it for employment and access to the social welfare system. Yet, black women lacked public sympathy from whites and political allies in public office in the mid-1970s.

The importance of the welfare mothers' movement and black women illustrates how the black family emerged as the proxy for black women in the late 1960s. Black women were visible to the extent that the state, segregationists, and even the black civil rights movement blamed them for black poverty. One of the key findings in Daniel Moynihan's infamous report, *The Negro Family: The Case for National Action*, was that persistent black poverty was due in part to matriarchy in the black family. Black women's employment undermined the traditional paternalistic way of life. Black women's employment did not provide any of the symbolic citizenship benefits of moral worth, dignity, or personal responsibility. Instead of being propped up as hardworking women who deserved social rights, the combination of gender and poverty shows how abstract characterizations of the worthy or unworthy poor fall apart when the variable of race is added to the equation.[14]

The Reagan era begins the start of neoliberal policy on a national level. When it came to welfare and AFDC, one immediate difference between Reagan and the three previous presidential administrations of the 1970s was Reagan's unapologetic implementation of white-private austerity. Nixon and Carter were still concerned about how the welfare state could achieve full employment. The most noteworthy reform effort was Nixon's Family Assistance Plan (FAP), which would have replaced AFDC with a guaranteed minimum income for everyone. Nixon's plan never made it out of the Senate, as white middle-class union members and business leaders rejected the plan's potential to undermine the existing social order. Carter also proposed a packaged AFDC reform that would have granted a guaranteed minimum wage while consolidating food stamps, AFDC, and disability insurance (SSI) with work-incentive programs. Although their reforms were rooted in stereotypes that the poor were lazy, they nevertheless were designed to achieve full employment. The Reagan administration had no such concerns. In an era of rising racial and economic insecurity, where elites from both political parties blamed New Deal–style social welfare programs and Keynesian economics for a decade of stagflation, elites assembled a thread of white-private austerity to drastically cut social welfare benefits.[15]

Reagan bypassed the issue of reforming welfare in favor of austerity measures to cut AFDC funding. Southern legislators had used austerity to defund public amenities rather than racially integrate them. On the heels of the Kemp-Roth tax cuts, Congress passed the 1981 Omnibus Budget Reconciliation Act, which eliminated all of the work incentives for AFDC recipients. The 30 1/3 rule and funding for childcare were gone, making work a disincentive for the poor. It also denied households who lost income because of a strike access to food stamps. It did increase the standard deduction on income taxes and authorized exceptional budgetary increases for the military. The economy was in a Federal Reserve–imposed recession. The need for AFDC increased as it was cut. Applying austerity measures to AFDC in 1981 could not have come at a worse time for poor families. This led to more families on welfare receiving fewer benefits, with each getting less. The total number of families needing AFDC still increased AFDC's budget, creating the impression that welfare spending was out of control.[16]

Every writer knows that compelling characters drive the narrative. So do politicians who routinely draw from popular narratives to round up support for their policy of choice. Elites and ordinary people tell stories as a means of communication to attract supporters and to help make sense of the world. In order to increase support for welfare reform, Clinton and the Republican Congress revived the Reagan-era character of the bad black woman: the welfare queen.[17]

Linda Taylor was the original welfare queen. She was arrested for welfare fraud in 1976. She used four aliases to collect $8,000. It wasn't just her crime that elevated Taylor from local Chicago-area criminal to the national representation of the welfare queen. It was how she looked and presented herself. She wore a fur coat and drove a Cadillac to the various welfare offices to pick up her checks. She was the dream of every antiwelfare conservative neoliberal: a living example of black-public welfare. Reagan seized on this story during his 1980 presidential run, retelling it over and over while inflating the amount of her crime. At one point, Reagan told audiences that she scammed over $150,000 a year from both welfare and Social Security.[18]

In 1996, Lillie Harden, an overweight, stout, 42-year-old dark-skinned black woman and mother of three became the new representation of the welfare queen. Dressed in an ill-fitting olive-green shirt, she was front and center at the signing of the Personal Responsibility Act. Harden's humble appearance was in stark contrast to the excess of Taylor's look. Whereas Taylor was a criminal scam artist bilking the system, Harden was cast as someone who simply refused to leave the system. The new welfare queen sat on the couch all day watching television. Welfare was her way of life. She was not personally responsible.[19]

The welfare queen did not cause elites and middle-class whites to suddenly reject welfare. The original use of and revival of the welfare queen in the 1990s illustrates how the links between blacks in general and black women in particular lurk behind neoliberal attacks against the welfare state. Public opinion polls conducted by the American National Election Study in the 1980s and 1990s indicate that the percentage of whites who thought welfare was a problem waned after Reagan's 1981 budget cuts. More whites thought poverty was a problem. Whites abruptly changed their view and once again thought welfare was a problem in 1992, especially among whites who believed that most blacks were lazier than most whites. Whites were in the middle of the tension between white-public and black-public. Elite whites supplied a plethora of negative images of black women to muster ordinary white support against the welfare state. Black women were simultaneously reproductively irresponsible, lazy, unwilling to work, and bad mothers. The image of the black 'crack whore' emerged in between the welfare queen stories as a way to criminalize black women's poverty and addiction. There has been no white welfare queen, and the hysteria over welfare once again declined after 1996.[20]

The 1996 Personal Responsibility and Work Opportunity Reconciliation Act (PRWORA) ended AFDC and replaced it with Temporary Aid to Needy Families (TANF). AFDC remained underfunded but stable until Bill Clinton promised to end welfare as we knew it when he ran for reelection. On the eve of the new debate over welfare reform, 38.9% of AFDC recipients were white, 37.2% were black, and 17.8% were Hispanic. Sociologists were debating if urban blacks represented some sort of underclass—a social class below that of the poor—or if a culture of poverty hindered poor blacks' ability to move into the middle class. Was welfare really an economic, political, or cultural problem in 1994? Or did it represent a political opportunity for an opportunistic neoliberal Democrat to rally the white middle class to advance his political career? The number of people receiving AFDC grew in the 1980s and early 1990s because the economy was awful for ordinary Americans. Elites enjoyed the fruits of tax cuts and high-yield bonds while the poor watched skilled and unskilled manufacturing jobs handed over to machines and computers and move to Mexico and then to Asia.

TANF drew on the same black stereotypes that informed other reforms. A time limit of 5 years was set to all beneficiaries because elite whites in Congress believed that the poor were lazy and that multiple generations of black families stayed on welfare because they viewed welfare as a way of life. TANF signaled a larger shift in the administration of welfare. As Soss, Fording, and Schram argued, TANF blurred the boundaries between the labor and welfare markets. A positive relationship exists between wages and benefit levels: they rise and fall together. TANF accomplished this by combining classic paternalist practices involved in monitoring welfare recipients with the neoliberals' project of creating market opportunities. A system of incentives that included time limits and a welfare recipient's willingness to participate in job-training programs replaced the politicized and still paternalistic system of AFDC. The cultural link between work and dignity was extended to include the link of independence that could only be found in a labor market inhospitable to low-skilled and unskilled workers.

When thinking about the long history of elite white power and welfare reform, one question that we should immediately ask is why it took so long to end AFDC. According the leading scholars on this subject, the link between black and welfare forged in the 1960s existed through the 1970s and 80s, yet the neoliberals did not overhaul AFDC until the mid-1990s. From Reagan to Clinton, the neoliberals have written policies and cut budgets but have always stopped short of eliminating means-tested programs. I would like to credit social movements and other political groups for forcing elite whites to keep it around, but there is no evidence that this is the case. This is where privatization comes in.

The Reagan-era cuts to AFDC triggered the privatization of social services. Privatization was not new in the 1980s. As I mentioned at the beginning of the chapter, private charities fought to limit all forms of assistance to middle-class white widows they classified as worthy. The surviving private charities were rare. The private charities that did survive became more professional, focused almost exclusively on children and family services, and relied on donations. There were virtually no private social services in the 1960s. Social work agencies were formed because of the increase in War on Poverty funds. The one exception in the 1960s is found in the Department of Labor, which contracted out job-training services as part of the bureaucratic reorganization of the OEO.

The systemic privatization of social services begins in the neoliberal era. The Reagan and George H. W. Bush administrations called on the nonprofit sector to take a lead in managing poverty. Bush described American civil society and the nonprofit sector as 'a 1000 points of light' for leading the struggle against poverty. Public expenditures to fight poverty were converted into grants, which nonprofits competed against one another for. By 1988, the federal government earmarked over 50% of social-service expenditures to the nonprofit sector. The number of nonprofits grew 59% from 1999 to 2009. The number of nonprofit firms receiving federal funds included religious organizations, like Catholic Charities, the AFL-CIO union to provide job training, and regional nonprofits like America Works that also provide job-training services. Wisconsin, Arizona, and Florida completely privatized their TANF services in the 2000s.

The privatization of social services included the entry of for-profit firms into the poverty market. For-profit companies include MAXIMUS and Affiliated Computer Services (ACS). MAXIMUS is a publicly traded company (it trades under the symbol MMS) that brought in over $2 billion in revenue in 2015. MMS administers social welfare benefits. ACS is a tech company that manages the electronic transfers of funds, including TANF benefit cards. Xerox acquired ACS in 2012. Instead of saving money, the entry of for-profit firms into the poverty market raised the costs of social services and led to charges of corruption, while also increasing the number of errors beneficial to the firms. Colorado contracted with MAXIMUS only to find that the cost of social services tripled once they were privatized. In 2006, the state of Indiana bought out their contract with MAXIMUS because of the costs combined with poor delivery of social services to needy families. Wisconsin, Tennessee, and Washington, DC, have all charged MAXIMUS with improperly billing for Medicaid reimbursements. The entry of for-profit firms into the market of poverty management dispels the myths of excessive public spending and government inefficiencies associated with the rhetoric of small government. Since a for-profit firm, especially one that is publicly traded, needs to make money, it simply costs the state more at the expense of beneficiaries to contract out to companies like MMS and ACS.[21]

The reemergence of privatization has to be understood in relation to the limits of austerity. Another reason why it took so long to end AFDC was that austerity had simply run its course by the early 1990s. There was nothing left to cut. Elite whites have historically used austerity to minimize the available public resources that target blacks. Austerity does not reduce deficits, but it does create new poverty while amplifying the existing negative effects of poverty. The sheer increase in the number of needy families going on and off AFDC enlarged the overall budget in spite of the reduction of individual benefit levels. Elite whites could not cut AFDC levels any lower without risking throwing all poor people off AFDC, including poor white families. Given that 70% of all welfare recipients are white, congressmen and congresswomen from poor white areas did not support additional cuts. Additional cuts also risked elite white and middle-class security, as impoverished populations become desperate to survive. Which leads us to the final answer: mass imprisonment.

A final reason why it took so long to end AFDC is found in the inverse relationship between social welfare programs and imprisonment— a relationship mediated by austerity and privatization. The inverse relationship between social welfare and imprisonment was more gradual than a drastic emergence from Reagan to Clinton. Elites became preoccupied with the relationship they created between blacks and crime in the early 1970s. This relationship was engineered by the Nixon administration's War on Drugs. I dedicate a substantial part of Chapter 7 to the relationship between the racist War on Drugs and imprisonment and Bill Clinton's characterization of young black men as a new breed of super criminal. Here, I want to discuss how elites' obsession with crime temporarily stalled changes to welfare policy.

State cuts to AFDC accompanied an increase in state spending on policing, building prisons, and costs associated with incarceration. Indeed, neoliberals actually pitched the privatization of prisons as a way to save money. For many states, imprisonment became economic policy in the

1980s and 1990s, especially in the economically depressed rural areas. Prisons create a handful of jobs that range from the initial construction to the subsequent staffing to the never-ending technological upgrades used to monitor prisoners. The number of federal prisons, state prisons, county jails, and parole officers created a job market that complemented social services' historical role around managing poverty. The maturation of the prison economy created a real material interest for rural middle-class whites on the continued racist zero-tolerance policing and imprisonment of racial minorities. Black-public crime was assembled in conjunction with black-public welfare. Elite white support for the penal aspect of the state and their complementary neglect of the social welfare aspect of the state drove AFDC to the point where it was simply no longer working.[22]

It should be noted that there are important differences in how systemic racism shaped the administration of local welfare policies in the era of TANF versus the era of AFDC.

Whites' explicit racial biases were tied to depoliticizing poor black families and deregulating eligibility criteria in the civil rights era. Urban blacks' AFDC eligibility was tied to voting for the city's Democratic machine. In rural areas, like Mississippi's Delta region, elite whites expected blacks to avoid involvement in the civil rights movement in order to remain eligible. James Cobb noted how in Mississippi, "at one Delta welfare office, a white worker reportedly warned a black mother: 'If you don't stop that freedom marching, I'm going to take your children from you.'" In most cases in Mississippi, the agrarian class continued their control over the economy and welfare offices well into the late 1960s. They implemented steep cuts via white-private austerity, justified by the poor's lack of personal responsibility. Mississippi Congressman Jamie Whitten explained why he rejected lowering the cost of the food stamp program: "When you start giving people something for nothing . . . I wonder if you don't destroy character more than you might improve nutrition." In 1964, they changed the formula to calculate food stamps. The poor were required to purchase food stamps, but they couldn't afford to, so the number of food stamp recipients in Leflore County and Sunflower County dropped by more than 50% in 1 year. Infant mortality increased in Mississippi, from 40.8 per 1,000 live births in 1946 to 55.1 per 1,000 live births in 1965.[23]

THE SEGREGATED WELFARE STATE 129

Whereas the informal eligibility requirements were distinct from formal eligibility criteria in the civil rights era, they became one and the same under TANF. States were responsible for creating their own policies to determine who was eligible for TANF. They also had to pay a greater percentage of the costs. Shifting the costs to the states helped create geographic disparities in how much assistance a poor family in Virginia received compared with a poor family in New York. The greatest disparity was between the $120 a month a poor family received in Mississippi and the $555 a month a poor family received in California. However, variations between states had more to do with the proportion of minority residents than the proportion of costs. Studies show that right after TANF became the law, states with the smallest proportions of blacks and Latinos and progressive civil rights law had the most generous benefits. States with a high proportion of blacks had minimal benefits. Neoliberal elites may not like welfare, but they tolerate it as long as it secured the political cooperation of marginalized whites.[24]

The reemergence of the black family in political discourse differs from how elites pathologized the black family in the 1960s. Whereas discussions of black women pivoted around larger 'social problems' of matriarchy and then onto black welfare queens as scam artists, the black family reemerged as the site of state-led racist political intervention. Since the 1990s, at various points in time, we find local elite white policy makers obsessed with the notion that welfare recipients are drug addicts. They invest public resources into new technologies such as drug-testing kits. They rarely find any welfare recipient who tests positive for drugs. They end up as expensive political theater designed to rile up middle-class white support for the neoliberal project. Nevertheless, the drug tests are designed to be humiliating and act as a deterrent for those in need of public assistance. Additional technologies designed to keep cash out of the hands of presumed drug addicts on welfare include the electronic benefits cards. We can also measure the reemergence of the bad black family in welfare state politics via foster care. Social workers try to keep poor white families together. In contrast, they break up poor black families at an alarming rate. The number of black and Hispanic kids in foster care is disproportionately high compared to the total population of black and Hispanic children. The percentage of black children in foster care has actually decreased from 32% in 2005 to 24% in 2014. It's still alarmingly high. In contrast, the percentage of Hispanic children in foster care has increased from 18% in 2005 to 22% in 2014. The percent of white children has remained constant: 41% in 2005 and 42% in 2014.[25]

Another difference is the staffing of local welfare offices, especially the social workers in the field responsible for making decisions on who does and doesn't get assistance. In the past, elite whites set policy, controlled budgets, and staffed local welfare offices. They still set policy and control budgets. There were many reported cases of male social workers abusing the power of the position by demanding sex in exchange for benefits. Today, the majority of local welfare administrators and social workers are black women, and social workers in general tend not to have an explicit racial bias against poor black women. The white racial frame and language of white-private is not exclusive to whites and continues to influence what appears to be a racially neutral administrative practice.

The main difference is how PRWORA encourages privatization. According to a study by the US Department of Health and Human Services titled "Privatization of Welfare Services," PRWORA "has encouraged outsourcing by lifting restrictions that had placed eligibility determination off-limits for privatization." Whereas state regulations created a system of mutual dependence between nonprofits and the state throughout the 1980s, PRWORA has deregulated welfare to empower the private sector. Under the current TANF policy, the private sector can create individual personal responsibility plans, enforce sanctions, and issue vouchers for housing and childcare. The relationship between the market and the privatization of welfare is readily found in mental health and substance abuse programs that are subjected to what health insurance and Medicaid will cover, which is currently limited to cognitive behavioral therapy. The unprecedented levels of privatization of the American welfare state place the poor at the mercy of the labor market, the viability of nonprofits that depend on government grants, and for-profit companies to deliver social services while in pursuit of a profit.[26]

In sum, TANF was the result of a longer process triggered by black inclusion in the 1960s and 70s that subsequently triggered austerity

THE SEGREGATED WELFARE STATE 131

measures designed to tank the AFDC program and the coinciding rise of privatization to take the financial burden of welfare off the hands of the state. By the 21st century, the traces of TANF's racist origins are masked by what appears to be the racially neutral process of privatization. Nevertheless, it once again shows how the language of neoliberalism needs a bad black citizen to activate support for the neoliberal project. The proof is found in how benefits levels vary by state based on the proportion of the total black population.

Social Welfare and the 21st Century White-Private Welfare State

On the eve of the 21st century, it appeared that Clinton's signature neoliberal welfare policy was a success. The number of families receiving means-tested programs declined 12% by 1999. This should be an expected outcome of any social welfare policy with time limits that ranged from 3 to 5 years depending on the state. Any data that indicated a reduction in the number of TANF recipients in the late 1990s was tainted by two additional factors. The first was the development and expansion of the technological sector. Although it resulted in a bubble, the tech sector did drive a brief period of historic economic growth. The second was related to the sheer number of people in prison—almost two million by 2000. Official unemployment data does not include those no longer actively looking for work or those imprisoned, which artificially deflates the official unemployment rate. Although sociologists and economists focus on metrics like structural employment, defined as the percent of the total population employed, and wage growth, the official unemployment rate continues to drive policy decisions. And when America entered another recession, another war, and then a great recession to start off the 21st century, it was ill equipped to handle the crises of bloated prison budgets, limited TANF budgets, and the increasing need for UI.

Neoliberalism creates a situation where social services work only when the need is limited. The Great Recession increased the need for unemployment and welfare. Barack Obama signed a bill that extended unemployment benefits from 26 weeks up to potentially 99 weeks based on how bad a state's unemployment was and the willingness of states to fund their share of unemployment benefits, but only after a prolonged ideological fight between the Democrats and Republicans, who insisted on more austerity. Not all states maxed out their share of the contribution. It's important to note two things regarding UI in the aftermath of the Great Recession. First, in spite of ideological differences over UI's effect on the American work ethic, the federal government and many states extended the length of time one could receive UI because unemployment insurance protects the national economy from any subsequent economic downturns that also affect elite whites. Second, and most important, UI was not privatized. In fact, UI benefited from the Extended Benefits program Congress passed in 1970. The Extended Benefits program gave Congress the authority to provide additional weeks of UI to those who exhausted their 26 weeks. And because UI remained a white-public program designed to protect the white-private labor market, it could be expanded to respond to economic downturns. Neither federal nor state governments can make the necessary adjustments when social services are privatized. Nonprofit and for-profit firms rely on government contracts and grants that cover future rather than present estimations of need. According to a study by the Urban Institute, the nonprofit response to the Great Recession was to cut benefits, jobs at the agency, and the number of programs offered to the poor—the exact opposite of what is needed in a recession.

In spite of the cuts and continued privatization of social services, we did see an expansion of the number of Americans receiving disability benefits (SSI) in the white-private welfare state. The number of Americans receiving SSI payments from 2001 to 2011 increased by 68.9%. The expansion of disability insurance is related to the downturn of the labor market and TANF. Just like prison inmates, the number of people who receive disability insurance is not counted toward the official unemployment numbers. As the time limits for receiving welfare began expiring around 2001, a fair number of people were simply unemployable, meaning they did not have the necessary skills—technical or personal—to remain in the labor market. It's pretty cheap to place the poor on disability. Just like TANF benefits, SSI payments are extremely low. The formula to calculate SSI benefits is one-third of one's highest 5-year earning period. In 2016, the average yearly SSI stipend was $13,980. The official poverty rate for a single person in 2016 was $11,880 and $20,160 for a family of three.[27]

THE SEGREGATED WELFARE STATE   133

Despite the dismal benefit amounts, the sheer number of SSI recipients led to an increase in the overall budget. The numbers of SSI applicants and awards have slightly declined between 2012 and 2016. We can credit part of the drop to the subsequent economic recovery. However, we can also credit the decline of applications due to the increase in middle-class complaints that too many undeserving whites were receiving SSI. In this case, the elite response to the political backlash was found in judges cracking down on award decisions. The process of applying for disability isn't complicated, but it's not exactly easy either. That's why a cadre of lawyers specializing in disability insurance exists to guide applicants through the process of applying for SSI and appealing a judge's decision. The process basically goes like this. You make a claim, backed by a medical doctor, that your disability prevents you from working. A judge will determine if you are unable to find suitable work. The state employs an occupational specialist to help the judge make this decision. The occupational specialist matches your job with its corresponding census occupational category. In this case, your disability that is preventing you from working has to reflect your occupational category. Of those receiving DI, 33.8% do so for back pain. Neoliberals and many ordinary Americans have cried foul at the number of undeserving people receiving SSI, echoing the chorus of Americans singing the song of corruption to VA pensions in the early 1900s. From 2011 to 2015, the number of new applicants declined by 16.2% and number of new awards declined by 24.3%. Nevertheless, there were still over 8.9 million Americans who received SSI in 2015, an increase of 3.8%.

So why haven't elites targeted SSI like they did AFDC? It may be that they have started the process given the increase in the number of new claims that are denied that began in 2011. It may be that elite whites have some compassion and do not want to kick off citizens who face severe disabilities. But SSI remains a white-public program and has not yet faced significant benefit cuts, time limits, or having aspects of SSI privatized. This is somewhat surprising given that blacks were 22.7% of working-age SSI recipients and 30% of the child SSI recipients in 2009. Blacks were twice as likely to receive DI and four times as likely to receive SSI in the late 1980s and 1990s as well. Yet, the racist attacks against the welfare state only targeted AFDC. The drastic increase of

SSI started in 2001. There are not many studies of the racial disparities or the expansion of SSI. What we do know is that the Bush administration stopped collecting data on the race and ethnicity of SSI applicants. Whether intentional or not, this new color-blind policy makes it difficult for neoliberals to define SSI as a black-public program. Looking at the increase in SSI from 2000 to 2010, Sandy Wong found an association between a large percentage of whites at the county level and SSI benefits. Thus, the available data supports the theory that the language of white-public protects SSI from austerity and privatization and allows for the expansion of SSI in the white-private neoliberal state.[28]

The failure of elites to link disability and unemployment insurance with black-public allowed for the expansion of these specific welfare state programs even within the white-private welfare state. This indicates the limits of analyzing the welfare state in terms of a racially neutral framework of the deserving or undeserving poor. Welfare state programs that support the undeserving white poor were not privatized, remained white-public, and were eligible for expansion when necessary. Added to these disparities regarding the disbursement and administration of welfare state benefits, we find that racism via the strategic deployment of the language of black-public is needed to activate neoliberal reforms. The language of neoliberalism provides a better theoretical understanding of how America's social welfare system formed than distinctions between deserving and undeserving poor.

The language of neoliberalism explains the paradox of the simultaneous expansion of the welfare state and the rise of a neoliberal state I introduced at the beginning of the chapter. The rapid inclusion of blacks into AFDC in the late 1960s and 1970s created the conditions for elites to pass drastic austerity measures aimed at AFDC while simultaneously drastically cutting taxes for elite whites. In light of the revenue shortages, elites encouraged the privatization of social services to replace public agencies. Rather than a contraction of social services or a contraction of the state, the privatization of social welfare created a new network of nonprofit and for-profit agencies. Black-public social welfare programs are a major obligation of the state that was deemed wasteful, too expensive, and a detriment to the American work ethic by elite white politicians, yet, the market around *poverty services* emerged as good business

THE SEGREGATED WELFARE STATE 135

for elites. The neoliberal project transformed poverty from a horrible condition into a lucrative market.

Notes

1. Monica Prasad, 2016, "American Exceptionalism and the Welfare State: The Revisionist Literature" *Annual Review of Political Science* 19 (May): pp. 187–203.
2. Michael B. Katz, *In the Shadow of the Poor House: A Social History of Welfare in America, 2nd Edition* (New York: Basic Books, 1996).
3. Margaret Somers and Fred Block, 2005, "From Poverty to Perversity: Ideas, Markets, and Institutions over 200 Years of Welfare Debate" *American Sociological Review* 70 (2): pp. 260–287.
4. Theca Skocpol, *Protecting Soldiers and Mothers: The Political Origins of Social Policy in the United States* (Cambridge: Harvard University Press, 1992), p. 7.
5. Gwendolyn Mink, "The Lady and the Tramp: Gender, Race, and the Origins of the American Welfare State" pp. 92–122 in *Women, the State, and Welfare*, edited by Linda Gordon (Madison: University of Wisconsin Press, 1990).
6. On the link between Unemployment Insurance and unemployment, see Robert Lieberman, *Shifting the Color Line: Race and the American Welfare State* (Cambridge: Harvard University Press, 1998), p. 178.
7. For a discussion on how whites continue to support Unemployment Insurance, see Martin Gilens, *Why Americans Hate Welfare: Race, Media, and the Politics of Antipoverty Policy* (Chicago: University of Chicago Press, 1999).
8. Lieberman, *Shifting the Color Line*, pp. 127–128, 136.
9. Joe Soss, Richard C. Fording, and Stanford Schram, *Disciplining the Poor: Neoliberal Paternalism and the Persistent Power of Race* (Chicago: University of Chicago Press, 2011), p. 93.
10. Jill Quadagno, *The Color of Welfare: How Racism Undermined the War on Poverty* (New York: Oxford University Press, 1994).
11. Gilens, *Why Americans Hate Welfare*, 3; William Julius Wilson, *When Work Disappears: The World of the New Urban Poor* (New York: Alfred A Knoff, 1996).
12. The historical precedent of black women working in social work and teaching professions was well established as the only professional jobs available to black women since the 1940s. It was a contentious subject within the black nationalist movement. In a speech at Morgan State College, Stokely Carmichael sarcastically asked the audience of black women if they wanted to pursue careers as social workers to "keep the kid in the ghetto" (see Hohle, *Black Citizenship and Authenticity in the Civil Rights Movement*, pp. 123–124 for more on this debate). On the physical toll, health dangers, and presence of black women in the southern poultry processing centers, see LaGuana Gray, *We Just Keep Running the Line: Black Southern Women and the Poultry Processing Industry* (Baton Rouge: Louisiana University Press, 2014). On the history of black women's employment see Enobong Branch, *Opportunity Denied: Limiting Black Women to Devalued Work* (New Jersey: Rutgers University Press, 2011).
13. On the history of the welfare mothers' movement, see Susan Handley Hertz, *The Welfare Mothers' Movement: A Decade of Change for Poor Women?* (Washington, DC: University Press of America, 1981) for an excellent ethnographic account of a welfare mothers' movement in Minneapolis; Quadagno, *The Color of Welfare*, Chapter 5; Premilla

Nadasen, *Welfare Mothers: The Welfare Rights Movement in the United States* (New York: Routledge, 2005); Martha Davis, 1996, "Welfare Rights and Women's Rights in the 1960s" *Journal of Policy History* 8 (1 January): pp. 144–165.

14. For the debates surrounding the black family and the Moynihan report, see Hohle, *Black Citizenship and Authenticity in the Civil Rights Movement*, p. 58.

15. Brian Steensland, *The Failed Welfare Revolution: America's Struggle Over Guaranteed Income Policy* (Princeton, NJ: Princeton University Press, 2009).

16. Details of the 1981 Omnibus Bill located at www.congress.gov/bill/97th-congress/house-bill/3982

17. For examples on how political elites tell stories to round up political support, see Ronald Jacobs and Sarah Sobieraj, 2007, "Narrative and Legitimacy: Congressional Debates about the Non-Profit Sector" *Sociological Theory* 25 (1) (March): pp. 1–25.

18. For an in-depth look at Linda Taylor's life, see Josh Levin's article titled "The Welfare Queen" at slate.com. Article located at www.slate.com/articles/news_and_politics/history/2013/12/linda_taylor_welfare_queen_ronald_reagan_made_her_a_notorious_american_villain.html

19. Barbara Vobejda, "Clinton Signs Welfare Bill" *Washington Post*, 23 August 1996, located at www.washingtonpost.com/wpsrv/politics/special/welfare/stories/wf082396.htm

20. Survey data reported in Soss, Fording, and Schram, *Disciplining the Poor*, p. 70.

21. For a summary of the problems surrounding the privatization of social services, see Nick Surgey and Katie Lorenze, "Profiting from the Poor: Outsourcing Social Services Puts Most Vulnerable at Risk" published 8 October 2013, originally published at prwatch.org, locate at www.prwatch.org/news/2013/10/12264/profiting-poor-outsourcing-social-services-puts-most-vulnerable-risk

22. Loic Wacquant describes the growth of prisons in this period as going through a vertical and horizontal expansion to capture the number of citizens imprisoned and on parole and the number of new prisons built during this time frame. See Wacquant, *Prisons of Poverty*, pp. 55–131.

23. James Cobb, 1990, "Somebody Done Nailed Us on the Cross: Federal Farm and Welfare Policy and the Civil Rights Movement in the Mississippi Delta" *Journal of American History* 77 (3 December): pp. 912–936, 924, 932.

24. For a summary of the research on the perception of who is on welfare and state disparities, see Chapter 8 in Gilens, *Why Americans Hate Welfare*.

25. Soss, Fording, and Schram, *Disciplining the Poor*, p. 58; the most recent foster care statistics are available through the Children's Bureau. See "Foster Care Statistics 2014" March 2016, located at www.childwelfare.gov/pubPDFs/foster.pdf

26. For the argument on how privatization led to government intrusion in the 1980s, see Michael Lipsky and Steven Rathgeb Smith, 1989–1990, "Nonprofit Organizations, Government and the Welfare State" *Political Science Quarterly* 104 (1): pp. 625–648; US Department of Health and Human Services, "Privatization of Welfare Services", located at https://aspe.hhs.gov/legacy-page/privatization-welfare-services-review-literature-chapter-ii-current-state-social-service-privatization-147441

27. See selected data from Social Security's Disability Program, located at www.ssa.gov/oact/STATS/dibStat.html

Patricia P. Martin and John Murphy, 2014, "African Americans: Description of Social Security and Supplemental Security Income Participation and Benefit Levels

THE SEGREGATED WELFARE STATE 137

Using the American Community Survey" Social Security Office of Retirement and Disability Policy, Research and Statistics, 2014. Note NO. 2014–01, located at www.ssa.gov/policy/docs/rsnotes/rsn2014-01.html

28. Patricia Martin, "Why Researchers Now Rely on Surveys for Race Data on OASDI and SSI Programs: A Comparison of Four Major Surveys" Social Security Administration, Social Security Office of Retirement and Disability Policy, Research and Statistics, January 2016; Sandy Wong, 2016, "Geographies of Medicalized Welfare: Spatial Analysis of Supplemental Security Income in the US, 2000–2016" *Social Science and Medicine* 160 (July): pp. 9–19.

5

THE NEOLIBERAL METROPOLIS
RACIAL SEGREGATION, SUBURBANIZATION, AND GENTRIFICATION

A curious issue arose in the wake of the Great Recession. Recent college graduates and young people, dubbed millennials by people who name generations, are no longer buying houses. Instead, they are opting to either rent or live with their parents until they can pay off their student loans and other consumer debt. Some have attributed the change in homeownership to the effects of the Great Recession. The Great Recession was the result of a housing bubble caused by banks that sold derivatives made up of packages of risky mortgages that promised no risk and high returns. Once the real estate speculation ended and the bubble popped, banks were left holding property that was no longer valuable. In turn, property values nosedived and ordinary Americans were left with underwater mortgages. Many simply walked away from their homes. Over the past 10 years, urban planners who identify with the school of new urbanism have become aroused at the sight of developers converting former factories and empty warehouses into some combination of lofts, market-rate apartments, ground-level retail storefronts, office space, and boutique hotels. They refer to this type of development as mixed use, although they ignore Jane Jacob's insistence that mixed use meant a mix of old and new buildings that could support a diversity of social classes and racial and ethnic groups, not just consumer choices. Some have gone so far as to dub this the 'return to the city movement'. So, have young people forgone the American dream of homeownership? Have the shackles of student loan debt prohibited young people from starting their adult lives? Has there been a shift in cultural preferences from homeownership to loft living? Not exactly. Young people are split over wanting to live in trendy, upscale urban neighborhoods or the outer suburbs. So they're still buying homes, they're just not buying starter homes in the neighborhoods where their parents typically bought their first homes.[1]

There is more to the question of declining homeownership among millennials, and it has to do with why they are only opting for one of two types of neighborhoods. Let's take a look at data readily available through the US Census on where different racial groups live. The 2010 Census showed that for the first time in US history more than 50% of all racial groups live in the suburbs. There is a difference in which suburbs whites and minorities live in. Blacks and Latinos are more likely to live in the inner-ring suburbs, whereas upper-middle-class whites overwhelmingly live in the outer suburbs, which are almost exclusively composed of other well-to-do whites. When we link the data together, what we find is that white millennials are avoiding living in the older and racially integrated inner suburbs. And since they cannot afford the 3,200-square-foot McMansion in the outer-ring suburbs or the house in the gentrified urban neighborhood, they either rent or remain at their parents' home until they can afford to purchase a home in a white-private neighborhood. The issue of millennial homeownership is not a story of student loan debt or new urbanism. It's another story of residential segregation.[2]

The racial segregation of American cities has been an ongoing process since the turn of the 20th century. The legacy of American slavery tethered blacks to southern plantations immediately after the Civil War. Freed slaves were forced back onto the plantations via the convict-lease system at the end of reconstruction. In 1900, 80% of blacks still lived in the South and in rural areas. However, by 1970, 80% of blacks lived in urban areas. The rapid movement of blacks to urban areas in the 20th century was largely due to the industrialization of the American economy. The mechanization of agriculture eliminated the need for cheap and labor-intensive farmwork. The combination of factory jobs due to

140 THE NEOLIBERAL METROPOLIS

the wartime economy combined with the myth of less racism in the North directed southern black migration patterns to New York, Chicago, Philadelphia, and Detroit. It also directed rural black migration patterns to Birmingham, Alabama; Atlanta, Georgia; and Jackson, Mississippi. Blacks found neither good jobs nor less racism in the North or in the city. Instead, blacks entered a living pattern Massey and Denton characterized as American Apartheid: the persistence of racial segregation that amplifies the social problems that come with poverty.[3]

Racial segregation is more than just the forced concentration and subsequent social isolation of poor and working-class blacks and Latinos in America's ghettos. The making of American metropolitan areas in the neoliberal era also meant the racial segregation of whites in specific urban neighborhoods and suburbs. Once we move beyond the city limits, America's suburbs, ex-burbs, edge cities, and small towns were basically all white until the turn of the 21st century. James Loewen called these all-white areas "sundown towns"after the white threat "Nigger, don't let us catch you here after the sun goes down." Although the majority of the black and Latino population resided in the suburbs by 2010, 65% of suburban residents were white. The rise of black and Latino suburbanization obscures two key facts: the fastest-growing suburbs are the outer suburbs, which are basically all white and wealthy, and over half of American cities are now majority minority.[4]

Residential segregation provides a spatial home for the neoliberal project. Whereas past generations of whites fled actual instances of racial segregation, today a generalized racialized insecurity exists among ordinary whites. On the one hand, elite whites never left the city. Elite white institutions like private schools ensured that the children of elites attended schools with other wealthy white children. They have barricaded themselves in gated communities and luxury apartments guarded by private security firms, championed private user fees to pay for services they use instead of tax dollars to pay for services everyone uses, and backed the militarization of the police force. On the other hand, working-class whites also never left the city. They couldn't afford to. Deindustrialization and the decline of good-paying unions made it so working-class whites could not afford to move to the suburbs. The old white working-class neighborhoods became the places of gentrification in the 1990s and 2000s. The process of gentrification reinvigorated the old neighborhood racial boundaries that symbolically marked a neighborhood as white and allowed suburban elites to triumphantly return to the neoliberal city.

The neoliberal metropolis is an elaborate network of economically and racially segregated settlement spaces. This chapter focuses on the causal role of white-private spaces that maintains the symbiotic relationship between racial segregation, gentrification, and suburbanization. The socio-spatial approach emphasizes the causal importance of economic, political, and cultural interests to determine land use. Social space is a contingent process mediated by racism, elite economic and political interests, and privatization. Mark Gottdiener outlined an understanding of urban space that was the result of both vertical and horizontal practices, resulting in multinodal and multicentric regional development, instead of a single city center that dominates regional growth and living arrangements. The vertical practices capture the relations between the state, financial capital, real estate elites, and businesses on urban space. The horizontal practices capture the importance of culture, as well as the relations between residents and neighborhood associations. Thus, the neoliberal metropolis is a multinodal network made up of heterogeneous racialized settlement spaces.[5]

Racial Segregation and the Spirit of Racial Zoning

There is nothing natural about residential segregation even though combinations of social class, ethnicity, and race have always divided our cities. Over the course of the 20th century, there was a shift from legal means to an economic logic to maintain racial segregation. Legal forms of segregation were a feature of white-public spaces. Jim Crow laws legally segregated public life and created a checkerboard pattern of racial segregation in southern cities. The checkerboard pattern captures how blacks and whites lived side by side in southern urban areas. Since all schools and public facilities were racially segregated, as well as everyday public life, blacks living in close proximity to whites did not threaten the white power structure. Black women worked in the homes of elite white families. They cleaned white homes, cooked food for white families, did white people's laundry, and took care of elite white kids. The absence of public transportation meant that blacks walked to work. The Jim Crow legal and economic structure of southern cities didn't necessitate a pattern of neighborhood segregation like in the North.[6]

Northern cities used a system of racial zoning laws that separated whites from blacks from immigrants in order to maintain all-white neighborhoods. Racial zoning laws existed within a larger regulatory field of land use. A regulatory field of land use comprises planners, residents, businesses, and the state, which determine the use and physical form of the urban environment. To deregulate a regulatory field of land use means to change the criteria that determine who and what can occupy a given space. These criteria reflect specific elite cultural and material interests. The material uses reflect the how zoning laws separate urban areas into industrial and residential zones and the height of buildings. The cultural uses reflect how cities maintain property values and designate some areas as historic districts to allow homeowners access to special tax credits. The combined material and cultural interests over zoning laws were central to the creation of residential segregation via the legacy of racial zoning laws.

Racial zoning laws accompanied comprehensive zoning laws in the early 1900s. The racial boundaries varied by city. Some cities racially zoned by block, while other cities zoned by ward or district. Although American cities were planned to some degree prior to the Civil War, it was not until the progressive planning movements that elite whites thought they could solve social problems by redeveloping cities. Los Angeles and New York used zoning laws to prevent the industrial and garment factories from spreading into the wealthy white neighborhoods. Since immigrants and the white working class resided in the factory zones and zones of transition, keeping factories out of elite areas meant keeping poor whites, immigrants, and blacks out of elite areas. Although there were no Jim Crow laws in the North, northern and western cities used a combination of direct and indirect racial zoning practices to create residential segregation.[7]

Southern cities also used racial zoning laws to reinforce residential segregation despite the existence of Jim Crow laws. Blacks were beginning to make some economic and social gains after the turn of the century. The use of racial zoning laws in cities was a response to the

THE NEOLIBERAL METROPOLIS   143

growing number of black residents in cities in the upper southern rim, like Louisville, Richmond, Atlanta, and Baltimore. Silver argued that racial zoning laws sprang up in relation to increases of 30–50% in the black population and had little to do with economic concerns, "Racial zoning in southern cities was as much a foundation for overall land use regulations as were regulation of the garment industry in New York City or encroaching industrial uses in Los Angeles." Baltimore was the first city to develop a comprehensive set of racial zoning ordinances to reinforce segregation. Baltimore's mayor argued that the city needed racial zoning laws because "blacks should be quarantined in isolated slums in order to reduce the incidents of civil disturbances, to prevent the spread of communicable disease into the nearby white neighborhoods, and to protect property values among the white majority." Other southern cities quickly followed. Jim Crow laws alone no longer ensured segregated white-public spaces.[8]

Racial zoning laws existed until 1917, when the Supreme Court ruled in *Buchanan v. Warley* that racial zoning ordinances were illegal. Although racial zoning was outlawed, the spirit of racial zoning continued to shape American cities. Unlike European states, which have relied on direct planning from the state, America has historically followed indirect planning. Indirect planning means setting policy instead of formal state planning. In turn, indirect planning creates multiple opportunities for finance, elites, real estate, and land speculators on the regional, metropolitan, and state level to organize social space. The practice of enforcing residential segregation was split horizontally between city planners and a network of real estate elites, homeowners associations, and block clubs. The available federal funds targeted for urban renewal did not accompany any regulations or oversight as to how or where the money was spent. Local elites relied on urban planners to organize cities around black-public and white-private spaces after the *Buchanan* ruling.[9]

A growing liberal business class comprising a network of local political elites, bankers, and real estate developers replaced industrial elites after World War II. In turn, they began remaking cities to reflect the economic and cultural interests of the liberal business class. They folded racial zoning laws into new strategies of privatizing public space and deregulating land use. This was evident in how urban planners created land clearance zones. Land clearance zones meant demolishing slums and removing people from residential neighborhoods adjacent to the central business district. Land clearance zones followed the neighborhood and ward lines originally established by racial zoning. For example, Atlanta's business class deregulated zoning laws by rezoning land adjacent to the central business district as low density. It was a black neighborhood. This land was already zoned for residential purposes. The new zoning ordinances changed it to commercial land use in the 1950s, allowing for the construction of a luxury hotel and a civic center. The city forced the black families to move on the basis that this social space was now reserved for commercial use. Atlanta's elite white business class used urban development money to relocate black families to existing segregated black neighborhoods. They also deregulated land use codes to construct highways that also traced the existing lines of racial segregation. The construction of the Westview Parkway in Atlanta followed an old racial zoning line between a black and a white neighborhood. Atlanta also deregulated housing codes to standardize construction materials and make workplaces safer. This ended up increasing the cost of constructing new homes and made tearing down slums more cost effective than constructing new low-income housing.[10]

The spirit of racial zoning is also found in a technique known as 'redlining'. Redlining involves banks refusing to grant mortgages and home equity loans to prospective homebuyers in black neighborhoods. The rationale for redlining came from the creation of the Federal Housing Association (FHA), a federal agency created through the National Housing Act of 1934. The FHA provided federal mortgage insurance but only to homes that could obtain a 'high favorable rating'. A high favorable rating meant that there was an absence of 'adverse factors' that jeopardized housing values. FHA guidelines defined racial integration as an adverse factor: "The more important among the adverse influential factors are the ingress of undesirable racial or nationality groups." The FHA made exceptions so as not to infringe on elite white privileges, such as excluding the "occupancy of domestic servants of a different race domiciled with an owner or tenant." The 1935 guidelines extended what constituted an adverse factor to include "a lower class of inhabitants." Furthermore, FHA guidelines formally endorsed racial covenants in

THE NEOLIBERAL METROPOLIS 145

decisions regarding insuring a home. Racial covenants prohibited the sale of white homes to blacks and were an integral early practice to maintain segregated neighborhoods.[11]

The result of the FHA underwriting guidelines was an overtly racist method of defining which areas were deemed worthy of mortgage insurance. Banks mapped out the city into green, blue, yellow, and red zones to target areas they deemed worthy of investment. The green areas were the suburbs, the blue areas were desirable white neighborhoods, yellow areas were the declining neighborhoods most likely to be racially integrated, and the red neighborhoods were the worst neighborhoods. The redlined neighborhoods were predominately black. Bankers and real estate elites used redlining simultaneously with land clearance zones to create the bad neighborhoods they claimed their maps only represented. Denying blacks access to loans ensured that slumlords controlled the rental market. Denying blacks access to lines of credit ensured that blacks did not have the funds to paint, repair porches, or replace roofs and windows. Since banks only issued loans to green and yellow areas, the invisible hand of the market was actually a visible white hand pointing the way to the suburbs.

The vertical racial zoning practices were linked with the horizontal racial zoning practices of white neighborhood associations and real estate elites. The civil rights movement's initial focus on desegregating public spaces initiated a tremendous backlash from whites. Although the fight over school desegregation provided much of the political theater during the civil rights era, school desegregation existed in a larger network of neighborhoods segregated by race and class. Thus, the fight over schools was simultaneously a fight over neighborhoods, pitting working-class whites against blacks. School desegregation was not as much of a threat to elites as it was to working- and middle-class whites, but elites enjoyed using publicly funded segregated golf courses. The importance of horizontal racial zoning practices emerged at the limits of deregulation and thus began the experiment of privatization.

Privatization is the method of controlling resources and public space through nonprofit and for-profit organizations. Creating white-private urban spaces exists alongside deregulation. Zoning deregulations alone can ensure placement. But it takes white-private deregulation and privatization to force relocation and displacement. Kevin Kruse showed prior to the process of white flight and suburbanization, whites symbolically and materially abandoned integrated public spaces. Whites who could not afford to move to the suburbs embraced privatization. They stopped using public pools and public transportation and subsequently no longer supported using public funds to maintain public facilities. A market for private cars, backyard swing sets, and private pools developed around the racist practice of privatization. In Atlanta, working-class whites organized through local neighborhood and property owners associations to work with bankers and the Homeowners Loan Corporation to help redline neighborhoods. To keep the peace between whites, Atlanta's mayor persuaded blacks to move to black neighborhoods rather than working-class white neighborhoods. Thus, privatization overcame class differences between elite whites and middle- and working-class whites because privatization linked all whites into the embryonic neoliberal project via residential segregation.[12]

The spirit of racial zoning explains how elite whites shaped the composition of the neoliberal city, carving out spaces for commerce and residential spaces stratified by race and class. The long-term effect was the concentration of wealth in elite white areas, racialized insecurity in middle- and working-class white areas, and blacks and poverty in black neighborhoods. Massey and Denton connected the Great Depression with the economic downturn in the 1970s to show how additional economic changes are historically "confined primarily to poor black neighborhoods." The Great Depression wiped out black-owned banks and insurance companies, black newspapers folded, and factories near black neighborhoods closed. Despite gains during the civil rights era, including affirmative action and school desegregation, they were not enough to overcome deindustrialization, job loss, and the real wage loss since 1973. Thus, the spirit of racial zoning laws created multiple settlement spaces to set up not only the neoliberal city but also the neoliberal metropolis.[13]

White Flight and Suburbanization

Today, more Americans live in the suburbs than in cities or rural areas. Less than 9% of Americans lived in the suburbs in the 1920s. This number grew modestly to 15% by 1940, before accelerating in the 1950s to the present day. The acceleration of whites moving to the suburbs is known as white flight. Although the suburbs have historically been all white, we have to be careful not to typecast all suburbs as free from social problems, as wealthy or middle class, or even as all white. Gottdiener noted that by the mid-1970s Suffolk County, NY began experiencing many of the same urban problems as cities, including the growing concentration of poverty, environmental contamination, traffic congestion, commercial strip malls, and racial segregation. Stratification between working- and middle-class whites, black ghettos, and Latino barrios has existed within the suburbs from the start.[14]

The history of suburbanization and white flight started in the 1930s. Its origins lie in a series of white-public banking deregulations that paved the way for the mass subsidization of suburban white-private homes. In addition to the 1934 National Housing Act, the federal government also passed the 1934 Veterans Administration Act (VA) and the 1935 Banking Act. The banking act deregulated the state's ability to subsidize credit markets by providing public funds to private banks by giving the Federal Reserve the authority to change interest rates. The VA Act created FHA mortgage insurance and the amortization of loans. The amortization of loans allowed the homebuyer to pay off the principle and interest over time and extended the life of the mortgage from five to 20 and eventually 30 years. As I noted above, the FHA established guidelines on where banks and insurance companies should and should not loan money. The advantages of homeownership for whites multiplied. Not only does owning a home build equity and grants one access to home equity loans, federal tax laws allowed for homeowners to deduct the interest on their home loans and local real estate taxes. This is an example of upward redistribution of wealth, as more expensive homes receive larger tax deductions. As white homes grew, so did white middle-class wealth.[15]

An elite white network made up of suburban planners, private builders, developers, and banks defined the regulatory field of the suburban land use. Local white elites formed land development corporations. Land development corporations bought up large swaths of rural land for future housing and strip plaza development. Since the suburban business and political elites were one and the same and local land development

148 THE NEOLIBERAL METROPOLIS

corporations were connected to statewide urban development agencies, speculating on land was a low-risk investment. As the suburban housing market matured, elites created a market around upgrading to new and larger homes. Local political elites deregulated zoning laws by the practice of up zoning or exclusionary zoning. Exclusionary zoning meant expanding low-density land use: more square footage, no multifamily homes, bigger backyards, bigger front yards, and more room between homes. This made subsequent suburban development wealthier and whiter. The links between suburban banking and international finance also grew in the 1970s. Suburbanization was fueled by private capital through the bond market, real estate development, and the private funding of industrial expansion. Banks linked the suburbs to global finance, as large banks bought up local banks in the growing and profitable suburbs. This gave white suburban homeowners and developers ample access to credit markets at the same time cities, New York City in particular, were on the brink of bankruptcy.[16]

Zoning, finance, regressive tax cuts, and informal tax exemptions alone do not explain the systemic racial exclusion of blacks and other minorities from the suburbs. Nor does it explain why whites ran like animals from a forest fire to the suburbs in the neoliberal era.

White flight is practically synonymous with suburbanization. Real estate developers used tactics like block busting to drive up white racial insecurity and drive down housing values. White racialized insecurity grew in relation to integrated schools more so than crime or property values. Suburban developers marketed suburban living to whites based on racially coded language of safe schools in the mid-1950s. Safe schools meant white schools, and since the suburbs were basically all white, they would not be affected by the *Brown* decision. This almost changed in the early 1970s. The federal government issued a mandate via the 1969 *Alexander* decision to desegregate schools with "all deliberate speed." Whites decided to leave the cities rather than send their children to integrated schools. In Detroit, local leaders filed a lawsuit, arguing that desegregation should extend beyond municipal lines and be carried out on a metropolitan basis. The 1974 *Milliken v. Bradley* decision stated that busing to racially balance schools could not exceed municipal boundaries. The suburbs were clearly marked as white-private, safe from racial pollution.

The popular imagination of the homogenous white middle-class suburbs never matched the reality of suburban life. Blacks and other racial minorities have always lived in the suburbs, albeit in limited numbers and confined to limited neighborhoods. Black real estate brokers guided blacks to the formally rural suburban tract as far back as the 1930s. By the 1950s, about 2.5 million blacks lived in the suburbs. Nevertheless, blacks and Latinos have experienced segregation within the segregated suburbs. In part, this was self-directed. Black peer group and organizational networks marked some parts of suburbs safe and appealing for blacks. Blacks who could afford to move to the suburbs sought out areas with a preexisting black population to avoid white violence and ridicule. The suburbs appeared all white because the first black families to move to the suburbs made themselves invisible to whites for their own protection. Increased black suburban visibility prompted whites to flee the inner-ring suburbs. As early as the 1970s, the formerly white suburb of Compton, California, became majority black, only to become majority Latino by the 1990s. Other inner-ring suburbs like Ferguson, Missouri (outside of St Louis), and Euclid, Ohio (outside of Cleveland), became majority black starting in 2000. Hispanic population growth has driven suburban growth in the Sunbelt and metropolitan areas in the southern rim, particularly Nashville, Charlotte, and Raleigh, as well as cities like Houston and Miami. A technicality in the US census that defined Latinos as white allowed Latino families to get around racial covenant laws. But the recent growth of Latinos in the suburbs is due to immigration and access to construction and unskilled service sector work. The black and Hispanic inner-ring suburbs are, unsurprisingly, poorer relative to the majority white inner-ring suburbs.[17]

Suburbanization in the neoliberal era has further advanced the neoliberal project of privatization. Orange County, California was the location for the formation of modern-day conservatism in the 1970s. Yet, the advancement of neoliberalism in the suburbs is not due to racial and class homogenization of the first wave of postwar suburbanization. It's due to racial integration, specifically, the selective inclusion of good black citizens, and the shrinking white middle class. Blacks and Latinos increasingly sought refuge from concentrations of urban poverty. By 2000, over half of all Hispanics lived in the suburbs. By 2010, over half of all blacks lived in the suburbs. Yet, many of the inner-ring suburbs became poorer and subsequently darker. Elite whites responded with a renewed call of privatization to create exclusive white-private spaces, such as gated communities and the development of outer suburbs.[18]

The decline of the inner-ring suburbs began in the 1980s. Their decline was due to a combination of a housing market driven by suburban sprawl, an aging physical infrastructure, deindustrialization, and racial integration. Inner-ring suburbs are suburban areas that butt up to municipal lines. They are typically the oldest suburbs made up of the modest, single-family homes that range from 750 to 900 square feet. In contrast, new suburban development in the outer suburbs feature houses around 2,200 square feet. The start of the neoliberal era amplified the process of deindustrialization and, for the first time, hit the white middle and working class, subsequently impacting the suburban housing market.

The process of deindustrialization combined with the introduction of neoliberal monetary policy, a.k.a. the Volcker Shock, kept working- and middle-class whites in place. Deindustrialization eliminated many of the good-paying union jobs that made the white middle class possible to whites without college degrees. It also drove down wages in the trade unions, such as electricians, plumbers, and carpenters, who are dependent on new housing startups. Wages declined while job insecurity rose. The Volcker Shock raised interest rates to their highest levels ever. This made getting a mortgage difficult for any family that could not afford the high-interest mortgage payments. It slowed down homebuying and the practice of trading up to larger houses. It also forced many working- and middle-class whites to essentially stay in place for the first time since the civil rights era.

Although credit markets loosened in the 1990s as the Federal Reserve lowered interest rates, the unionized factory jobs did not return. This left the white working class in place in areas with declining housing values and middle-class whites fiercely clinging to their dwindling white privilege. For whites who were unable and in some cases unwilling to sell their homes and trade up to the larger homes in the outer suburbs, the inner-ring suburbs became more diverse. However, diversity was limited to an increase in the black and Hispanic populations to go along with working-class whites. White elites were not there. In turn, white

THE NEOLIBERAL METROPOLIS   151

racialized insecurity fueled renewed privatization strategies as whites that could no longer flee the limited racial integration of the suburbs. This pattern mirrors the period of racial integration of city neighborhoods in the 1950s, where white-private homeowner associations championed the rights of property owners and whites stopped using public amenities. The difference between then and now is there are no longer the legal mechanisms of racial zoning laws or racial covenants to enforce segregation. Only the market is left. Consequently, whites began to lean on the neoliberal market to protect their white spaces. White flight from the racially integrated inner-ring suburbs replaced white flight from the cities beginning in the 1990s and continuing into the 2000s.

Suburban elites have created a series of white-private spaces to distance and insulate themselves from blacks, Hispanics, and poor whites. Although we find the same pattern of whites invoking privatization in response to racially integrated spaces, privatization in the neoliberal era is different from the privatization that set up the neoliberal era. One difference in privatization in the 1990s was that white-private was targeted at public and private spaces as opposed to just public spaces. Cities have continued to privatize public space, via security cameras, permits, and the sale of parks and valuable waterfront space to developers. But in the suburbs, privatization has targeted existing white-private homes and white-private communities. Whereas homeowners associations advanced privatization after whites refused to pay for public services they no longer used, contemporary homeowners associations have linked white-private with notions of security and exclusion. As Frug noted, homeowners associations still use privatization as their "right to exclude", but the right to exclude is practiced through a myriad of intermediary links indirectly linked with race. Homeowners associations set their own rules and regulations on age minimums, number of inhabitants, types of flowers permitted in the garden, the collection of user fees for road maintenance, and trash collection and dictate whether you can park in your driveway or if you have to park your car in the garage.

The distinctive white-private settlement space in the neoliberal era is the gated community. Gated communities are exactly what their name entails. They are upscale suburban developments guarded by some type of gate: iron, brick, or electric. Some include 24-hour manned guardhouses and intercom systems that connect gates with the guardhouses. Gated communities began showing up in the late 1980s as developers marketed the enhanced security features to elite whites and wealthy retirees. The features of gated communities quickly spread to the white middle class. Blakely and Snyder called the rise of gated communities "forting up", as the white middle class continued to flee racially integrated schools and depreciating home values in the inner-ring suburbs. With the exception of New York City and Chicago, gated communities are more likely to be found in the South and the West than the rest of the United States. Gated communities in the South and West are the white response to the increased Hispanic suburbanization.[19]

White-private homes in the outer suburbs are linked to white-private suburban business and industrial parks. Central business districts and the highways systems that connect downtowns to the suburbs are still important. But the multinodal metropolitan region is driven by the development of suburban business districts and office parks. Access to these private parks is through a single road or entrance, possibly guarded by a private security guard manning a small white security booth. They are not on public transportation routes. Developers fight to restrict buses from picking up and dropping off passengers on their property. The probability of elite whites interacting with or encountering someone different from them is low. In 2010, affluent whites lived in suburbs that are 72.4% affluent and white.[20]

In sum, the history of suburbanization and white flight linked the white middle class with elite whites to facilitate the expansion of the neoliberal project. The combination of ever-shifting forms of racism and ever-shifting federal banking and monetary policy to create white-private markets around housing allowed for the renewal and revival of privatization. Recently, some scholars have used the term 'black flight' to describe black suburbanization. This implies that blacks are fleeing from dangerous cities and marginalized blacks the same way whites fled all blacks. 'Black flight' is a misleading term that obscures the systemic racist elements that guide suburbanization. White flight is still the dominant pattern creating multiple tiers of residential segregation, between whites and blacks, between working-class blacks and Latinos, and most important, between elite whites and everyone else. The question of black suburbanization in the neoliberal era has to be understood in relation to the black ghetto and white gentrification.

The Black Ghetto

The black ghetto was already an established institution in cities by the time the civil rights movement took an interest in residential segregation after the passage of the 1965 Voting Rights Act. Although early 20th-century black migration is typically understood as south to north, it was actually rural to urban. In 1910, 73% of blacks lived in rural areas. By 1960, 73% of the black population lived in urban areas. Northern cities like Chicago, New York, and Philadelphia saw their black populations grow. But so did southern cities like Atlanta, Georgia, and Birmingham, Alabama, and western cities like Los Angeles. Regardless of which city blacks migrated to, an all-black neighborhood was waiting for them when they got there. Northern cities like New York and Philadelphia had all-black neighborhoods by 1910. Indeed, Du Bois's seminal work, *The Philadelphia Negro*, documented the social conditions of Philadelphia's Seventh Ward, an all-black neighborhood that dated back to America's colonial era.[21]

The state subsidized the creation of the black ghetto just like it did with white suburbanization. They are each one side of the same coin. On the one hand, racial zoning laws, racial covenants, and the formal and informal practices of redlining geographically separated whites from blacks. On the other hand, these same racist practices contained blacks in urban areas whites no longer desired to occupy. The difference is the deregulation of banking and series of tax incentives that created a market for white-private homes allowed for whites to choose where they wanted to live. Blacks had little choice. Slums became overcrowded as the proportion of the urban black population continued to grow within the limited black settlement spaces. Available housing for upper- and middle-class blacks was distributed along the periphery of the ghetto or working-class white neighborhoods. Whites responded to integrated neighborhoods with privatization. However, privatization did not create the contemporary black ghetto. Black-public urban renewal policies and public housing did.

To understand how urban renewal policies created the contemporary black ghetto, we have to follow the relationship between elite whites,

154 THE NEOLIBERAL METROPOLIS

housing, suburbanization, and the redevelopment of the central business district. America had a slum problem following the Great Depression. The existing housing stock of cities was old, and there were not enough houses to accommodate demand. White suburbanization was a solution that created another problem: getting whites from the suburbs to where the professional and manufacturing jobs were. This required the construction of highways. Funded by the federal government, municipal and state officials built an elaborate highway system connecting the suburbs to the central business districts. The highways were built on the periphery of black neighborhoods, cutting them off physically and symbolically from the business districts. What happened when existing black neighborhoods were in the way? Elites demolished them and relocated the residents to public housing.

Urban renewal policies focused on the construction of public housing. Between 1940 and 1970, the federal government funded the demolition of 500,000 slums and built 900,000 public housing units. In turn, the black and minority population in public houses increased from 25% to over 60%. Public housing was spending to segregate. Public housing was segregated. Fearing that integrated public housing would create racial problems, local housing officials set aside separate public housing for whites and blacks. In the Commodore Perry Projects in Buffalo, New York, the black projects were literally across the street from the white projects. But the larger implication was the concentration of blacks and poverty in a single location.[22]

Residential segregation and the black ghetto helped to give rise to the politics of black authenticity and black nationalism in the late 1950s and early 1960s. Although Marcus Garvey popularized black nationalism via his back-to-Africa movement, black nationalism was historically an urban black political project. Its roots dated back to the Detroit of the 1930s. What made black nationalism an urban movement was more than just location. The unique physical and cultural landscape of the black ghetto shaped black experiences and social problems. The various black nationalist groups were the only social movements mobilizing around issues disproportionate to the urban black community: slum dwellings, slumlords, poor schools, police brutality, a lack of jobs, a lack of health care, addiction, rodents, and cockroaches. The black nationalists' focus on urban social problems inadvertently made urban problems black problems.[23]

A series of race riots across America's cities in the late 1960s cemented urban poverty with black and Latinos. The riots in Watts, Newark, and Rochester were prompted by police brutality, not black aggression. As Feagin and Hahn noted, it was not just marginalized blacks committing violence and rioting. Two parties were involved in the "ghetto revolts." This same pattern of blaming marginalized blacks for violence emerged in riots over school integration in Boston. White parents attacked black children, not the other way around. The combination of the unequal distribution of state resources to urban areas and the race riots changed the image of poverty in America. The face of American poverty was no longer rural and white. It was urban and black. In the neoliberal era, changes to and then the eventual elimination of federal antipoverty funds, the War on Drugs, tough-on-crime policing, and the withdraw of the labor market from the black ghetto created the representation of the dangerous and downtrodden city that elites claimed they were protecting the middle class from.[24]

The black ghetto has undergone an important transformation in the neoliberal era. The paradox of continued residential segregation at the same time as new forms of racial civic inclusion has transformed the black ghetto from the communal ghetto to the hyperghetto. As Wilson noted, the communal ghetto was single race but multiple classes. The outmigration of middle-class blacks made possible by the civil rights movement inadvertently destabilized the black ghetto by removing families and black role models. Wacquant dubbed the new black ghetto as the hyperghetto, in part because its demographic composition is single class and single race. However, Wacquant also showed how the hyperghetto has made the ghetto into a permanent and quintessential American institution. The formation of the hyperghetto resulted from neoliberal reforms that tied racism, the labor market, and the state together. Chicago, the birthplace of American urban sociology and Jane Addams's Hull House, is the home to some of the most destitute and dangerous black neighborhoods that some residents affectionately called Chi-raq. Whereas actual attempts at racial integration once prompted demands for privatization, the hyperghetto feeds national white racial insecurity necessary

156   THE NEOLIBERAL METROPOLIS

for renewed calls for more neoliberalism. In this case, the hyperghetto may be worlds apart from America's suburbs, but they each remain one side of the same neoliberal coin.

Gentrification

The growth of outer suburbia and gated communities and hypersegregation are the dominant spatial patterns in the neoliberal era. Starting in the 1980s, urban sociologists identified another spatial pattern of note: gentrification. The term 'gentrification' actually dates back to the 1960s, when Ruth Glass coined the term to describe the influx of a 'new gentry' into London that was displacing working-class Londoners. Neil Smith argued that gentrification and the rehabilitation of cities have become synonymous since the 1990s. The original gentrifiers were professional developers, landlords, and middle-class whites who returned to white working-class neighborhoods. They focused on rehabilitating old houses and buildings and converting abandoned warehouses into lofts. By the 1990s, developers and real estate elites relied on tax credits and state investments to construct new buildings to drive the rent gap. The rent gap is the difference between the cost of a structure and the potential ground rent. Theoretically, the cost of buildings and land investment drops to a point that it becomes profitable for redevelopment. One of the offshoots of uneven development is that redevelopment in one part of the metropolis drives down the value of land in another part of the metropolis. Today, a combination of real estate speculation and white-private state investment widens the rent gap. In the process, the original residents are either physically or symbolically displaced. They are physically displaced when they can no longer afford the new rents or, in the case of homeownership, higher property taxes and assessed values of the home and are forced to move. They are symbolically displaced when they no longer feel a sense of belonging in the neighborhood. The sensation of symbolic displacement can be city- or metropolitan-wide, as trigged by investment in one area and disinvestment in another.[25]

To the layperson's eye, gentrification may appear as urban renewal. After all, the restoration and reuse of old buildings and the streets being filled with people, specialty shops, and trendy restaurants are better than unoccupied buildings and empty streets. However, when we peek behind

THE NEOLIBERAL METROPOLIS   157

the curtain of gentrification, what we find is a complex relationship between finance, the state, and racism.

Before moving on, let me clear up some common misconceptions of gentrification. First, unlike suburbanization and residential segregation, gentrification is not a universal feature of all cities. Gentrification is primarily a characteristic of global cities like New York, London, Toronto, San Francisco, Atlanta, and Chicago, to name a few. Gentrification is not a major social problem of midsized cities in the old industrial Northeast, a.k.a. the Rust Belt, the Midwest, or the old agricultural South. Midsized cities struggle with issues of abandoned neighborhoods, soil contamination due to heavy metals, water contamination due to lead and PCBs, and crumbling sewer systems. Second, neighborhoods are not gentrified because of new restaurants and shopping districts. Nor is it the result of local real estate elites using state money to transform dying central business districts. Gentrification requires both the influx of economic capital, captured through the networks that link real estate elites, finance, and a connection with a romanticized artistic or bohemian culture.

The third popular misconception is that gentrification is the process of whites displacing blacks. This is simply not the case. On the one hand, a white-in, black-out movement would certainly fit with this book's overarching theory. Research indicates that a racial threshold of about 40% predicts whether or not that neighborhood will experience gentrification. Neighborhoods with a black or Hispanic population that exceeds 40% do not gentrify. The neighborhoods that are gentrified or are in the process of becoming gentrified are the neighborhoods that were populated by working-class whites and immigrant families who never left. Urban sociologists use terms like 'embourgeoisment' to describe how gentrification is actually elite white neighborhoods that have enjoyed the influx of financial capital and increasing property values. If gentrification were the process of whites moving into black neighborhoods, then the black ghetto would theoretically disappear. Instead, racially segregated neighborhoods have remained consistent and in some cases, exist side by side to gentrified neighborhoods.[26]

Once we move away from the misconceptions of gentrification, we immediately see that gentrification is another form of residential

158   THE NEOLIBERAL METROPOLIS

segregation in the neoliberal city. The link between racism, finance, and bohemian culture indicates that the same combination of vertical and horizontal urban development that explained racial zoning of cities and suburbia also explains why elite white areas of the city are gentrified. Since we have to start somewhere, let's start with bohemian culture and the creative class.

Since elite whites already populated selective city neighborhoods, bohemian neighborhoods provided the perfect urban location for real estate elites in the 1980s to sell to Wall Street's young white urban professionals, also known as yuppies. Bohemian neighborhoods are defined in relation to their nonconformist ideas, expressed through art, sexuality, and the rejection of capital expressions of conspicuous consumption. Yet, bohemia has always been an elite white cultural expression, a critique of conspicuous consumption that does not jeopardize elite white privilege. 'Bohemia' is a French term that the 19th-century writer Henri Murger used to describe Parisian neighborhoods populated by starving artists. Richard Lloyd argued that what we know as bohemia is the result of a "cumulative mythology of past bohemias." The 19th-century poet Charles Baudelaire was the embodiment of the mythology of bohemia. Known as the cursed poet, Baudelaire was censured over his poems about vampires and lesbians, which offended French public morality. He was bisexual and caught syphilis from a prostitute. He also lived off of a generous inheritance that allowed him to pursue his poetry. The beats in New York's Greenwich Village are the anchor for the mythology of American bohemia. Jack Kerouac attended the elite prep school Horace Mann in the Bronx before moving on to Columbia. William Burroughs was the son of a wealthy St. Louis family whose fortune was made in manufacturing key-operated adding machines, a precursor to the battery-powered calculator and electric cash register. The beats were able to experiment with culture because they had the financial means to do so. But experimenting with cultural norms is much different than breaking from elite white culture rooted in systemic racism.[27]

Elite whites who gentrify old bohemian and formerly working-class white neighborhoods are not the same as elite whites who reside in the outer suburbs. Richard Florida calls the new white elite "the creative class." Regarding urban development, he argued, "They [the creative class] gravitate to the indigenous street-level culture found in SoHo, Greenwich Village, and parts of Brooklyn and Jersey." He distinguishes the creative class from other social classes based on occupations supposedly in creative fields, like technology, finance, and design, and their desire for cultural diversity. Florida uses occupational census data to define members of the creative class and cities that have high concentrations of the creative class. In doing so, Florida ends up sampling the dependent variable: he identifies successful cities first and then selectively mines the data to indicate what makes the cities successful. For example, he includes finance but not teaching as a "creative occupation" but does not tell us what makes a given occupation creative or uncreative. Unfortunately, Florida also ignores both the history of systemic racism in his explanation of the rise of the creative class and urban development. The creative class is the pop bourgeoisie of the neoliberal era, whose consumer and living choices reproduce systemic racism across racialized settlement spaces.[28]

Hyperghettos and gentrified neighborhoods coexist in today's global city. New York City scored high on Florida's creative indexes. In 2010, New York City was also home to the largest gap between the rich and the poor in the United States. As the *New York Times* described it, "Household incomes in Manhattan are about as evenly distributed as they are in Bolivia or Sierra Leone—the wealthiest fifth of Manhattanites make 40 times more than the lowest fifth." New York's median income of $49,461 was not just below the national average but substantially below the $68,700 income cap that qualifies one for public housing in Manhattan. The median income gap does not take wealth into account. How is it possible for such drastic forms of economic inequality to exist in the same place? Take the specific tax advantages for investment bankers. Investment bankers and hedge fund managers enjoy a special tax advantage that classifies their income as capital gains rather than earned income. This allows the highest earners to pay a lower tax rate than the working and middle class. It's not the creative class that drives cities. It's neoliberal tax policy based on the logic of the upward redistribution of resources.[29]

The logic of white-private-gentrification provides the cultural and material link that defines 21st-century urban development. As Max

Rousseau showed, "loser cities" caught in the web of declining populations, job loss, low-skilled workers, and a stigmatized city image have resorted to embracing gentrification policies to attract white middle-class residents, a social group all but absent from postindustrial cities today. Gentrification policies include sending signals to property developers that the city is open for business. Aided by a combination of federally funded HUD programs like HOPE VI, Empowerment Zone, Enterprise Community, and Renewal Community that ran from 1993 until 2010, cities were able to demolish public housing, offer tax breaks, dole out grants, and provide technical assistance to businesses. The upward redistribution of public resources to businesses is designed to purchase payrolls by giving companies lucrative tax credits to remain or relocate, regardless of how much the jobs pay or the effects new businesses have on existing local businesses. All cities, states, and county Industrial Development Agencies (IDAs) learn to play the neoliberal development game or risk falling even further behind. It's a game with no winners except elite whites.[30]

The logic of white-private gentrification links real estate speculation and privatized social welfare. Twenty-first-century cities are increasingly dealing with the problem of affordable housing and homelessness. Housing vouchers have all but replaced public housing. Housing vouchers allow the poor to live anyplace that a landlord is willing accept the housing vouchers. And landlords are willing to rent to tenants with housing vouchers. Vouchers guarantee a revenue stream and allow the landlord to charge a premium above what the voucher pays. Housing vouchers have actually made the problem of affordable housing worse. In some cities, the difference in rent between a poor and a rich neighborhood is only $200 to $300. Although the vouchers are a better alternative to the Robert Taylor–style housing complexes that were demolished under the HOPE VI program, they have created a market for companies and hedge funds to purchase houses in distressed neighborhoods in bulk. Companies rely on local city officials to ignore housing code violations and housing court judges and are more than willing to evict tenants rather than find resolutions to keep people housed. As Desmond pointed out, black women are more likely to be evicted than any other racial or gender demographic. Privatized social welfare anchors

THE NEOLIBERAL METROPOLIS   161

the black and poor in specific neighborhoods and reinforces the hyper-ghetto as other parts of the city continue to develop.[31]

The dual existence of gentrification and racial exclusion also shapes a citywide sense of belonging. A sense of belonging captures one's attachment to the community, through feeling comfortable within the urban landscape. The opposite of belonging is feeling excluded even if one is allowed to enter public space. Gentrification involves various types of cultural exclusions. Planners and local elites design amenities around idealized types of citizens they want in the city. Trendy and upscale retail establishments and restaurants replace local businesses that once catered to the needs of locals. Whites view art festivals, the installation of bike lanes, and the creation of dog parks differently than blacks and Hispanics. Although blacks who reside in neighborhoods that are early in the gentrification process don't mind rising property values and the unrelated decline in crime, they don't see these 'new urbanism' amenities as reflecting their interests.[32]

The neoliberal metropolis is a white-private settlement space comprised of a network of hyperghettos, inner- and outer-ring suburbs, gentrified neighborhoods, and multinodal central business districts. Elite whites were the key actors in assembling the neoliberal metropolis. Financial elites, state planners, and real estate elites remade cities and the surrounding suburbs in the 1970s and 1980s to reflect the needs of neoliberal capitalism. Global cities like New York and Chicago became the home of financial capitalism. Financial capitalism requires computers, telecommunications, and data storage. In the 1980s, the telecommunication structure was fax machines. By the late 1990s, it was access to high-speed Internet connections, data storage, modems, and computer processers to conduct data analysis. By 2010, financial firms began using supercomputers to place thousands of trades a millisecond before a rival firm places the same trades. Regardless of the changes in technology, location still matters: these supercomputers still need to be in close proximity to the New York Stock Exchange to get that millisecond advantage. These financial elites bought condos in Manhattan and rehabbed brownstones in Brooklyn. Location is everything.

The logic of suburban growth was organized around a duality of white-public financial deregulations and white-private homes. When linked

THE NEOLIBERAL METROPOLIS

with the rest of the neoliberal metropolis, specifically the formation of the black ghetto, the metropolitan regions became organized around the white-private suburbs and the black-public city. The crime, poverty, and physical decay that assembled racialized insecurity became cemented with black and the city. In order to mask the obvious racism to each other, whites deployed a white racial frame to police geographical boundaries via the defense of property values, good schools, and safe neighborhoods. As Robert Beauregard argued, as early as the 1950s whites' "fear of racial pollution" fundamentally changed America's sociological view of cities: "Whereas once cities might have been symbolized by great factories and towering office buildings, these images were displaced by black faces, poverty, and African-American slums."[33] White suburban America became a white-private safe space and a real location for the neoliberal project to connect elite whites with the white middle class.

The neoliberal project is activated by real instances of racial integration. As a number of blacks and Hispanics entered the suburbs in search of the American dream, elite whites responded with a renewed call to privatization. Whites did not just flee from images of bad blacks or fear of the black ghetto. They basically fled from all blacks. Gates sprung up around housing developments. As middle- and upper-class good black citizens entered the suburbs, the shopping mall, itself a replacement for downtown public shopping, closed. In turn, whites have sought large houses in the outer suburbs. They have sought out Victorian houses, brownstones, and Queen Annes in the white-private gentrified city, which is filled with expensive specialty boutique shops, trendy bars and restaurants, and white-private schools—islands of white-private security in the dangerous neoliberal city.

Notes

1. See Derek Hyra, 2015, "The Back to the City Movement: Neighborhood Redevelopment and Processes of Political and Cultural Development" *Urban Studies* 52 (10): pp. 1–21 for a characterization of gentrification as a return to the city movement; Jane Jacobs, *The Death and Life of Great American Cities* (New York: Vintage Books, 1992); M. Leanne Lachmann and Deborah L. Brett, "Gen Y and Housing: What They Want and Where They Want It" Urban Land Institute, 2014, located at http://uli.org/report/gen-y-housing-want-want/

2. John R. Logan, "Separate and Unequal in Suburbia" Census Brief prepared for Project US2010, 2014.

THE NEOLIBERAL METROPOLIS   163

3. Massey and Denton, *American Apartheid*.
4. James Loewen, *Sundown Towns: A Hidden Dimension of Racism* (New York: Touchtone, 2006); On the recent demographic changes to cities and suburbs, see William Frey, "Melting Pot Cities and Suburbs: Racial and Ethnic Change in Metro America in the 2000s" The Brookings Institute, located at www.brookings.edu/~/media/research/files/papers/2011/5/04%20census%20ethnicity%20frey/0504_census_ethnicity_frey.pdf
5. Mark Gottdiener, *The Social Production of Urban Space, 2nd Edition* (Austin, TX: University of Texas Press, 1994).
6. Joseph Crespino, *In Search of Another Country: Mississippi and the Conservative Counterrevolution* (Princeton, NJ: Princeton University Press, 2007).
7. James Scott, *Seeing Like a State: How Certain Schemes to Improve the Human Condition Have Failed* (New Haven: Yale University Press, 1999).
8. Christopher Silver, "The Racial Origins of Zoning in American Cities" pp. 23–42 in *Urban Planning and the African American Community: In the Shadows*, edited by June Manning Thomas and Marsha Ritzdorf (Thousand Oaks, CA: Sage Publications, 1997); Baltimore mayor quote located in Silver, "The Racial Origins of Zoning in American Cities."
9. On the decentered nature of urban planning, see Gottdiener, *The Social Production of Urban Space*.
10. Hohle, *Race and the Origins of Neoliberalism*.
11. FHA quotes located in the "Racial Content of FHA Underwriting Practices 1934–1952", located at the University of Baltimore, Langsdale Library, Special Collections Department.
12. Kruse, *White Flight*.
13. Massey and Denton, *American Apartheid*, p. 126.
14. Mark Gottdiener, *Planned Sprawl: Public and Private Interests in Suburbia* (Beverly Hills, CA: Sage Press, 1977).
15. On the history of New Deal–era banking reforms, see David M. P. Freund, "Marketing the Free Market: State Intervention and the Politics of Prosperity in Metropolitan America" pp. 11–32 in *The New Suburban History*, edited by Kevin Kruse and Thomas Sugrue (Chicago: University of Chicago Press, 2006).
16. See Gottdiener, *Planned Sprawl* on up zoning and exclusionary zoning in the suburbs.
17. Andrew Wiese, "'The House I Live In': Race, Class, and African American Suburban Dreams in the Postwar United States" pp. 99–119, 101 in *New Suburban History*, edited by Kevin Kruse and Thomas Sugrue (Chicago: University of Chicago Press, 2006); Bernadette Hanlon, 2009, "A Topology of Inner-Ring Suburbs: Class, Race, and Ethnicity in US Suburbia" *City and Community* 8 (3 September): pp. 221–249.
18. Lisa McGirr, *Suburban Warriors: The Origins of the New American Right* (Princeton, NJ: Princeton University Press, 2002).
19. Edward J. Blakely and Mary Gail Snyder, "Divided We Fall: Gates and Walled Communities in the United States" pp. 85–99 in *Architecture of Fear*, edited by Nan Ellin (New York: Princeton University Press, 1997).
20. See Gottdiener, Planned Sprawl on multi-nodal and multi-centric suburban development; Logan, "Separate and Unequal in Suburbia."
21. Karl E. Tauber and Alma Tauber, *Negroes in Cities: Residential Segregation and Neighborhood Change* (Chicago: Aldine Publishing Company, 1965); W. E. B. Du Bois, *The Philadelphia Negro: A Social Study* (New York: Oxford University Press, 2007).

22. Robert Beauregard, *When Urban America Became Suburban* (Minneapolis, MN: University of Minnesota Press, 2006), p. 81.
23. On the history of black nationalism in the civil rights era, see Hohle, *Black Citizenship and Authenticity in the Civil Rights Movement*, Chapter 4.
24. Joe R. Feagin and Harlan Hahn, *Ghetto Revolts: The Politics of Violence in American Cities* (New York: MacMillan Publishing, 1973). On the changing face of American Poverty, see Gilens, *Why Americans Hate Welfare*.
25. Ruth Glass, *London: Aspects of Change* (London: MacKibben and Kee, 1964); Neil Smith, *The New Urban Frontier: Gentrification and the Revanchist City* (New York: Routledge, 1996).
26. Jackelyn Hwang and Robert J. Sampson, 2014, "Divergent Pathways of Gentrification: Racial Inequality and the Social Order of Renewal in Chicago Neighborhoods" *American Sociological Review* 79 (4): 726–751; Thomas Maloutas, 2011, "Contextual Diversity in Gentrification Research" *Critical Sociology* 39 (1): pp. 33–48.
27. Christopher Mele, *Selling the Lower East Side: Culture, Real Estate, and Resistance in New York 1880–2000* (Minneapolis, MN: University of Minnesota Press, 2000); Richard Lloyd, 2004, "The Neighborhood in Cultural Production: Material and Symbolic Resources in the New Bohemia" *City and Community* 3 (4 December): pp. 343–372, 343.
28. Richard Florida, *Cities and the Creative Class* (New York: Routledge, 2005), p. 164.
29. See Sam Roberts, "Income Data Shows Widening Gap between New York City's Richest and Poorest" 20 September 2013, located at www.nytimes.com/2012/09/20/nyregion/rich-got-richer-and-poor-poorer-in-nyc-2011-data-shows.html?_r=0; See Amy O'Learly, "What Is Middle Class in Manhattan" *New York Times* 18 January 2013, located at www.nytimes.com/2013/01/20/realestate/what-is-middle-class-in-manhattan.html
30. Max Rousseau, 2009, "Re-Imagining the City Center for the Middle Classes: Regeneration, Gentrification and Symbolic Policies in 'Loser Cities'" *International Journal of Urban Affairs and Regional Research* 33 (3 September): pp. 770–788.
31. Mathew Desmond, *Evicted: Poverty and Profit in the American City* (New York: Crown Publishers, 2016); Richard Schweid, *Invisible Nation: Homeless Families in America* (Oakland: University of California Press, 2016).
32. Samuel Shaw and Daniel Monroe Sullivan, 2011, "'White Night': Gentrification, Racial Exclusion, and Perceptions and Participation in the Arts" *City and Community* 10 (3): pp. 241–264; Zheng Wu, Feng Hou, and Christoph M. Schimmele, 2011, "Racial Diversity and Sense of Belonging in Urban Neighborhoods" *City and Community* 10 (4): pp. 373–392; Derek Hyra, 2012, "Conceptualizing the New Urban Renewal: Comparing the Past to the Present" *Urban Affairs Review* 48 (4): pp. 498–527; Derek Hyra, *The New Urban Renewal: The Economic Transformation of Harlem and Bronzeville* (Chicago: University of Chicago Press, 2008).
33. Beauregard, *When Urban America Became Suburban*, p. 76.

6

RACISM AND THE NEOLIBERAL CRISIS IN AMERICAN EDUCATION

No politician has ever stood in front of a bank and proclaimed segregation forever.

American education seems to be in the state of a continual crisis. Americans pin their hopes on education to solve social problems. We believe we can educate ourselves out of poverty, racism, bad health, and debt. Since the 2000s, America has enacted federal education policy with names like "No Child Left Behind," "Race to the Top," and "the Common Core" designed to fix a broken educational system. Instead, research indicates that education is the key site of the reproduction of social hierarchies, specifically social class and racial hierarchies. The education crisis is typically described in racially neutral terms: low test scores, underperforming schools, or bad teachers. But where we went to school and where we send our children to school is an extension of where we live, our economic means, and in some cases, our religion—all of which are patterned by a long history of racism. The neoliberal solution to the crisis of American education is always the same: privatize the schools.

The privatization of schools is the funneling of public money to private schools, including nonprofit and for-profit schools. Contemporary forms of school privatization go by the name of school vouchers and charter schools. But privatization has a much longer history in American education. The effort to privatize public schools originated at the dawn of the civil rights era as southern states prepared for life after the 1954 *Brown v. Board of Education* decision. The privatization of schools waned in the 1970s as the Supreme Court set geographic boundaries that limited school desegregation to the municipal level, helped establish a numeric ratio that defined a school as segregated or integrated, and helped establish a system of magnet schools designed to minimize racial integration in order to keep whites in the cities. The return of privatization today coincides with the rise of charter schools in the gentrified city. Whites have returned to parts of the city only to find a limited number of majority-white public schools. White-private schools create majority-white schools within a majority-minority neighborhood and school district. White-private schools are extremely rare in suburban school districts, popping up only when a significant proportion of black or Hispanic residents exist in the suburban district.

The neoliberal project found a home in the never-ending school reform efforts. The school and the classroom became the symbolic and material home of white racial and economic insecurity. The language of neoliberalism connected white-private with schools, with profits, with union busting, with knowledge, and with fears of interracial sex. This all started with the events leading up to the *Brown* decision.

The Elite White Response to the *Brown* Decision

The NAACP and a young lawyer named Thurgood Marshall challenged the constitutional legality of *Plessy v. Ferguson*. In 1896, the Supreme Court upheld earlier segregation laws on the grounds that segregation was constitutional as long as the services and institutions were equal. The *Plessy* decision dealt with railroad cars, but it applied to schools as well. The NAACP appointed Marshall to lead their legal defense fund and pursue the fight for citizenship rights. Marshall replaced a former dean of Howard's law school, Charles Houston. Houston used an equalization strategy to chip away at southern states that could not or would not fund black schools the same as white schools. This laid the legal foundation for the *Brown* case, the basis that black schools were separate but unequal. Marshall challenged the outright legality of segregation, successfully arguing that all-white primaries were unconstitutional in

THE CRISIS IN AMERICAN EDUCATION   167

Smith v. Allwright (1944). All-white primaries essentially negated the black vote since the South enjoyed a one-party system and the Democratic primaries were the election. Marshall brought the *Brown* case to the Supreme Court in 1952. The *Brown* case was actually a collection of five cases dealing with school segregation. It's known as the *Brown* decision because of a combination of bravery, historical chance, and alphabetical order. Marshall and his team of NAACP lawyers used sociological and psychological studies to show the negative impacts of racial segregation, a novel approach in 1952. The Supreme Court justices were divided on the constitutionality of *Plessy* so they decided to rehear the case in December of 1953. On 14 May 1954, Supreme Court Justice Earl Warren, after much political negotiation with the prosegregation judges, declared in the majority opinion of the court that "separate educational facilities are inherently unequal."

Southern whites anticipated the *Brown* decision. They understood that any school desegregation case would disproportionately impact southern white power. Nearly 70% of the entire US black population lived in the South in 1950, and blacks were increasingly migrating from southern rural areas to southern cities. Jim Crow laws legally protected white-public schools from racial integration. But the preceding 80 years of systemic racism created stark differences between white and black schools. There were disparities in teacher salaries, the sizes of the buildings, the duration of the school day, and the number of grade levels in a single room. There were disparities in the length of the school year, in the number of busses to take the kids to school and back, and whether or not there were textbooks in the classrooms. White schools were consolidated into school districts while black schools remained independent schools. White schools had a school curriculum designed to prepare whites for entrance into the contemporary labor market while black schools still prepared blacks for the agricultural job market. Because employment options for the vast majority of blacks were restricted to the agricultural sector, many blacks simply dropped out of school. Mississippi's Jim Crow laws dictated that black and white schools even be at least two and half miles apart. The only way to keep the schools segregated was to get around the *Brown* decision, which meant creating an alternative to public schools. Southern whites found their alternative in privatization.

168   THE CRISIS IN AMERICAN EDUCATION

The Privatization of Public Schools After Brown

Elite whites in Alabama, Virginia, Mississippi, Arkansas, and Georgia organized official state commissions to get around the *Brown* ruling. Each state was influenced by the others' policy proposals and new legislation. Although they settled on a strategy to privatize their public schools, the privatization of schools spread in a nonlinear fashion. Some states even proposed spending more money on black schools in a desperate attempt to maintain legal segregation and to ward off black families sending their children to white schools. In all cases, elite and ordinary whites assembled a language of white-private as a strategy of maintaining control over the racial composition of schools.

Elite whites in Alabama were the most anxious and ambitious in their privatization plans. The Beatty Plan was the first plan to privatize schools in Alabama. It was proposed before there was verdict in the *Brown* decision. The Beatty Plan stated that parents had the right send their children either to a school "of his own race" or a "mixed school." A proposed Wilcox Amendment would have made it a criminal offense for teachers to encourage racial integration. Elites were not sold that the Beatty Plan guaranteed segregation. Therefore, Sam Engelhardt, president of the Alabama Citizens' Council and state senator, proposed his own plan, the School Placement Bill. Unlike the previous school segregation plans, the School Placement Bill relied on the language of white-private to link education with private companies. To support the bill, Engelhardt gave speeches where he emphasized how "private corporations operate every kind of service and business even schools and colleges. The only trouble is that there are not enough privately owned education institutions to accommodate all persons seeking education." The School Placement Bill proposed privatizing Alabama's school system so Alabama's schools would not be subject to the *Brown* decision. It proposed to eliminate state funds to public schools, repeal compulsory education laws, repeal teacher tenure, allow for public money to support K–12 private schools, and authorize county school boards to transfer public property to private schools. It also authorized schools to track students based on subjective measurements, like a student's home life, morals, social environment, and psychological ability. A bad family was code for black families. Alabama's governor Jim Folsom vetoed these

THE CRISIS IN AMERICAN EDUCATION 169

bills. Folsom couldn't overcome support for the bill that did authorize the privatization of Alabama's public schools: the Pupil Placement Act.[1]

The Pupil Placement Act gave Alabama the right to abolish public schools. Albert Boutwell, a legendary Alabama moderate segregationist and businessman, whose political career included being a state senator and mayor of Birmingham, had the political skill to move the school privatization bill through the Alabama state legislature. Boutwell was the quintessential southern white elite. The Pupil Placement Act authorized the state to give public money to private schools, to gift public facilities to private owners, and to give parents the choice to send their kids to racially segregated or integrated schools. It protected teacher tenure to minimize white opposition to the bill. The Pupil Placement Act removed of the word 'public' from the phrase 'public education' and the word 'segregation' from the state constitution and authorized "the state, city and county governments to sell or lease public parks to private operators, if necessary, in order to avoid integration by federal edict as has already happened in other Southern States." Immediately after Alabama passed the Pupil Placement Act, a local Montgomery parent group formed the Montgomery Private School Corporation. The Montgomery School Corporation's mission statement defined them as "a non-profit corporation to undertake providing our white children with segregated private schools when and if that should become necessary." Alabama's Pupil Placement Act remained in place until 1968.[2]

Virginia proposed school privatization plans at the same time Alabama was deciding the fate of public schooling in the Heart of Dixie. In 1955, Virginia organized the Virginia Public Education Commission, also known as the Gray Commission. The thrust of the Gray Commission was issuing vouchers to white families so that they could continue to send their children to white-private schools rather than integrated public schools. Virginia also authorized the Stanley Plan, named after Governor Thomas Stanley. The Stanley Plan gave the governor the power to withhold state money from any school that integrated. Whereas the Gray Commission allowed for public money to be indirectly transferred to private schools, the Stanley Plan eliminated all public funding from the integrated public school. Both plans stopped short of Alabama's full privatization option.

170   THE CRISIS IN AMERICAN EDUCATION

The Mississippi legislature gave the governor the power to abolish all public schools. Delta politician Walter Sillers was the primary author behind the bill to privatize schools, known as the 'last resort' amendment. It was known as the last resort amendment because whites in Mississippi were very good at using a variety of intimidation tactics that ranged from loss of a job to violence to prevent blacks from even seeking admission to white schools. Mississippi Legal Educational Advisory Committee (LEAC) member Maurice Black summed up the rationale behind the legislation to abolish the public schools: "If they [black students] are not in the public schools, they can't be integrated. . . . If they [the schools] are private, privately operated and privately owned, why the *Brown* decision won't apply here." If enacted, the private option gave the state the authority to approve charters for private school corporations, to give charter schools direct public money, and to give public money to the counties for the explicit purpose of funding scholarships for white children to attend private schools. The Citizens' Council supported the privatization of schools, assuring their members that the amendment would not "abolish *our* schools" (emphasis mine). There was some opposition to school privatization in Mississippi. Urban whites were concerned about the availability and quality of education and their ability to afford private schools even with the vouchers. The business class had real concerns about the quality of workers in the labor pool in a period of industrial and service sector expansion. But opposition voices from Mississippi's business class and urban whites were in the minority. Mississippi voters voted in favor of abolishing public schools by a two-to-one margin.[3]

The Georgia legislature formed the Georgia Commission on Education in 1953 to recommend steps to preserve racial segregation prior to the *Brown* decision. The commission recommended that Georgia privatize their schools; gave the state the right to abolish public schools, provide public grants to students to attend private schools, and lease public property to private schools; and permitted private school teachers to join the state retirement system. Because the federal government did not press the states to actually desegregate their schools, the various private options were rarely activated. Atlanta voluntarily desegregated their public schools in 1961. Atlanta's black population increased as blacks migrated from the surrounding rural areas to the city. Atlanta's black elite were gaining some local political power, and Atlanta's white business class famously said that they were too busy to hate. But the schools were desegregated in name only. Atlanta passed a school placement act known as 'the local option'. The local option gave school districts the option to continue offering public education or to privatize their schools. The local option included admission criteria, such as IQ tests and available classroom space, to determine if black students were eligible to attend an integrated school. It ensured that schools would remain segregated even as the proportion of Atlanta's black population continued to increase.[4]

Little Rock, Arkansas, briefly privatized their schools after Dwight Eisenhower sent federal troops to Little Rock in 1957. Eisenhower sent federal troops to Little Rock after Arkansas's governor, Orval Faubus, sent the Arkansas National Guard to stop the racial integration of Little Rock's Central High School. The city of Little Rock responded by closing all the high schools for the 1958–1959 school year. The Little Rock Private School Corporation immediately opened T. J. Raney High School as an all-white private school. The city gave the private school corporation money and a building. The Citizens' Council also raised approximately $175,000 for the school. Backed by the racially moderate business class, the local PTA groups fought the privatization of Arkansas schools all the way to the Arkansas Supreme Court. The Supreme Court ruled that closing the schools was illegal. Although T. J. Raney High School had an enrollment of 1,200 students, it was not viable without public aid, and whites could not afford the annual tuition of $15 per pupil to keep it open.[5]

The elite white response leading up to the *Brown* decision and after was to privatize public education in order to maintain racial segregation. The plan to create white-private schools was an early elite white strategy to create racial solidarity across class and geographical divisions. The series of school privatization bills did not explicitly mention race and were completely void of overt racist statements. Southern elites were not concerned with profits, funding, or the quality of schools. Privatization was advanced simply as a means to maintain segregation. Ever since, white-private has been the preferred solution to create new forms of racially segregated schools.

172 THE CRISIS IN AMERICAN EDUCATION

Austerity and Public Schools

The *Brown* decision mandated that all schools be equally funded. This required southern states to increase public spending to consolidate districts and bring schools up to modern standards. Integrated schools increased the cost of public schools and decreased support among segregationists to pay for them. There were initial attempts by some white business elites in Alabama and Mississippi to *spend to segregate*, increasing public funds to black schools in order to make them separate but equal. The white business elite hoped that an increase in school expenditures would improve the local workforce and keep them racially segregated. This did not negate the *Brown* decision, so they pursued school privatization. The integration of public schools reinvigorated white-private austerity. As I discussed in Chapter 3, one legacy of the power of white agrarians in the South was the system of regressive taxation. Regressive taxes paid for schools. Agrarians and industrial elites had a vested interest in a low-skilled and uneducated workforce to till the fields, move trees through the lumber mills, and operate machines in the factories. They did not support tax increases to fund any school. Rival elite whites were unable to pass legislation to standardize tax assessment practice. The opposite of tax increases and increased public funding was austerity.

Austerity is a moral approach to state budget making that seeks an equivalence of revenues and expenditures. It is also a method of exercising power and control over specific populations. One or more groups are going to be hurt when budgets are restricted, and some groups are going to benefit from the budgetary restrictions. Elite whites deployed a language of white-private austerity in relation to the use of white taxpayer money to fund black public education.

Austerity emerged as a parallel strategy during the debates over the school privatization acts in Alabama. Engelhardt rallied support for his school segregation plan by giving speeches to various white groups. Rather than argue for the merits of racial segregation or just focus on the rationale for privatization, Engelhardt argued that integrated public schools were an economic burden on whites. Engelhardt claimed, "In my county [Macon] we are spending $696,000.00 in 1953 on negro education. We are spending $85,000.00 on the white school system in

THE CRISIS IN AMERICAN EDUCATION   173

1953." The reason for the funding gaps was that 85% of Macon County residents were black. In a similar line of thought, Boutwell argued that integrated schools meant a larger state budget because whites would not support property tax hikes in order to pay for educating black children. He claimed, "The public in most if not all districts, would refuse to vote for the necessary taxes to sustain a program of compulsory integration." Boutwell used austerity to tie racial integration with the economic burden of whites *and* with the economic burden of the state.[6]

Mississippi's elites capitalized on the racialized anxiety of ordinary whites that stemmed from school integration to double down on their already existing practice of austerity. What was new was how segregationist groups that formerly fought for increased taxation to pay for schools abruptly changed their minds. When Mississippi's schools and other public amenities were white-public, there was movement to increase taxes to pay for white-public services. This changed after *Brown*. We can see this change in the Citizens' Council's opposition to taxes and spending white tax dollars on black children. A Citizens' Council fundraising letter stated, "The Mississippi public will not support with their taxation integrated schools nor will they allow their children to attend them." The letter also linked austerity with white tax dollars: "During the 1957–58 school session, the state of Mississippi, to mention just one example, paid a total cost of $23,922,209 for Negro public school education. It is figured conservatively that white taxpayers paid 90 percent of this amount." Money for all of Mississippi's public schools came from the sales tax and vice taxes on cigarettes. White Mississippians did not support issuing bonds to fund black schools, and black Mississippians did not support segregated schools even if more public money was allocated to black schools.[7]

Segregation Academies and the 1964 Civil Rights Act

The legislative framework for privatizing schools was in place by the late 1950s, but the privatization of schools was not a universal feature of southern education on the eve of the 1964 Civil Rights Act. Local white parent groups sought out privatization in areas where the local black population had some political power, the segregationist groups were weak, and the state had the economic means to operate a school

174 THE CRISIS IN AMERICAN EDUCATION

district without federal money. The more civil rights acts passed by the federal government, the more white children attended private schools. About 1.5% of Alabama primary and secondary students enrolled in private schools between 1939 and 1957. After the passage of the 1957 Civil Rights Act and Eisenhower's decision to send federal troops to Little Rock, enrollment in private schools in Alabama increased to 3.2%. Private school enrollment in Alabama again sharply increased from 3% to 7% in 1968, the year the federal government began to enforce integration by tying federal funding with compliance with the 1964 Civil Rights Act. In contrast, there was virtually no increase in private school enrollment in Mississippi. Mississippi continued to employ a combination of violence and economic sanctions to ward off blacks who were seeking out racially integrated schools. Or they simply ignored federal laws. In 1964, only 0.02% of black school children went to school with white children. In 1969, 88% of blacks still attended all-black schools.[8]

The 1964 Civil Rights Act changed the field of public education. Title VI of the 1964 Civil Rights Act tied federal school aid with desegregation of schools. Rather than facilitate racial integration, whites responded to the 1964 Civil Rights Act with more white-private schools and more white-private austerity. The result was segregation academies. The term 'segregation academy' refers to the all-white private schools that sprang up all over the southern landscape after the 1964 Civil Rights Act. Citizens' Council president William Simmons stated that the 1964 Civil Rights Act transformed public schools into "government schools." In response, the Citizens' Council organized a plan to create "free enterprise schools" to replace "socialized education." Racially integrated government schools were black-public schools. Only white-private schools could guarantee the continuation of racially segregated schools.[9]

Mississippi's Citizens' Council was at the front line in establishing segregation academies. The Citizens' Council opened their first school in 1964 in Jackson, Mississippi. They called it Council School No. 1. Tuition was $375 a year, with $185 of the tuition underwritten by public money. Twenty-two students enrolled in the first year, but enrollment grew to 260 students in the elementary and high school in 1966. The amount of public aid increased to $240 in 1968. Former governor Ross Barnett held a fund raiser, and two of Jackson's largest banks issued the

THE CRISIS IN AMERICAN EDUCATION 175

school a $600,000 loan. The Citizens' Council's white-private school system eventually grew to 12 separate schools. The number of white students enrolled in the Jackson public school system went from 21,000 to less than 9,000. In addition to the Citizens' Council–sponsored segregation academies, local Mississippi parent groups incorporated 55 private school foundations in 1966. Although there were 158 school foundations in 1970, only 100 or so were actually open and educating children. By 1973, there were 125 segregation academies open in Mississippi, about 40,000 white students transferred from public schools to a segregation academy. McMillen estimated that throughout the South, about 300,000 children were enrolled in some 300 to 400 segregation academies.[10]

Segregation academies began to spring up in Alabama starting in 1964. White parent groups led the movement to open segregation academies. This gave Alabama's segregation academies a distinct local flavor. For example, in February 1964, the Alabama State Board of Education authorized financial aid to parents of Tuskegee High School to enable white students to attend white-private schools. In 1965, Selma, Alabama, passed the "Freedom Choice Plan" in response to the admittance of 20 black children into the Selma public school system. Selma's Freedom Choice Plan rerouted public money to white groups to so that they could establish the white-private schools of the John T. Morgan Academy in 1965 and Meadowview Christian Church in 1971. It also began the era of the rise in popularity of Protestant religious schools as a means to maintain school segregation in the South. The state of Alabama did not implement a broad school integration program until 1971, in response to the 1969 *Alexander v. Holmes County* decision.[11]

The National Response to School Desegregation

The 1970 school year began the era of the nationalization of white-private schools. In 1969, the Supreme Court ordered in *Alexander v. Holmes County* that racial integration proceed with "all deliberate speed" and deemed the various school privatization and freedom of choice plans unconstitutional. The *Alexander* case involved 33 counties in Mississippi. In some ways, the South was a different place in 1970 than it was in 1950 or even 1960. Southern whites were increasingly moving to the suburbs. Southern cities lost their historic checkerboard pattern of racial segregation in favor of a northern style of residential segregation by neighborhood. Seventy percent of blacks lived in urban areas, and the black population in northern and western cities continued to increase in the shadow of the urban race riots of the late 1960s. In other words, the South increasingly resembled the North and the North increasingly began resembling the South. This was never so apparent as in the national response to school desegregation.

The issue that galvanized whites across the nation was busing students to achieve school desegregation. The Supreme Court ruling *Swan v. Charlotte-Mecklenburg County Board of Education* in 1971 stated that lower courts could bus students to achieve a racial balance in schools. The increasing uniform urban landscape defined by residential segregation meant than neighborhood schools were also segregated. Unlike legal markers of segregation, like racial zoning, redlining, and the whites-only signs posted above water fountains and on the schoolhouse door, residential segregation via market and economic forces is not illegal. Busing, which meant transporting white children to majority black schools and transporting black children to majority white schools, was a way to racially integrate schools and preserve racially segregated neighborhoods. A majority of white parents wanted their neighborhoods and schools to remain segregated. Elite whites capitalized on the increasing racial anxiety around school desegregation. Busing was now forced busing, and forced busing dominated the national education debates in the 1970s and early 1980s.

White-Private Deregulations: Forced Busing and School Desegregation in the North

George Wallace, the segregationist governor of Alabama, whose political career dated back to the 1930s and who was infamous for standing in front of the University of Alabama and proclaiming segregation forever and for sending the state police to the 1965 Selma to Montgomery march to assist the local sheriff in physically beating black protesters as they tried to walk across the Edmund Pettus Bridge, decided to run for president. Not once. Three times. He challenged Lyndon Johnson in the 1964 Democratic primaries and then ran as an independent in 1968

THE CRISIS IN AMERICAN EDUCATION   177

and once again in the 1972 Democratic primary. He never thought he'd win. But he understood that many ordinary whites did not support school integration. He saw the increasing white opposition to forced busing in the North as his big political opportunity. Integrated schools did not threaten elite whites and many middle-class whites. They already sequestered themselves in exclusive suburban enclaves and had the option of sending their children to private schools. Arthur Bremer shot Wallace five times in a failed assassination attempt during Wallace's 1972 presidential campaign. Wallace would spend the rest of his life in a wheelchair. That did not derail his political career or his political influence. Nixon admired Wallace's strategy of using of racism to draw white voters away from the Democratic Party. Pat Buchanan called this 'the Southern Strategy'. Wallace sat in his wheelchair on stage next to Ronald Reagan during Reagan's 1980 presidential campaign speech at the Neshoba County Fair in Mississippi, the speech where Reagan conjured up the spirit of past segregationists and declared his unwavering support for states' rights.

Wallace rode the topic of forced busing all throughout the 1972 Democratic primary. White voters in Michigan were especially receptive to Wallace. Mirel found a relationship between white Michigan voters who supported Wallace in the 1972 Democratic primary and voter rejection of a proposed 1972 property tax increase to pay for busing. A member of the Detroit white antibusing group Citizens Committee for Better Education summed up his rejection of using white-private taxes to support racial integration in Detroit: "If they have less money, they'll have less money to buy buses." Although Wallace didn't know it at the time, his influence over Michigan's white electorate would lay the foundation for the 1974 Supreme Court decision *Milliken v. Bradley*.

A parent group in Detroit, with the help of the NAACP, sued the state of Michigan in 1970. The point of the class-action lawsuit was to address Detroit's racially segregated school system. Black parents wanted better schools for their children. The defendant in the lawsuit was Michigan's governor William Milliken. The issue was over whether schools should be desegregated at the municipal or county level. After an appeal, the Supreme Court ruled in *Milliken v. Bradley* (1974) that suburban school districts did not deliberately discriminate against blacks

178   THE CRISIS IN AMERICAN EDUCATION

and were exempt from formulas to achieve racial balance in schools. Cities were still required to use busing to achieve racial balance in their schools. A subsequent decision, known as *Milliken II*, not only upheld *Milliken v. Bradley* but also stipulated that a school had to deal with the negative effects of segregation and that seeking integration was not enough. By exempting the suburbs from racially integrating their schools, *Milliken v. Bradley* gave white families a place that was void of working-class whites and blacks and the sense of racial security they longed for.[12]

The crisis of education in the North became a distinctly urban crisis after the *Milliken* decisions. Since education is always tied to where we live, the question became how to minimally integrate urban public schools to slow down white flight. Deindustrialization had the unintentional effect of keeping many working-class white families in the city. They did not have the economic means to move to the suburbs or send their children to private schools. The *Alexander* decision took the option of privatizing public schools off the menu of available segregation options. The northern elite white response was to use white-private deregulation to remake city schools. Northern white elites focused on the regulatory field of education because lower court decisions empowered state supreme court justices and municipal school boards to decide how students were assigned to schools. The 1968 *Green v. New Kent County, Virginia,* decision quantified racial integration by establishing a ratio between black and white students, faculty, and facilities. State supreme court justices quantified the criteria to define a school as integrated via pupil ratios that ranged from 30 to 50% black.

Northern urban schools were segregated across a complex array of zoning regulations, feeder systems, and historic white ethnic settlement spaces. Cities used zoning regulations to establish a district system for school placement. School administrators assigned students to a school based on what district their family lived in. The district system was not always synonymous with neighborhood boundaries. Districts could be gerrymandered to incorporate more blacks into a single district. Conversely, districts could be modified to create exceptions that let whites opt into white districts. School boundaries were hard for blacks and fluid for whites. There was also an institutional process of a feeder system. Feeder systems are when segregated elementary schools were linked with

THE CRISIS IN AMERICAN EDUCATION   179

segregated high schools. Busing threatened the segregated educational ecosystem because busing transgressed neighborhood boundaries. The result was a magnet school system that provided an incentive for whites to remain in the city via minimal racial integration and the preservation of racially segregated neighborhoods.

A magnet school system was a school system comprising a small set of elite schools followed by a second tier of specialty schools. Racist pupil placement tests were recast as criteria tests for admission to select schools. The small set of elite magnet schools were predominately white and middle class. Some cities achieved racial integration by busing white students to elite schools located in black neighborhoods. Other cities simply bussed poor whites and blacks between marginalized neighborhoods. Elite and ordinary white parents enthusiastically supported magnet schools. White parents liked majority-white schools. The growing business class liked elite schools that prepared students for employment in the neoliberal economy. Magnet schools were successful in some places and unsuccessful in others. In cities like Detroit, so many white families with children left the city that racial balance became a mathematical impossibility. The New York City magnet school system managed to create four elite schools and basically a series of all-black schools. In cities like Boston, whites fled racially integrated schools after a violent and prosegregationist response to stop busing failed. And forget coming back. White families kept leaving Boston. To put Boston's white exodus in a long-term perspective, the percentage of white children in Boston public schools decreased from 64% in 1970 to 35.5% in 1980 to 22.2% in 1990 to 14.7% in 2000 to 13% in 2012. The problem of education remained unsolved in the first two decades of the neoliberal era.[13]

Racism and Education in the Neoliberal Era

A federal judge ordered Cleveland, Mississippi, to desegregate their schools in May of 2016, some 46 years after the Alexander decision. At first glance, you may think, well, it's business as usual in Mississippi. And it's easy to pick on Mississippi. But 65% of black and Hispanic students attended racially segregated schools in New York City in 2016. Countless numbers of suburban school districts remain majority white by a very large margin. And this was one of 177 school desegregation cases the US Justice Department had in court in 2016. Cleveland had an open-enrollment system. No whites chose to enroll in the all-black East Side High School. Cleveland passed a plan to consolidate their two high schools into a single high school and their two middle schools into a single middle school. The Cleveland School District voted to appeal the ruling in July 2016. White parents worried that the consolidation plan would prompt white families to flee the school. In that same month, the Southern Poverty Law Center filed a lawsuit over how Mississippi funds their charter schools. The Mississippi Charter School Act allows charter schools to receive public funding. In the neoliberal era, charter schools have emerged as the white-private option to maintain school segregation.

Education may be the most salient issue that ties elite, middle-class, and a growing cadre of working-class whites to the neoliberal project. For whites, the issue is about maintaining majority-white schools in neighborhoods that are gentrifying or suburbs that are becoming racially diverse. This is not about the quality of schools, good and bad teachers, resources, or standardized tests. Although a market logic or profit motive lurks behind charter schools, money is not driving school privatization in the neoliberal era. Racism is. No one files a petition to create a charter school in majority-white suburbs or in rural areas. Privatization around schools has always been about control: the control of curriculum, the control of labor contracts, and the control over admittance criteria. Schools have become the most noticeable white-private space in the neoliberal city.

Charter Schools

Two weeks after Hurricane Katrina, the city of New Orleans fired 7,500 public school teachers. This happened in September of 2005 and was the first step en route to privatizing New Orleans's public school system. Ten years later, the entire New Orleans public school system was converted into charter schools. Arne Duncan, then Obama's education secretary, said that Hurricane Katrina was "the best thing that happened to the education system in New Orleans." New Orleans was home to some of the worst public schools in the United States. It was corrupt and by all accounts wasn't doing a very good job of educating students.

THE CRISIS IN AMERICAN EDUCATION   181

Louisiana had plans to take over some of the city's worst schools before the storm. Charter school advocates have pointed out that the massive privatization efforts worked, often citing metrics like increased graduation rates and improved test scores. Critics point out that the charter schools simply suspend and push out kids who don't do well, don't offer adequate special education services, and welcome the high dropout rates because they make the bad and underperforming students disappear from the data. What none of them point out is that the privatization of the schools was a way to prevent busing black students to schools in New Orleans' surrounding suburbs.[14]

Charter schools are publicly funded nonprofit or for-profit organizations. The debates around school privatization are centered on charter schools. The charter exempts the school from certain state and local regulations, the main ones being labor contracts with the teachers' union, length of school day, and length of school year. Minnesota was the first state to enter into a contract, or a charter, with an organization in 1991. In 1992, City Academy opened in St. Paul, Minnesota. By the start of the 2013 school year, there were 6,465 charter schools operating in 41 states and the District of Columbia, educating over 2.5 million children. For the 2013 school year, charter schools were 7.2% of all public schools serving 5.2% of all public school students. Although the majority of charter schools are freestanding not-for-profit schools, charter management organizations (CMOs) operate 15% of charter schools, and education management organizations (EMOs) operate 13% of charter schools.[15] CMOs are nonprofits that operate multiple charter schools, while EMOs are for-profits that operate multiple charter schools. Proponents of charter schools emphasize that charter schools provide choices: "Use charters to test new and creative strategies to expand choice and choices—while also respecting today's fiscal realities."[16]

The first question is whether or not charter schools improve education. It's not an easy question to answer. The best studies have returned mixed results. One study from the Center for Research on Education Outcomes (CREDO), located at Stanford, indicated that based on aggregate-level test scores, charter schools do better than public schools, but a lot of variability exists between charter schools. There is evidence that charter schools in predominately poor black neighborhoods do better than public schools in poor black neighborhoods, especially on metrics of high school graduation and the number of children who attend college. Moving from aggregate-level data to admissions tests and the educators and administrators who decide which children to admit and to exclude, we see that charter schools work as long as there are there are no problems. Charter schools enroll fewer children who need special education. Charter schools disproportionately suspend and expel black students and students with disabilities. Charter schools work as long as their students come from stable middle-class families, do not have a learning disability, pay attention in class, and do their homework! In this regard, charter schools work like private prisons and private social welfare. Private prisons work as long as violent offenders and inmates with physical and mental health issues are incarcerated in the state-run public facilities. Privatized social welfare works as long as there are no poor people.[17]

The second question is where are charter schools popping up? The answer is in areas where whites and racial minorities live side by side and share the same school district. While charter schools don't do much to improve education, they are very good at maintaining the history of racially segregated schools, or what one charter school think tank called "ethnocentric charter schools." Studies by the Brookings Institute and the UCLA Civil Rights Project have both indicated that charter schools are more racially and economically segregated than public schools. Racial and economic segregation in charter schools reflects the contemporary race and social class division in the neoliberal era. Racial and ethnic diversity in the classroom is driven by an increase in Hispanic and Asian students. Black and white students were basically no more likely to be in racially integrated schools in 2013 than they were in 1980. According to the UCLA study, "charter schools are more racially isolated than traditional public schools in virtually every state and large metropolitan area." Two trends stick out. The first is that 70% of majority black charter schools were 90–100% black. The second is how white students comprised a higher percent of charter school enrollment in urban areas. In other words, charter schools are ensuring that schools remain segregated in areas where public schools would otherwise be racially integrated.[18]

School Vouchers

School vouchers are a form of school privatization where the state uses public money to indirectly subsidize traditional private schools. A school voucher is basically a check from the state worth x amount of dollars payable to the private school of your choice. Traditional private schools include religious schools and private nondenominational schools. Similar to charter schools, the logic of school vouchers is based on the notion of choice. Advocates of school vouchers argue that parents should have the choice to send their children to whatever school they want regardless of their economic means. Ironically, this was the whole point of public education: giving a child an education regardless of his or her social class. However, advocates of school vouchers also draw on a once obscure paper published by Milton Friedman in 1955, right after the *Brown* decision and southern states granted locales the right to abolish public education. Friedman argued that school vouchers could reduce costs and improve education through increased competition. His was an example of the early use of the language of white-private, but the paper never had any influence over education policy makers.

School vouchers emerged as an alternative to abolishing public schools after the *Brown* decision. Georgia passed a Tuition Grant Law in 1955 that gave school vouchers to white families so that they could send their children to an all-white private school rather than a racially integrated public school. Eighty-three percent of white families who received school vouchers from the Tuition Grant Law already had their children in private schools. Georgia gave black families tuition grant subsidies to send their children to college out of state. The state issued over a 1,000 grants totaling $186,000 to subsidize white students' private school tuition in 1962. Hundreds of the grant recipients lived in the all-white sections outside of Atlanta. School vouchers were popular with elites and some middle-class whites because they received all the benefits of the tuition grants. Working-class whites couldn't afford private schools even with the vouchers. Georgia's Tuition Grant Law remained on the books until 1967.[19]

Fourteen states and the District of Columbia have some kind of school voucher program. Rather than a field of competition leading to better schools, as school voucher program advocates predicted, school

184   THE CRISIS IN AMERICAN EDUCATION

vouchers created the conditions for widespread corruption. Milwaukee, Wisconsin, was the first school district to implement a school voucher plan in 1990. Less than 10% of students in Milwaukee use the voucher program. Milwaukee's voucher program has been riddled with corruption and scandals, including a school that received money for students who never attended, the use of physical discipline, and schools refusing to release academic data. Florida used a school voucher program from 2006 to 2010 but ended the program because of widespread corruption, including one school that was housed above a liquor store. White-private schools in Louisiana that receive vouchers teach creationism in science class.[20]

School vouchers have been effective at creating racially segregated schools. Data and studies on the allocation of school vouchers and admittance or rejections based on race are scarce. States and schools refuse to supply the data. Where data does exist, we find the predictable pattern of how a white-private school voucher program is funneled to white families. Indiana actually does provide data on their school voucher program. The total cost was about $54 million for the 2015–16 school year. From the 2011–12 school year to the 2015–16 school year, the percentage of whites receiving school vouchers in Indiana's program increased from 46% to about 61%. The proportion of blacks receiving school vouchers in Indiana's program from the same time period actually dropped from 24% to 13%. The proportion of Hispanics remained somewhat constant, dropping from 20% to 18%. Sixty-one percent of voucher recipients for the 2015–16 school year lived in the city, down from 69% in 2011, whereas the number of vouchers from suburban areas increased from 16% to 22% in the same time frame. Cleveland began a school voucher program in the 1996–97 school year. Roughly two-thirds of the Cleveland students who received school vouchers for the 2000–01 school year never attended a public school. Ohio started their school voucher program called EdChoice in 2006. Ohio spent $117 million in 2015 on school vouchers to students attending a school that fails to meet state testing benchmarks. The 2014–15 data indicated that white students in Ohio disproportionately received a school voucher to attend a private school. Whites were 64.3% of Ohio's EdChoice expansion, a program that issued 3,600 vouchers to low-income students

THE CRISIS IN AMERICAN EDUCATION   185

whether they are attending low-performing schools or not. School vouchers are appealing to white families living in mixed-race urban and suburban areas.[21]

Not all private schools accept school vouchers and school voucher programs do not stipulate any mandates on private schools to accept students who apply. Private schools have the leeway to reject applicants for any reason. It feeds into the draw and mystique that surrounds white-private schools. This mystique emanates in part from a circular reasoning tied to meritocracy: the children of families who can afford to pay for private school receive a better education than children in public schools, which allows their children to obtain entrance into elite colleges and earn high incomes. You don't read stories in the newspaper about failing private schools, only requiems for the value of a Catholic school education as more and more Catholic schools shutter due to falling enrollment. The mystique surrounding private schools is a way to mask the structural aspects of systemic racism.

Elite private schools embed a hidden curriculum to teach elites what it means to be elite. Khan showed that elite boarding schools used to emphasize entitlement: the sense that you are superior to others based on your heritage and social class. The sense of elite entitlement was crucial to create social bonds between elites. Khan argued that contemporary elite boarding schools teach a hidden curriculum of privilege. Privilege emphasized how to act in the world. It links the notion of elite with generic values like hard work and personal accomplishments. Although elite universities are still overwhelmingly white, they are becoming more racially and ethnically diverse while simultaneously becoming more class homogenous.

Private schools help their children learn to value diversity even though the children's day-to-day lives are full of children just like them. White children learn how to value diversity as they learn privilege. The emphasis on diversity is designed to enrich the lives of young white children. It has replaced the emphasis of integrating schools to better the lives of young black children. Diversity helps elite white children learn how to interact with minorities so that they will be better CEOs, lawyers, teachers, and managers of firms in the future. Diversity also grants the private school some immunity to charges that they employ racist admission practices. Schools want some racial difference but not too much. As the previous chapter on where we live and the present chapter on where we go to school indicate, whites abandon neighborhoods and schools once a racial integration threshold is passed. Whites value diversity so long as actual relations with minorities are restricted to a minimal number of racially nonthreatening bodies. And therein lies the appeal of white-private schools in the neoliberal era.[22]

The neoliberal crisis in education in 2017 was the same crisis in education in 1954: integrated schools. It is a white-private crisis activated by real instances of racial integration. The original wave of school privatization after the *Brown* decision was confined to the parts of southern states with a sizable black population. Places like northern Alabama, which sits on the base of Appalachia, or places on the coastline of the Gulf of Mexico or the Atlantic Ocean did not have significant minority populations and thus were not places where we found the local school districts activating the private option. Places with a strong segregationist movement also did not activate the private option because they used violence and fired their black employees if they attempted to send their children to the white school. Northern cities did not have a sizable black population until the mid-1960s. Even then, a combination of residential segregation and feeder schools kept blacks in black schools. In 1968, 42.7% of black students in the Northeast were in were schools that were 90% to 100% black. White flight was a threat to the viability of urban school districts in the 1970s. This led to the creation of magnet schools, elite and specialized schools based on minimal amounts of minority students to keep whites in the city. Once the racial balance of magnet schools tipped too far into the black, as the proportion black and Hispanic school-aged children increased, whites reached back into the old segregationist's bag of tricks. The result was the return of white-private schools in the form of charter schools and school vouchers. In 2011, the number of black students in the South attending hypersegregated schools was 34.4%, while 51.4% of black students in the northeastern schools attended hypersegregated schools. Regardless of the deregulatory or privatization strategy involved, the crisis of American education over the last 60 plus years has been the crisis of racial integration.[23]

THE CRISIS IN AMERICAN EDUCATION   187

The notion that the crisis in education is a white-private crisis is not meant to downplay some of the key problems in our educational system today. School systems continue to grow their administrative budgets at the expense of instructional budgets and invest in dubious technology and pedagogical practices, like replacing books with tablets and chalkboards with Smart Boards. A real question is whether or not superintendents and school boards make these investments to help children or further their own careers. Property taxes are still the basis to pay for public education. In turn, rural white schools remain underfunded. Urban schools, the school systems where you find the overwhelming of majority black and Hispanic schools, are almost completely reliant on state and federal aid to remain open. School privatization does not fix any of these problems. Sociologists have produced a myriad of studies over the years that document the persistent problem of dysfunctional schools in poor black neighborhoods. Instead, white parents have mobilized to form charter schools and opt out of standardized tests. When black schools are defined as underperforming, they are ignored. When white schools are defined as underperforming, white parents mobilize to eliminate the criteria used to define their schools and children as average or underperforming.

Privatization is the preferred white solution to the problem of racially integrated schools. It was the alternative to massive resistance, white flight, and paying a private school tuition. Whites could not simply walk away from public schools the same way they could stop going to an integrated park, pool, or golf course or stop using public transportation. Outside of the for-profit charter schools, there is a distinct absence of a profit motive behind school privatization. Real estate elites and building owners profit off of rents, but the charter schools are overwhelmingly nonprofit organizations. A political debate currently exists around school vouchers because they funnel public funds into private schools through families who already have the means to pay for the schools. But this debate will eventually wane if the vouchers allow white students to escape integrated schools. And if and when it does happen, we can expect the complete privatization of public school districts with sizeable black and Hispanic populations.

Schools are arguably the key link between elites and ordinary whites. The only public entities whites interact with more than public schools

188   THE CRISIS IN AMERICAN EDUCATION

are roads and running water. White ambivalence to issues of racial equality ends at the schoolhouse door. The outcome is the establishment of a cultural chain of a white-private education that is superior to either a white-public or black-public education. The broader effects of the continual political struggles create the racist pretext to privatization and austerity that changed the underlying meaning of public education. Public is devalued because it is linked with black. In the neoliberal era, integrated public schools become black-public schools associate with poverty, danger, and waste rather than something that contributes to the collective good.

Notes

1. Memo on the Beatty Plan for maintaining separate schools, by William Henry Beatty, 12 July 1954, The Sam Engelhardt Papers, Alabama Department of Archives, Montgomery Alabama (hereafter cited as SE); Speech to Support School Bill, SE Box 4 Folder 8; "Suggested Plan for the School System if Supreme Court Abolishes Segregation"; Carl Grafton and Anne Permaloff, *Big Mules and Branchheads: James E. Folsom and Political Power in Alabama* (Athens, GA: University of Georgia Press, 1985), p. 186.
2. Ibid.; Montgomery Advertiser, "Special Session to Wipe Out Public School Unlikely Now", *Montgomery Advertiser* 9 September 1954; Montgomery Advertiser, "Outlook on School Bills Shaky as Deadline Nears" *Montgomery Advertiser*, 1 September 1955; The Alabamian August 1956 volume 1, no. 2, SE Box 15 Folder 1; Pupil Placement Acts became the method of keeping schools segregated all over the South and were not found to be unconstitutional until the 1968 *Green v. County School Board of New Kent County* case.
3. Yasuhiro Katagri, *The Mississippi State Sovereignty Commission: Civil Rights and State's Rights* (Jackson, MS: University of Mississippi Press, 2001), xxxii; "Why Should the Amendment to Abolish Public Schools to Prevent Integration be Passed, located in Citizens" Council 1954–55, dated 11/22/1954, Mississippi Department of Archives and History.
4. Neil McMillen, *The Citizens' Council: Organized Resistance to the Second Reconstruction, 1954–1964* (Urbana: University of Illinois Press, 1971), foot note, 73; Harold Paulk Henderson, *Ernest Vandiver, Governor of Georgia* (Athens: University of Georgia Press, 2000).
5. McMillen, *The Citizens' Council*, 16; Quoted in Charles Bolton, *The Hardest Deal of All: The Battle Over School Integration in Mississippi, 1870–1980* (Jackson, MS: University of Mississippi Press, 2005), 69; pp. 278–282.
6. Tuscaloosa News, "Engelhardt Introduces Bill to Abolish His Macon District" 14 July 1955, p. 25; "Report of Alabama Interim Legislation Committee on Segregation in the Public Schools" Jim Folsom Papers, Reel 41, Box 32, Folder 3.
7. Ibid.; Pamphlet, "The Educational Fund of the Citizens' Council: Published in Greenwood Mississippi" Citizens Council Publications, 1952–1960, MDAH; Bolton, *The Hardest Deal of All*, 76; Bolton, *The Hardest Deal of All*.

THE CRISIS IN AMERICAN EDUCATION   189

8. Crespino, *In Search of Another Country*, 1; Grafton and Permaloff, *Political Power in Alabama*, 198; Luther Munford, 1973, "White Flight from Desegregation in Mississippi" *Integrated Education* 11: pp. 12–26.

9. McMillen, *The Citizens' Council*, 300, 303.

10. McMillen, *The Citizens' Council*, 301; Bolton, *The Hardest Deal of All*, 177; Michael W. Fuquay, Summer 2002, "Civil Rights and the Private School Movement in Mississippi, 1964–1971" *History of Education Quarterly* 42 (2): pp. 159–180, 167; McMillen, *The Citizens' Council*, p. 302; Crespino, *In Search of Another Country*, p. 200; Fuquay, "Civil Rights and the Private School Movement in Mississippi, 1964–1971," p. 176; McMillen, *The Citizens Council*, p. 302.

11. Grafton and Permaloff, *Political Power in Alabama*, 198; J. Mills Thorton, *Dividing Lines: Municipal Politics and the Struggle for Civil Rights in Montgomery, Birmingham, and Selma* (Tuscaloosa and London: The University of Alabama Press, 2002); See Thorton, *Dividing Lines*.

12. Jeffery Mirel, *The Rise and Fall of an Urban School System: Detroit: 1907–1981, 2nd Edition* (Ann Arbor: University of Michigan Press, 1999), 350; Ibid., p. 349.

13. US Census, Boston Public Schools, 2012; Katharine Seelye, "4 Decades After Clashes, Boston Again Debates School Busing" *New York Times*, 4 October 2012, located at www.nytimes.com/2012/10/05/education/new-boston-busing-debate-4-decades-after-fervid-clashes.html

14. For Arne Duncan see "Education Secretary Duncan Calls Hurricane Katrina Good for New Orleans Schools" *Washington Post*, 30 January 2010, located at www.washingtonpost.com/wp-dyn/content/article/2010/01/29/AR2010012903259.html; for overview of New Orleans and it critics see Andrea Gabor Op-ed, "The Myth of the New Orleans School Makeover" *New York Times*, 22 August 2015, located at www.nytimes.com/2015/08/23/opinion/sunday/the-myth-of-the-new-orleans-school-makeover.html?_r=0

15. Ibid.

16. Because charter schools receive public funding, they are classified as public schools. Schools with a paid tuition requirement are classified as private schools. These numbers do not include college and university students; Quote located at http://files.eric.ed.gov/fulltext/ED491210.pdf

17. The Center for Research Education Outcomes, "National Charter School Study" Stanford University, 2013, located at http://credo.stanford.edu/documents/NCSS%20 2013%20Final%20Draft.pdf; United States Government Accountability Office (GAO), "Charter Schools: Additional Federal Attention to Help Protect Access for Students with Disabilities"June 2012, GAO-12–543, located at www.gao.gov/products/ GAO-12-543; UCLA Civil Rights Project, "Charter Schools, Civil Rights, and School Discipline: A Comprehensive Review" 2016, located at www.civilrightsproject.ucla.edu/resources/projects/center-for-civil-rights-remedies/school-to-prison-folder/federal-reports/charter-schools-civil-rights-and-school-discipline-a-comprehensive-review; Mark Berends, 2015, "Sociology and School Choices: What We Know after Two Decades of Charter Schools" *Annual Review of Sociology* 41: pp. 159–180.

18. Erica Frankenberg, Genevieve Siegel-Hawley, and Jia Wang, 2010, *Choice without Equity: Charter School Segregation and the Need for Civil Rights Standards* (Los Angeles, CA: The Civil Rights Project/Proyecto Derechos Civiles, 2010), located at www.civilrightsproject.ucla.edu; Grover J. Whitehurst, Richard V. Reeves, and Edward

Rodrigue, "Segregation, Race, and Charter Schools: What Do We Know" Brookings Institute, Center on Children and Families, October 2016.

19. Calvin Trillin, *An Education in Georgia: Charlayne Hunter, Hamilton Homes, and the Integration of the University of Georgia* (Athens: University of Georgia Press, 1992), p. 47; Kruse, *White Flight*, p. 171.

20. Valerie Strauss, "The New Push for School Vouchers at State, Federal Levels" *Washington Post*, 12 February 2014, located at www.washingtonpost.com/news/answer-sheet/wp/2014/02/12/the-new-push-for-school-vouchers-at-state-federal-levels/?utm_term=.6242b019e42e

21. Indiana Department of Education, Office of School Finance, "Choice Scholarship Program and Annual Report: Participation and Payment Data" April 2016, located at www.doe.in.gov/sites/default/files/news/2015-2016-choice-scholarship-program-report-final-april2016.pdf; Bill Bush, "White Students Disproportionately Use Ohio School Voucher Program" *Columbus Dispatch*, 17 August 2016, located at www.dispatch.com/content/stories/local/2016/08/28/white-students-disproportionately-use-ohio-school-voucher-program.html

22. John D. Skrentny, *After Civil Rights: Racial Realism in the New American Workplace* (Princeton, NJ: Princeton University Press, 2014), p. 10.

23. Niraj Chokski, "The Most Segregated Schools May Not be in the States You'd Expect" *Washington Post*, 2014, located at www.washingtonpost.com/blogs/govbeat/wp/2014/05/15/the-most-segregated-schools-may-not-be-in-the-states-youd-expect-2/ (last accessed 31 December 2014).

7

WHITE-PRIVATE VIOLENCE
POLICE BRUTALITY AND
MASS INCARCERATION

Blame it on those hot summer nights. That's what the *New York Times* did in an article about the 1967 Roxbury Riots. The hot summer weather can take quite the toll on the body, especially during a riot. For two black women who "swiped a huge television set from an appliance store" and struggled to carry the television down the street and then up the front steps and into the front room of their Roxbury home, the only thing more unbearable than the heat was their discovery: "Damn! All that work and it ain't even a color set." It could have been worse. They could have been the black women the police dragged from the city's welfare office protesting the indiscriminate removal of black mothers from their right to receive public assistance that triggered the riot. But then again, that may have already happened to them. The *Times* reporter never followed up on the secondhand story of the two women and the heavy black-and-white television set.

It seems that every instance of a racial uprising or a so-called race riot happens in relation to an instance of police brutality. Police brutality is not the cause of the riots. Police brutality is part of an existing network of racial inequalities that include economic discrimination and residential segregation. Cities like Watts, Newark, and Rochester became synonymous with race riots in the late 1960s. They didn't become synonymous with police brutality. In the same 1967 article about the Roxbury Riots, the *Times* reporter asked why the riot started. The answer was "Too many policemen, the Negroes said, and not enough jobs and decent houses." Fast-forward 50 years later, police brutality exists in an almost identical network of racial inequalities in Ferguson, Cleveland, Baltimore, and New York.

One constant feature of the neoliberal era has been the expansion of the criminal justice system in relation to the racialized insecurity of white America. As we've seen in the previous two chapters, privatization emerged as the preferred strategy to reclaim intimate spaces where flesh-and-blood bodies interact, like schools and neighborhoods, on behalf of whites. However, privatization has its limits. White-private schools and white-private gated communities may protect elite whites from blacks and other poor groups, but they cannot protect elites from themselves. Neoliberal economic and political policy has increased inequality to the extent that it became a threat to elite white power. At the limits of white-private, we find the state willing to use the police to protect elite white interests.

This chapter looks at the meta history of the most explicit form of elite white control: using the state's autonomy over the means of violence to selectively target the black population. The centralization of police violence is relatively new and started with a move to criminalize black protest affiliated with the civil rights movement. Prior to the civil rights movement, white violence toward blacks was decentralized across a network of local police and white supremacists groups. It was during the civil rights movement that the state began to centralize police power, first by limiting white violence against the civil rights protesters and second, by actively criminalizing black movements through FBI, CIA, and COINTELPRO programs. This pattern continued in the 1980s and 1990s. The Reagan and Clinton administrations produced a comprehensive federal policing policy that targeted and imprisoned black men. There is a direct link between the racial coding of drug laws and the privatization of prisons to an indirect pattern of private parole and arbitration.

The Two-Pronged Criminal Justice System

Reconstruction Era

Slavery was abolished in 1865. On paper, the end of American slavery was a significant blow to elite whites. The system of slave labor used to pick cotton for domestic and foreign export made many bankers, factory owners, shippers, and farmers wealthy. Freed black slaves could now own property, establish businesses, and enter public life. It was perhaps this last sentiment, the ability of blacks to enter and walk freely in public, that prompted a general violent white reaction against blacks. Although elite whites could no longer control black movement in public space, they still controlled Congress and state legislatures and access to capital and credit. It is in relation to the loss of white-public space where we find the development of a two-pronged criminal justice system.

The two-pronged criminal justice system was a system of white-sanctioned violence disbursed across the state and white civil society. Although it was primarily aimed at blacks, poor whites and whites sympathetic to racial equality or the unions were also caught up in the violence. The state-backed criminal justice system included judges, prisons, and the police. This prong of the criminal justice system protected capital by enforcing contracts and ignoring workers' civil citizenship rights. It protected elite white interests by negating contracts with Native Americans, as well as using the military to relocate Native Americans off of lands rich in nutrients and commodities like iron, coal, and timber to the dry and arid Midwest. It protected elite whites by refusing to prosecute white violence against blacks. Finally, the 13th Amendment that abolished slavery and involuntary servitude also included the clause that exempted involuntary servitude as a punishment for crime. As Davis argued, the black codes replaced the slave codes via the selective criminalization of violations like breach of contract, vagrancy, possession of firearms, and insulting gestures when blacks committed the violation.[1]

White civil society made up the second prong of the criminal justice system. Whereas the state was the core of the criminal justice system, white civil society served as the periphery and shadow criminal justice system. In an ideal world, civil society is the space between the state and the family where common interests are realized through debate, and places like churches and town hall meetings level the playing field between competing social classes. For Alexis de Tocqueville, white Kansas represented the idealized civil society. He would have arrived at a different conclusion about democracy in America if he had stayed in the tenements in New York or ventured down south. Civil society in urban centers and the rural South organized a system of violence to enforce racial and ethnic boundaries. The overlapping white networks between the state and civil society created systemic racist violence against blacks.

White civil society provided the institutional location for a shadow system of criminal justice. The system of criminal justice included antiblack and anti-immigrant groups. No other American group represents the use of racial violence on the periphery like the Ku Klux Klan. In 1865, a handful of former Confederate soldiers in Tennessee formed the first Klan. They were one of a handful of racist white organizations that included the White League and the Knights of the White Camellia. The first Klan was not well organized. They existed in an assemblage of local chapters held together by a shared history, a shared geography, racism, and a disdain for Republican carpetbaggers that rivaled their disdain for blacks. Although the first rendition of the Klan only lasted 5 years, the impact of their 5-year reign of terror lasted for generations.

The type of violence that periphery groups like the Klan exercised is known as a 'spectacle of violence'. Michel Foucault defined a 'spectacle of violence' as a dramatic and ritualized form of violence that seeks to control populations through fear. We see the dramatic aspects of violence in how the Klan policed the newly freed black slaves: the white hoods, riding horses in the night, burning crosses. These dramatic effects became terrifying to blacks because that conjured up memories and emotions linked with terror. Lynching was a ritual. Angela Davis defined lynching as an "extralegal institution that surrendered thousands of African-American lives to the violence of ruthless racist mobs." Du Bois captures the Klan's spectacle of violence in *Black Reconstruction*. Du Bois quoted General Carl Schurz at length, who, along with Ulysses Grant and Harvey Watterson, was sent by President Andrew Johnson to report on the conditions of the post-Civil War South. Schurz reported that the Klan was comprised of

> Armed bands of white men [who] patrolled the county roads to drive back the Negroes wandering about. Dead bodies of murdered Negroes were found on and near the highways and byways . . . [hospital] reports of colored men and women whose ears had been cut off, whose skulls had been broken by blows,

whose bodies had been slashed by knives or lacerated with scourges.

Returning Confederate soldiers met a black man on the public highway. "They first castrated him, and afterwards murdered him in cold blood." An 18-year-old black woman arrived at a hospital after she was "bucked and gagged" with gashes on her back "as large as my little finger. . . . It may have been larger" because she could no longer spin cotton at 8 months pregnant.[2]

The federal government exercised the legal power of the state to end the first Klan. It was not an act of benevolence or social justice to protect the rights of former slaves. Rather, it was the consolidation of elite white power on the national level. As Du Bois noted, this was the instance of the unification of "Big business, super-finance, and the southern planters" that restarted the southern planters' control and exploitation over black lives. Du Bois noted that "the Democrats promised to 'guarantee peace, good order, protection of the law to whites and blacks': or in other words, exploitation should be so quiet, orderly, and legal as to assure regular profit to Southern owners and Northern investors." The unification of northern and southern elite whites paved the way for the convict-lease system. The convict-lease system was the legal practice of leasing prisoners to companies for a fee. Although the same companies that relied on slave labor to remain profitable, like cotton plantations and mines, were the primary beneficiaries of convict leasing, northern companies also leased convicts to lay down rail tracks. The black codes flipped the racial composition of US inmates upside down, thus providing a steady supply of forced black labor. David Oshinsky argued that the convict-leasing system was worse than slavery because companies literally worked blacks to death. In addition to exhaustion, malnutrition, and dysentery, blacks died of "shackle poisoning" as the shackles broke the skin around the ankles and opened the body to bacterial infection. The convict-lease system was practiced by southern states into the early 20th century. Texas did not abolish convict leasing until 1928.[3]

The end of the period of reconstruction accidently created the demand for black convict-lease labor via the new 1890 southern state constitutions. The 1890 southern state constitutions capped interest rates that banks could charge and began the era of legal segregation known as Jim Crow and the one-party system that lasted for more than 60 years. However, it was the economic turmoil from the long depression that tied elite whites with ordinary whites in relation to a new demand for cheap black labor. The depression that lasted from 1873 to 1879 is referred to as the 'long depression' because it is the longest period of economic depression in global history. The long depression depressed global commodity prices, making convict leasing the only way for companies to remain in business. While Jim Crow laws restricted access to the limited state resources to whites, they further opened up the criminal justice system to blacks, whose forced labor was instrumental in building America.

The solidification of a white-public culture created the conditions for another shadow criminal justice system in the early 20th century. Echoing the events of 1865, a second shadow criminal justice system developed in relation to the increased political power of northern blacks associated with the New Negro Movement and the Harlem Renaissance. Inspired by Du Bois, the New Negro Movement refers to a group of writers, activists, and public intellectuals who shared an interest in racial and class equality in Harlem. Whereas the state fused 19th-century periphery white violence to the state under the convict-lease system and Jim Crow laws to consolidate elite white power, the early 20th-century shadow criminal justice system arose in relation to middle-class whites trying to protect their access to state resources. Elite and ordinary whites worried about the growing population of blacks in Harlem, Detroit, and Chicago. They feared black political power. The white response to the New Negro Movement was the second Ku Klux Klan.

The 1915 film *Birth of a Nation* helped to nationalize the Klan's popularity. It was based on Thomas Dixon's novels *The Clansmen and the Leopard's Spots* and *The Traitor*. Dixon was more than just an author. He was a public intellectual who briefly served in North Carolina's General Assembly and briefly served as a minister in New York City. His friends included John Rockefeller and Theodore Roosevelt. The film *Birth of a Nation* told a racist story through a heroic narrative of the Klan saving white society from blacks. The most explicit scene featured Klan members saving a white woman from a black rapist, whom they promptly hung.

WHITE-PRIVATE VIOLENCE

Although black-on-white violence was as rare as a two-headed chicken, elite whites drew from white racist fears to fan the flames of periphery white violence.

The second Ku Klux Klan was a national white supremacist movement. It was organized through fraternal organizations and Protestant churches. Nancy MacLean estimated that about five million middle-class whites, organized through 4,000 chapters, were located throughout the United States. The Klan was especially popular in Midwestern and western states that lacked Jim Crow laws to legally protect white-public spaces. The second Klan did not restart lynching. Lynching never stopped. From 1882 to 1934, lynch mobs murdered more than 5,000 people, almost all black. One person was prosecuted. Indeed, the police ignored and encouraged white violence toward blacks in riots in New York, East St. Louis, and Chicago. The rise of the second Klan reestablished a mechanism of violence to protect the white economy from racial integration. Migrant black workers who migrated from the southern plantations seeking employment in the northern factories could not avoid white violence.[4]

Thus, from the end of slavery to the eve of the civil rights movement, a dual criminal justice system existed to protect the interests of white elites. The end of slavery made blacks a political and economic threat to global capitalism. The arm of the criminal justice system associated with the state expanded the definitions of criminality specifically tied to blacks in order to force blacks back onto the plantations and into mines. The arm of the criminal justice system associated with white civil society ensured that a spectacle of systemic violence existed to informally protect white-public spaces. The two arms of the criminal justice system fused elite whites with middle-class whites. Whereas Foucault saw the abrupt end to the spectacle of violence in France, American systemic racism ensured that a rational and ritualized violent criminal justice system existed simultaneously.

Civil Rights Era

The civil rights era ended the Jim Crow period. The *Brown* decision made the *Plessy v. Ferguson* statute of separate but equal unconstitutional. In addition to the demand for racial integration, the Montgomery bus boycott tested the two-pronged system of criminal justice that legitimated state-sanctioned white violence. As elite whites entered into a period of collective confusion against the latest black movement to demand equal rights, the use of periphery violence inched closer to the state core.

One reason peripheral white violence began to fuse with the state was the formation of a new segregationist organization: the White Citizens' Council. By the mid-1950s, the Klan had retreated to the margins of southern life. While there were still Klan chapters in and around the few industrial cities and rural areas, they were more of a symbolic threat than actual one. The White Citizens' Council, which quickly became known as just the Citizens' Council, was soon the central organizing hub of segregationists and big business. Citizens' Council chapters sprang up all over the Deep and Upper South. By May 1957, there were approximately 300,000 members of the Citizens' Councils who raised over $2 million to fight racial integration. Citizens' Councils differed by state. In Mississippi, they were the main practitioners of violence. In Alabama, members of the Citizens' Councils were local elites, including businessmen, mayors, and state senators. They preferred economic sanctions, like firing blacks from their jobs, denying them credit, and evicting them from their homes to dramatic public violence.[5]

Another reason that white violence moved closer to the state was the rise of good black citizenship. Good black citizenship made nonviolent protests meaningful. After all, blacks were nonviolent before the civil rights movement and had little to show for their political struggles. Movement leaders like King not only also refused to respond violently and clash with police and whites, they also refused to lash out with emotionally charged rhetoric that reflected black stereotypes. This confused elite whites and their nonelite white allies. They were used to blacks backing down from their demands for equality when threatened with violence. They were used to always being in the right, no matter what they did or how they did it. This began to change during the Montgomery bus boycott. When a group of local whites bombed King's house, King did not lash out. In fact, he calmed down a situation that was rapidly escalating into a full-fledged riot. King symbolized the new political representation of black citizenship that put the spotlight on peripheral white violence.

WHITE-PRIVATE VIOLENCE

The various civil rights movement's demonstrations hastened the fusion of peripheral white violence with the state. This was not a linear process. Voter registration drives did not create the violent white response the movement needed. Nor did all southern locales provide the movement with a bad white response. SNCC found no success when they went to Albany, Georgia, and were confronted by a sheriff named Laurie Pritchett. Pritchett instructed his police officers to use minimal violence, especially when the media were present, to neutralize the movement's strategy of establishing a good black / bad white binary to highlight racial injustice. The movement found their bad white adversary in other locales, most famously in Birmingham and Selma, Alabama. Birmingham had two nicknames—the Magic City and Bombingham. The former came from its rapid industrial growth at the turn of the twentieth century. The latter came from the history of Birmingham-area Klan members bombing black homes, black-owned businesses, and black churches. By 1963, the only magic trick Birmingham had left was making black people disappear. Between 1947 and 1953, white supremacists set off over 50 bombs in black neighborhoods to dissuade blacks from pushing for neighborhood and school integration. Bombings were so common and ignored by Birmingham officials that local racist Robert Edward Chambliss was affectionately known in the community as "Dynamite Bob."[6]

The spectacle of violence in Birmingham and Selma was possible because peripheral white violence fused with the state. In Birmingham, the link between the state and peripheral violence was through one person: Eugene "Bull" Connor. Connor had a long history of using violence against labor protests and against local black elites and had direct connections with the local Klan. David Vann, a political rival of Connor's, eventual mayor of Birmingham, and the closest thing you could find to an elite white moderate in Birmingham, spoke openly of the relationship between the Klan and local elite whites. Vann stated that Birmingham had the largest membership of Klansmen in the United States and that the Klan's political importance should not be underestimated: "I'm told that, [as] a fact, that a person who was running for office, if they were not supporters of the Klan, they couldn't get elected." Vann alluded to how many Klan members were professionals who joined every organization to get elected. Concerning the police, Vann stopped short of saying that the Klan and the police were one and the same, just that "Well, I don't think they were one in the same, but I'll say this. . . . I really think there were probably informers that informed for the police department and FBI."[7]

In Selma, peripheral white violence was formally linked with the state in two ways. The first was through Dallas County Sheriff Jim Clark. He deputized a local white posse that ranged between 300 and 500 men, dressed them in old army fatigues, and armed them. The second was through George Wallace. Wallace deployed the state police to stop the civil rights movement's march from Selma to Montgomery. The march was supposed to highlight black voter disenfranchisement in the South. Combined, the deputized white posse and state police unleashed a spectacle of violence that surpassed the violence in Birmingham. The state police, local sheriff's office, and the white posse attacked the civil rights protesters with tear gas, electric cattle prods, and batons as they attempted to cross the Edmund Pettus Bridge—a bridge named after a Confederate general. The spectacle of violence was broadcast nationally over network television. The federal government did not send in troops to protect the protesters until after the violence found its way into the antiracist white community: whites killed James Reed, a white minister, after he left a local diner with blacks, and Violet Liuzzo, a white activist from Michigan while she was driving a black civil rights worker from Selma back to Montgomery.

The movement of white violence on the periphery to the state core during the civil rights era created the conditions for systemic racism to become the singular logic of America's criminal justice system. Rather than being eliminated, white violence became state violence directed at blacks. This is evident in the urban race riots, Richard Nixon's War on Drugs, and the expansion of the FBI's COINTELPRO program of the late civil rights era and early 1970s.

Although there were many issues simmering beneath the surface in Watts, California, like its declining physical infrastructure and the disappearance of job prospects for blacks, the event that ignited the most significant race riot in the second half of the twentieth century was police brutality. Although blacks had endured peripheral white violence since reconstruction, systemic police brutality was relatively new, and it

WHITE-PRIVATE VIOLENCE

grew as the urban black population grew. The near all-white police forces took it upon themselves to police the symbolic and geographic boundaries between black and white neighborhoods with violence, via beatings and what police call 'pretext stops', stopping someone over a minor traffic violation, like a broken taillight on a car, to justify a broader police inspection. In black neighborhoods in northern and western cities, it was either the absence of the police force or a violent police response.

Nixon's southern strategy drew on whites' racial insecurity to expand the presence of the FBI into the black community. Nixon and Patrick Buchanan saw the political opportunity in George Wallace's presidential campaigns in 1968 and 1972. Wallace emphasized issues like forced busing to draw the support of middle- and working-class whites. Nixon added one important element to the southern strategy: the War on Drugs. Nixon declared a War on Drugs to associate blacks and antiwar protesters with drugs, violence, and disorder. According to John Ehrlicman, a Nixon advisor on domestic affairs, the Nixon administration

> Knew we couldn't make it illegal to be either against the war or black. But by getting the public to associate the hippies with marijuana and blacks with heroin, and then criminalizing both heavily, we could disrupt those communities. We could arrest their leaders, raid their homes, break up their meeting, and vilify them night after night on the evening news. Did we know we were lying about the drugs? Of course we did.[8]

Armed with a new strategy to target his political enemies, Nixon increased the number of federal drug control agencies, instituted mandatory sentencing of two to 10 years, and made no-knock warrants legal. In 1973, the Drug Enforcement Administration replaced the Bureau of Narcotics and Dangerous Drugs.

New York's Rockefeller Drug Laws illustrate the expansion of rational state violence into the black community. Passed in 1973 and named after former New York State governor Nelson Rockefeller, the Rockefeller Drug Laws instituted mandatory prison sentences for drug sales, extended the length of sentences for drug offenses, and converted the sale of heroin and cocaine to Class A felonies. First-degree murder is a Class A felony in New York State. Until 1973, New York used drug treatment and therapy to fight addiction. Rockefeller viewed these programs as expensive and ineffective. As Kohler-Hausman showed, Rockefeller ignored advice from drug treatment experts: "His proposal was deliberately antispecialist, and the flagrant rejection of modern, social scientific knowledge was a key part of its appeal." The late civil rights era made using overt racial connections politically problematic for elite whites. Kohler-Hausman viewed elite framing of the Rockefeller Drug Laws as "efforts to protect the public" from "the addict" and "the drug dealer." Although she correctly noted how the addict and drug dealer were code words for black and Hispanic in New York, law and order police strategies were linked with black-public, not separated from the public. Black-public created white support for draconian drug laws because it contrasted the white-private homes and communities as needing protection from black-public crime, violence, addiction, guns, and gangs.[9]

In order to get broad support for the new drug laws, Rockefeller selectively worked with local black elites in Harlem. The new assemblage of racial inclusion that started with the civil rights movement allowed for narrow inclusion and broad marginalization of black life in the post-civil rights era. Local black elites and middle-class blacks wanted the state to do something to save their declining city neighborhoods. Fighting crime was the only issue elite whites put on the negotiating table. As Alexander argued, "Conservatives could point to black support for highly punitive approaches to dealing with the problems of the urban poor as 'proof' that race had nothing to do with their 'law and order' agenda." Drawing in black support hardened the links between black and public by putting a black face on the victim and the perpetrator.[10]

Finally, the federal government fused peripheral white violence with the state via the expansion of the COINTELPRO program. The federal government used global issues to rationalize the expansion of the federal criminal justice system. The FBI organized a counterintelligence program dubbed COINTELPRO to eliminate all left-wing political movements in America. It was formed in 1956 under the direction of J. Edgar Hoover to target communist groups. Hoover expanded the program to include the anti–Vietnam War movements, prodemocracy

WHITE-PRIVATE VIOLENCE

movements, the American Indian Movement, and of course, the black nationalists.[11]

Hoover and COINTELPRO's main focus was Oakland's Black Panther Party. Huey Newton and Bobby Seal formed the Black Panthers in 1966. They were inspired by the work of black nationalists in SNCC working in rural Alabama, who formed a political party called the Black Panther Party to run black candidates in local elections. The Black Panthers' political and community work focused on providing health care and other social services to the black community. Their public appearance, which consisted of black leather jackets, sunglasses, military-esque postures, and openly legally carrying guns, fed into the white elite fantasies of all blacks as criminals. In contrast to the civil rights movement associated with King, the Black Panther Party wanted to be racially threatening as an expression of the politics of black authenticity. Hoover called the Black Panthers the "Greatest threat to Internal Security." Of 295 COINTELPRO programs that the FBI admitted to conducting, 233 were aimed at the Black Panther Party.[12]

COINTELPRO was not the first time the federal government organized a formal program to stop the civil rights movement. The US Justice Department Community Relations Service (CRS) studied the civil rights movement's strategies in the mid-1960s. The CRS consulted local municipalities on how to police the civil rights protests. Unlike Hoover's obsession with destroying the entire movement, the CRS drew from Pritchett's policing model and urged a good white response to prevent the movement from filing federal lawsuits. Furthermore, the FBI created the Ghetto Informant Program (GIP), which ran from 1967 to 1973, to collect information on urban black communities. Similar to the days of the Klan, they did not target white supremacist groups, despite the federal government listing the Klan on the federal terrorist list. Thus, COINTELPRO was the culmination of state efforts to incorporate peripheral white violence. The Nixon administration criminalized black protests in particular and urban black communities in general.[13]

The fusion of peripheral white violence with the juridical aspects of the criminal justice system happened in relation to the civil rights movement. The Nixon administration used black-public crime to criminalize urban black politics by associating the black nationalists and the politics of black authenticity with urban blight and poverty. Although imprisonment rates did not increase in the early part of the 1970s, the foundation for the state to mobilize against racial minorities was set during the late civil rights era. The era of mass imprisonment begins in the neoliberal era.

Mass Imprisonment in the Neoliberal Era:
Prisons, Austerity, and Privatization

Imprisonment rates grew sharply after Ronald Reagan became the 40th president of the United States in 1980, despite no real increase in crime rates. Reagan drew from the black-public protest-crime link established by Nixon to justify implementing two key neoliberal policy objectives to the criminal justice system: austerity and privatization. The result was a combination of increased drug arrests, an increase in federal money to build prisons, cutbacks to federal antipoverty programs, the start of private prisons, and a link between US global and domestic policy. In short, the era of mass imprisonment involved the state creating the same marginalized black population that it eventually imprisoned.

Austerity involves drastically reducing or eliminating public money for social services and antipoverty programs. Despite the rhetoric of small government, Reagan paired reductions in antipoverty funds with increased federal spending on prisons. The Reagan administration took its cue from the Nixon administration. Between 1970–75, Nixon changed the formula to determine how the federal government supplied anti-poverty funds to cities. Under Johnson's War on Poverty program, the federal government provided project grants to fund urban renewal proj-ects in cities and Head Start programs in schools. Nixon replaced the federal project grants with block grants and lowered the levels of general revenue sharing. In 1981, the Reagan administration cut funding to AFDC, housing assistance, and school lunches despite the increase in need for these services. On top of eliminating Urban Development Action Grants, the 1986 budget included a 9% cut in housing assistance, mass transit, and urban infrastructure.

Reagan made the black-public crime link the central cultural assem-blage behind a series of crime bills in the 1980s. In contrast to Gerald Ford and Jimmy Carter, Reagan began the precedent of making executive orders and omnibus crime bills a part of domestic policy. Reagan signed three major executive orders in 1984 and two more in 1986. Each crime bill explicitly drew from the racist links between the War on Drugs and blacks to increase money for prisons, create minimum sentences for drug offenses, and created sentence disparities between crack and powdered cocaine. Sentence disparities over cocaine and crack reflect the social class and racial differences in cocaine use. Powdered cocaine is expensive. Crack is cheap, but it weighs more. To make crack, you have to cook cocaine in water and baking soda, which gives it the rocklike appearance it's nicknamed after and adds mass. Prison sentences were determined by weight, so poor blacks and whites were sent to prison for a longer time than upper-class white drug dealers and addicts. When Reagan took office, there were 329,821 people in federal and state prison. When he left office in 1988, 627,600 people were in federal and state prison, an increase of 90%.[14]

The 1990s continued the trend of mass imprisonment. Federal prisons were operating at 146% capacity, while state prisons were at 131% capacity. America elected Clinton as president under the guise of a new Democrat and amid another recession. As I discussed in Chapter 3, Clinton took the neoliberal turn to places Reagan could only dream, ending AFDC and Glass-Steagall. Predictably, imprisonment rates continued to soar in the 1990s, driven by three key developments: the new penal ideology, the 1994 omnibus crime bill, and imprisonment as a form of economic development in distressed areas.[15]

The first new addition was embedding black-public crime into a new penal ideology. Loic Wacquant points out penal policy in the 1990s was driven through the fusion of neoliberal and neoconservative thinks tanks, and thus, the "private sector makes a decisive contribution to the conception and implementation of 'public policy." These included the Cato Institute, American Enterprise Institute, and Manhattan Institute. The conservative think tanks fused social-psychological research that argued crime is triggered by urban disorder, things like broken windows and abandoned cars, with racist ideas of the danger of integrated public space. Rudolph Giuliani put these ideas into police practice and, in turn, made broken windows theory and zero tolerance standard policing strategies and dubious theories taught in criminal justice courses. Led by New York

City Police Chief William Bratton, Giuliani increased the police budget by 40%, hired an additional 12,000 officers, and implemented new technologies designed to statistically track bad behavior. By 1996, New York was making about 1,000 arrests per week for minor drug offenses.[16]

The new penal ideology provided a national and global model for elite whites to reclaim public space. The new policing lexicon and police practice was organized around the black-public/white-private binary. Zero-tolerance policing specifically targets groups on the margins, such as the homeless, squatters, addicts, poor blacks, and poor Hispanics, because they have the least amount of resources to fight back. The rates of police brutality spiked in the 1990s, increasing by 60% during the Giuliani era. The apex of police brutality in New York City was the plunger rape incident. In 1997, four New York City police officers responded to a call about a melee outside a Haitian nightclub in Brooklyn. They apprehended Abner Louima and took him back to the precinct known as 'Fort Tomb'. The four officers took Louima to the public bathroom, beat him, and threw him on the floor. Then two officers held him down while Officer Bruder proceeded to shove the wooden handle of a plunger in and out Louima's rectum, before shoving the blood- and shit-covered handle into Louima's mouth. The officers threatened to kill Louima if he told anyone. The extent of police violence in 1997 rivaled the peripheral white violence in 1867.

The racist portraits of black and Latino criminals that hung in the background of racially integrated public spaces continued to shape whites' preoccupation with crime in spite of declining crime rates. Clinton's New Democrat coalition epitomized the selective inclusion of local black elites at the expense of blacks on the margins. Clinton's approach to federal criminal justice reform was redefining bad blacks as career criminals who were responsible for the majority of crime. He noted, "Gangs and drugs have taken over our streets and undermined our schools. Every day, we read about somebody else who has literally gotten away with murder." Hillary Clinton reiterated the link between bad blacks and career criminals by extending the association to children:

> They are not just gangs of kids anymore. They are often the kinds of kids that are called "super-predators." No conscience,

no empathy. We can talk about why they ended up that way, but first we have to bring them to heel.

It was against this backdrop that the New Democrats lined up to support the 1994 Violent Crime Control and Law Enforcement Act. The 1994 crime bill expanded the death penalty, lengthened prison sentences through 'truth-in-sentencing laws', eliminated federal funding for inmate education, increased funding for new prisons, increased funding for 100,000 new police officers, and established sex offender registries.[17]

Finally, the construction of prisons and mass imprisonment became economic policy in the 1990s. Prisons were built in depressed rural white areas. They replaced factories and the network of farms and food processing plants that make up agribusiness. Prisons as economic policy connected the state with Wall Street. Investment banks, like Goldman Sachs, financed the construction of federal and state penitentiaries. The construction of prisons as economic policy has been characterized a recession-proof economic policy. The state has an insatiable desire for putting the poor in prison. Prison budgets continue to rise to employ corrections officers, sergeants, lieutenants, captains, supervisors, social workers, and wardens. However, a local economy based on prisons and schoolteachers does not produce goods and services that can produce surplus value to build local economies around. There is also an important political side to using mass imprisonment as economic policy. The inmate population counts toward the local population census count, and with the exception of Maine and Vermont, prisoners are not allowed to vote. This gives conservative white rural populations a greater say over state and federal legislation than racially diverse urban areas.

By the late 1990s, social critics were lamenting the rise of the prison-industrial complex, built on the racist black-public crime link of black criminality, welfare mothers, and racist police practices. As Silverstein noted,

> The prison industrial complex is not a conspiracy, but a confluence of special interests that include politicians who exploit crime to win votes, private companies that make millions running or supplying prisons, and small town officials who have turned to prisons as a method for economic development.

Angela Davis added consumers, informational technology (IT) firms, lobbyists, private manufacturers, and academics to the ever-expanding list of beneficiaries of mass imprisonment. Wacquant characterized the expansion of America's penal system in the 1990s in terms of its vertical and horizontal expansion, to capture the number of new prisons, new prisoners, and longer sentences, and the drastic increase of parole and probation. The racist stereotypes that lurk behind crime rival only inter-racial sex in conjuring up middle-class white fears. Elite whites were able to consolidate white political support around mass imprisonment while creating a market around poverty. All the time, crime rates have stayed the same since 1971.[18]

Privatizing the Criminal Justice System

The black-public crime link that was established in the 1960s and 1970s set the stage for the privatization of the criminal justice system from the 1980s through the turn of the century. Although white racialized insecurity of public life that drove the process of mass incarceration continued into the 21st century, it does not explain how other aspects of the criminal justice system have been privatized. Privatization is fundamentally about control. Elite whites have linked privatization with existing neoliberal values of austerity and emerging global problems to tighten their grip on the state. As the criminal justice system is further privatized, blacks, poor whites, and Hispanics experience the erosion of their citizenship rights. Let's consider some of the emerging trends toward the privatization of the criminal justice system that result from the expansion of the white racial frame and language of neoliberalism.

Privatization of Prisons

The privatization of prisons started after the 1983 Supreme Court Ruling *Grubbs v. Bradley*, which declared Tennessee's overcrowded prison system to be unconstitutional. The *Grubbs* ruling forced Tennessee to make a decision. Should they build more jails and increase the state budget at a time that Republican and southern Democratic legislatures demanded austerity? Should they move away from the War on Drugs, which was filling the jails at a historic rate? Tennessee had a third option: privatize their prisons. It was not a coincidence that Correctional

Corporation of America (CCA), America's first prison corporation, was founded in Tennessee in 1983. The total percent of inmates housed in private prisons has remained in the 7–8% range since the 1990s. Yet, the number of inmates in private prisons continued to increase at the turn of the 21st century. The US Department of Corrections estimated that 76,100 inmates were held in private prisons in 2000. This number increased to 92,200 in 2013, before dipping to 91,200 in 2014, an increase of about 20% since 2000. The number of inmates in federal prisons grew even faster. There were 9,400 inmates in privately run federal prisons in 2000. That number grew to 31,900 in 2013 before also dipping to 30,500 in 2014, for a staggering 224% increase. The rise in the number of inmates in privately run federal prison is because the federal government is responsible for all offenders in the District of Columbia, which was 49% black according to the 2014 census estimate. In August 2016, Obama ordered the Justice Department to begin phasing out the use of private prisons on the federal level, with the exception of immigration and customs enforcement. A month after Donald Trump took office, Attorney General and longtime segregationist Jeff Sessions reversed Obama's directive to end the privatization of prisons on the federal level.

Private prisons make money off incarceration. Their business model is to pay the state for the right to its prison budget. Private prisons argue that they can manage prisons more efficiently than the state, so they make their money on the difference between the cost to run the prison and the state budget. On closer inspection, private prisons are profitable for reasons that have nothing to do with efficiency. They have contracts with states that specify minimum occupancy rates of 90%. They only house level-1 offenders, low-risk and nonviolent offenders who require less supervision and less medical care. Violent inmates are housed in public federal and state prisons. Finally, private prisons are nonunion, allowing them to pay guards far less than public unionized prisons. As Michael Hallet noted, "Prisoners are no longer profitable solely for their labor, but also now for their bodily ability to generate per diem payments for their private keepers." Private prisons make money off a never-ending supply of prisoners that come from the growing pool of surplus labor in the neoliberal era.[19]

Private prisons proved to be a profitable endeavor for investors, but the continued privatization of the criminal justice system is not driven by nor is it sustained by profits alone. On the one hand, imprisonment has always been a means of social control and reproducing elite power. Prisoners are denied the right to vote and access to means-tested benefits. The majority of prisoners are young, less than 35 years old, people who missed out on early employment and educational opportunities that allow young people to build a career. On the other hand, the black-public crime link has served as a key ideological vehicle for neoliberalism. The creation of bad black and bad Latino subjects since the 1980s has fueled the representation of crime as a racial threat that does not exist. In turn, white-private is further embedded in middle- and upper-class white political culture, allowing for a generalized acceptance of neoliberal privatizing strategies.

Privatization of Parole

In 2000, the National Center for Policy Analysis (NCPA), a neoliberal think tank whose organizational goals are to "develop and promote private, free market alternatives to government," published a white paper titled "Privatizing Probation and Parole." The white paper addressed the growing market potential of parole with an estimated 600,000 convicts expected to be released from prison in 2000. Their argument was simple. The existing public parole system was corrupt and broken; it was inefficient. They cited statistics that "criminals under government supervision commit 15 murders a day" and provided a list of hand-selected cases of convicts who raped women while on parole. The image of a rapist convict on parole reoffending is a common black-public trope in the language of neoliberalism. As I noted earlier, it was a story line in the pro-Klan film the *Birth of a Nation*. It was also a central narrative in the 1988 presidential race between Vice President George H. W. Bush and Massachusetts governor Michael Dukakis. Down in the polls, Bush wanted to make Dukakis look soft on crime and seized an opportunity with Massachusetts' furlough program that granted prisoners weekend releases. The Bush campaign released what is known as the 'Revolving Door Ad'. It starred Willie Horton, a convicted murderer serving a life sentence who never returned from his weekend furlough. Instead, Horton

WHITE-PRIVATE VIOLENCE 211

kidnapped and raped a white woman, before eventually being apprehended in Maryland. Horton's mug shot, his eyes sunken, nostrils flared,
and mouth slightly agape as an unkempt beard gingerly clung to his
crooked jawline, stared out of the television and into the homes of millions of middle-class whites.[20]

Privatized parole is when that state grants a company the right to
collect fees directly from the probationers. It also goes by the name of
"offender-funded programs" because people arrested for misdemeanors
pay for the 'right' not to go to jail. Although parole is the primary feature
of companies like Sentinel Offender Services, Judicial Correction Services, and Providence Community Correction, they also provide a range
of services to the local courts. These additional services include drug
tests and supplying electronic monitoring devices like ankle bracelets.
The privatization of parole has been driven and aided by the growth of
digital databases and GPS technology. The police have used ankle bracelets since the 1960s to track the whereabouts of parolees via radio signals.
Contemporary ankle bracelets link the private parole companies with
the makers of GPS devices and satellites. SCRAM systems ankle bracelets combine GPS surveillance with biometrics to track alcohol consumption. Private parole companies also provide classes with titles like "Moral
Recognition Therapy" that promise to give offenders "higher stages of
moral reasoning . . . thereby reducing recidivism." Offenders pay for
each of these services, on top of monthly supervision fees and the cost
of the original fine. According to a report published by Human Rights
Watch, these monthly costs can run into hundreds of dollars. For the
poorest American citizens who are subjected to privatized probation
because they already lacked the financial means to pay for various traffic
infractions and other misdemeanors like disorderly conduct, even a
$100-a-month fine is financially unattainable.[21]

Ten states allowed for privatized probation in 2000. That number grew
to 12 by 2014, as cash-strapped counties and states, crippled by their
own proausterity and antitax policies, desperately sought out any type
of revenue. Although the Supreme Court ruled in *Bearden v. Georgia
1983* that it was unconstitutional to jail someone who does not have the
ability to pay a fine, private probation allows the companies to work with
the courts to jail anyone who cannot pay the company. Georgia sits at

the epicenter of the privatized parole movement. In 2013, 648 Georgia courts assigned over 250,000 people to private probation companies. This netted probation companies more than $40 million in revenue. No one should be surprised to find Georgia here. Led by the white business class, Georgia was one of the southern states that pioneered privatizing schools and public services used by blacks in the 1950s.[22]

The privatization of parole follows the precedent of the two-pronged criminal justice system established during the reconstruction era. The difference is that the fusion of peripheral white violence with the state now consists of a system of symbolic violence involving courts and debt collectors. Whereas the convict-lease system chartered blacks to companies to produce commodities, the privatization of parole places the poor in a situation best characterized as debt servitude. Parolees are revenue generators making up for public revenue lost to discourses of austerity. Private parole is more akin to the creation of a regressive tax on the poor who commit misdemeanors so minor that the courts don't feel it is worthy their time and cost. Indeed, Hendricks and Harvey showed how blacks disproportionately endure new forms of monetary punishment. A 1% increase in the black population is good for $82,213 in local revenue through fines. In turn, they astutely point out that municipalities now

> rely heavily upon fines and fees as the lifeblood of government and this money is generated along racial lines, communities of color end up financing significant portions of the very institutions (e.g., police department, court system) that are responsible for their own racial subjugation.

Monetary punishment is typical of the neoliberal way of directing the upward redistribution of wealth: taking money from the poor and giving it to the wealthy. It's vampire capitalism masquerading as law and order.[23]

Privatization of Arbitration

Arbitration is the process of resolving a dispute between two parties instead of going to court. The two parties select a neutral third party to make a legally binding decision instead of a judge. It's popular in

WHITE-PRIVATE VIOLENCE   213

labor and business disputes, which is why elites have pursued the privatization of arbitration. Privatized arbitration involves private companies providing arbitration services for businesses. Private arbitration is a shadow civil court. It is still a method of deciding disputes between businesses and citizens over issues that range from discrimination at the workplace to personal injury lawsuits, except that citizens do not have the right of appeal. Legal scholar Myriam Gilles describes private arbitration as amounting to "the whole-scale privatization of the justice system." Unlike the privatization of parole, which draws from a language of black-public, the process of privatizing arbitration relies on the expansion of the white-private racial frame. Specifically, it draws heavily from how white-private is embedded into the notion of being a good white. Unlike blacks and bad whites, good whites can trust elites, businesses, and the state, right?[24]

The growth of privatized arbitration started in 2011. The Supreme Court allowed companies to insert clauses into employee contracts that banned class-action lawsuits. Personal injury attorneys and lawyers who specialize in class action lawsuits have been the thorn in the side of businesses for some time. Through the process of defending the public's right to safety, which is legally guaranteed in existing regulations, regulations that the state refuses to enforce, class actions are one of the few available mechanisms to limit elite white power. The private arbitration system gives businesses almost total control over their employees, yet, as *New York Times* reporters Silver-Greenberg and Corkey noted, "Little is known about [private] arbitration because the proceedings are confidential and the federal government does not require the cases to be reported." What we do know is that businesses choose a single arbitrator and pay other employees to testify in their favor, and businesses almost always win.[25]

Private arbitration is the most explicit example of how systemic racism affects black and whites. Whereas the privatization of parole represents how marginalized citizens are stripped of their right to due process and left to the mercy of elite white courts, the privatization of arbitration is the middle-class losing the right to due process. Elite whites have always controlled the courts. Take a quick glance at the Supreme Court, and you will find nine judges from the Ivy Leagues who specialized in white-collar law. However, private arbitration also exemplifies how the expansion of white-private masks its racist origins. Privatization provides businesses optimal control over all labor, regardless of race or class. Yet, because privatization is embedded with positive associations of what it means to be white, especially generic attributes of personal responsibility, middle- and upper-class whites inadvertently support a system that is rigged against them. As white-private continues to expand into the criminal justice system, the racial identification with neoliberalism has come back to haunt middle-class whites.

The War on Drugs, the War on Terror, and Police Brutality

The start of the 21st century has continued the trend of mass imprisonment that escalated in the 1980s. A central thread that ties racism with mass imprisonment and police brutality in the 21st century is the War on Terror. George W. Bush declared a War on Terror after a few Saudis affiliated with the terrorist group al-Qaeda crashed two planes into the World Trade Center and one into the Pentagon. They tried to crash a second plane into the Pentagon but were thwarted by passengers, who ultimately crashed the plane into a grassy field in Pennsylvania. On the global front, Bush ordered an invasion of Iraq, despite no evidence that they were involved in the attack or that they harbored weapons of mass destruction. On the domestic front, the Bush administration used terrorists groups to advance an aggressive police policy toward American citizens of color. The start of the 21st century did not invent the process of linking global conflicts with domestic police policy. The process of assembling new forms of racial inclusion accompanied the expansion of black-public crime to other racial and ethnic minorities. After 9/11, it was Arabs, Persians, and all Muslims. In the 1980s, it was Hispanics.

The United States expanded the link between the domestic War on Drugs to Latin America in the 1980s. America has long viewed Latin America as their territory. The 1823 Monroe Doctrine stated that further European attempts to colonize Latin America would be considered an act of aggression toward the United States. The spirit of the Monroe Doctrine established the precedent for US political and economic intervention in Latin America. Latin America became an experimental laboratory for neoliberal policies in the 1980s and 1990s. America's economic involvement in Latin America is known as the Washington Consensus, a tip of the hat to the neocolonial ties between North and South America. The histories of US-Latin American relations are more complex and nuanced than I can do justice to right now. But one thing that US intervention in Latin America did was create the conditions to criminalize Hispanics and Latinos at home.

The origins of the Washington Consensus are found in Mexico's debt crisis. As David Harvey showed, the global financial crisis of the 1970s hit Mexico especially hard. The demand for Mexican products and oil declined. Mexico borrowed money from US investment banks to stay solvent. The Volcker Shock drove up interest rates on Mexico's debt. Mexico declared bankruptcy in 1982. This did not sit well with elites. Backed by the US Treasury, World Bank, and IMF, the United States set out to restructure Mexico's economy to reflect an idealized neoliberal state. The World Bank granted Mexico a loan in 1984, its first loan to a country. The loan came with the caveat that Mexico had to restructure its economy. The economic restructuring of a national economy by banks was unprecedented. Austerity policies gutted state budgetary expenditures toward urban infrastructure, transportation, water, health care, and trash collection. As Harvey said of Mexico's poor:

> It is a moot point whether we call this the restoration of the creation de novo of class power. . . . Their [the peasantry] lot became markedly worse as wealth accumulated both within Mexico and beyond in the hands of a small group of magnates backed by their financial and legal apparatuses of power.[26]

The US-led economic restructuring of Mexico created two representations of American Latinos. One was of the illegal immigrant who drained the American social welfare system. As Arturo Santa-Cruz notes, Mexican migration to the United States is patterned by historical context, proximity, and the regional concentration of Mexican-Americans in addition to economic reasons. Ninety-eight percent of all Mexican migration is to the United States. The link between racism and Mexican migrants extends back to the Depression era, as Santa-Cruz noted,

"Already since the 1930s, it became evident that in addition to the misfortune of having to abandon one's home to seek a better life, Mexicans who migrated also suffered exploitation and racism across the border." Between 1965 and 1983, 83% of the roughly 28 million Mexican migrants returned home. What changed was US border policy in relation to Mexico's economic collapse, where Santa-Cruz argued, "the relationship between migration and national security began to take shape." Reagan claimed that America lost control over its borders. The US response was to increase the number of border patrol officers and to detain illegal workers. Mexican migrants were criminalized under the umbrella of national security.[27]

The other representation was the international drug smuggler. To be fair, the global cocaine trade does originate in Latin America. One reason is climate. Coca production requires a natural tropical climate with low altitude, 1,600 to 6,500 feet above sea level. The other reason is social. A coca harvest is more profitable than soy or rice. It's also more predictable because the coca plant is not as susceptible to drought as rice or soy, just the global demand for cocaine. Latin American drug kingpins used the state-backed military to monopolize the international networks that connect the coca fields with domestic markets in the United States. Panama's former dictator Manuel Noriega and Colombia gangster Pablo Escobar became the face of the 1980s drug trade, prompting America to link their domestic War on Drugs to Latin America. American gangs like the Crips, Bloods, and Latin Kings relied on their Latin American connections for drugs and guns. These connections linked marginalized black communities with marginalized Hispanic communities and, in the process, tied Hispanics with black-public crime. In the Reagan and first Bush eras, the percent of Hispanics in federal and state prisons grew from 9.9% in 1979 to 12.6% in 1986 to 16.7% in 1991.[28]

The post-9/11 era ushered in a new wave of state violence that linked the global War on Terror with policing. The expansion of the black-public link to the fear of Muslims allowed the neoliberal project to continue the assault on social programs that started in the 1980s and 1990s. As Hallet argued, "The trend toward spending more on security and less on social welfare has only been exacerbated by September 11 and the War in Iraq." The Bush Administration used global terrorism to reorganize US immigration policy. Similar to the US response to Mexican migrants in the 1980s, immigration services became militarized and criminalized. Immigration and Naturalization was renamed the Bureau of Immigration and Customs and is housed under the Department of Homeland Security. Privacy rights were abolished after the US government allowed the FBI to obtain private communications via text messages and email. The introduction of color-coded threat levels reinforced the racialized paranoia toward all groups. Instead of combating terrorism via its causes, elite whites in the United States seized on the opportunity provided by 9/11 to expand police presence.[29]

The war on terrorism and increased militarization of the police expanded to everyday police practice. After 9/11, the New York City Police Department combined antiterrorist practices with broken window theory in a practice known as stop and frisk. Rather than fight terror, it simply harassed blacks and Hispanics riding the subway on their way to work. Ninety percent of the five million people stopped in New York City since 2002 were black or Hispanic. Rather than fight terror, stop and frisk was another white-private strategy to police integrated public space and make everyday life for blacks unbearable. The federal government has transferred tanks, armored trucks, mine-resistant vehicles, planes, helicopters, M-16 assault rifles, and grenade launchers to local police around the country. In response to the increased public awareness of police brutality thanks to the Black Lives Matter movement, states have outfitted the police with digital body cameras.[30]

The expansion of black-public to include Hispanics and Muslims masks the fact that actual domestic terrorists in the United States are conservative, Christian-fundamentalist, antigovernment white men. Since 9/11, the majority of US domestic terror attacks have come from white right-wing extremists. Prior to 9/11, the majority of US domestic terror attacks came from white right-wing extremists. The most dramatic was Timothy McVeigh and Terry Nichols, who blew up a federal building in Oklahoma City with a rental truck filled with fertilizer, killing 168 people, including 19 children in the building's day-care center. Other white conservative right-wingers have shot up Jewish day cares and assassinated abortion and family-planning doctors. No war on terror has been declared against the white Christian right. American prisons are not filled with white terrorists. Similar to the days of Klan lynching and whites exploding bombs in black churches and the homes of civil rights leaders in the South, the white terrorist gets a free pass.

America's criminal justice system sits alongside America's educational systems as a place where it's fairly easy to measure racism in the neoliberal era. The Bureau of Justice Statistics readily provides raw data on the sheer number of black and Hispanic men and the growing number of black and Hispanic women behind bars. Instances of racist police brutality have become commonplace. But the legacy of America's racist criminal justice system goes back much farther than the era of mass imprisonment.

The origins of America's modern criminal justice system began after the Civil War. Elite whites viewed former black slaves as a threat to their economic system, which relied on unpaid labor, and political system based on white-public life. The state mobilized to protect its agricultural, industrial, and financial sectors through the convict codes and institution of Jim Crow laws. Groups like the Klan used violence to intimidate blacks while groups like the Citizens' Council used economic sanctions to prevent blacks from getting involved in the civil rights movement. Ordinary whites were also active participants in the use of violence to maintain racial segregation. They supported the centralization of violence on the federal level because the FBI targeted the black nationalists. They've supported mass imprisonment on the grounds that they needed protection from black super predators. They've supported privatized parole on the grounds that the poor and the criminal are a moral and economic burden on society. It is impossible to separate systemic racism from America's criminal justice system.

The days of America's two-pronged criminal justice system are also connected to the expansion of the present-day neoliberal criminal justice system. The fusion of the legal arm of the criminal justice system with white peripheral violence during the civil rights era set the stage for mass incarceration in the neoliberal era. Elites have used the language of neoliberalism to create the conditions for the subsequent expansion of the white-private criminal justice system. Elites used the white-private-austerity link to gut social welfare and antipoverty programs by securing the consent of ordinary whites. It made the inverse relationship

WHITE-PRIVATE VIOLENCE

between funding for social services and funding for prisons possible. At the turn of the 21st century, elites have linked ordinary whites' racist fears of integrated public spaces with policing, terrorism, and the negation of privacy rights. The expansion of the neoliberal criminal justice system is based on whites' assumption that the criminal justice system only targets blacks and Hispanics and that they will be OK because they are white. The neoliberal project now expands to places like parole and probation that directly impact poor whites and arbitration, which impacts the civil rights of middle-class whites.

Notes

1. Angela Davis, *Are Prisons Obsolete?* (New York: Seven Stories Press, 2003), p. 28.
2. Ibid., p. 25; W. E. B. Du Bois, *Black Reconstruction: An Essay Toward a History of the Part Which Black Folk Played in the Attempt to Reconstruct Democracy in America, 1860–1880* (New York: Harcourt, Brace and Company, 1935), pp. 671, 672.
3. Du Bois, *Black Reconstruction*, pp. 684, 692; David Oshinsky, *Worse Than Slavery: Parchment Farm and the Ordeal of Jim Crow Justice* (New York: Free Press, 1996).
4. Nancy MacClean, *Behind the Mask of Chivalry: The Making of the Second Ku Klux Klan* (New York: Oxford University Press, 1994), p. 10; Joe Feagin, *Racist America: Roots, Current Realities, and Future Reparations, 3rd Edition* (New York: Routledge, 2014), p. 57; Joe Feagin, *The White Racial Frame: Centuries of Racial Framing and Counter-Framing* (New York: Routledge, 2013), p. 83.
5. Hohle, *Race and Origins of American Neoliberalism*, p. 19.
6. Hohle, *Black Citizenship and Authenticity in the Civil Rights Movement*, pp. 69–73; Glen Eskew, *But for Birmingham: The Local and National Movements in the Civil Rights Movement* (Chapel Hill: University of North Carolina Press, 1997); Diane McWhorter, *Carry Me Home: Birmingham, Alabama: The Climatic Battle of the Civil Rights Revolution* (New York: Touchtone, 2002).
7. David Vann, Oral History Project, conducted 2 February 1995, Birmingham Civil Rights Institute.
8. Quote located in Dan Baum, "Legalize It All: How to Win the War on Drugs" *Harper's Magazine*, 18 April 2016, located at https://harpers.org/archive/2016/04/legalize-it-all/
9. Julilly Kohler-Hausman, 2010, "The Attila the Hun Law: New York's Rockefeller Drug Laws and the Making of a Punitive State" *Journal of Social History* 44 (1 Fall): pp. 71–95, 73, 80.
10. Michelle Alexander, *The New Jim Crow: Mass Incarceration in the Age of Colorblindness* (New York: The New Press, 2012), p. 42.
11. Ward Churchill, *'To Disrupt, Discredit, and Destroy': The FBI's Secret War Against the Black Panther Party* (New York: Routledge, 2005).
12. Quoted located in ibid., p. 83.
13. Randolph Hohle, 2009, "The Rise of New South Governmentality: Competing Southern Revitalization Projects and Police Responses to the Black Civil Rights

Movement 1961–1965" *Journal of Historical Sociology* 22 (4 December): pp. 497–527; David Garrow, *Bearing the Cross: Martin Luther King, Jr. and the Southern Conference Leadership* (New York, Quill, 1986); Tim Weiner, *Enemies: A History of the FBI* (New York: Random House, 2012).

14. US Department of Justice. Bureau of Justice Statistics. Prisoners in 1994, August 1995.

15. Wacquant, *Prisons of Poverty*, p. 51.

16. Ibid., 10–17, 11.

17. "20 Years Later, Parts of Major Crime Bill Viewed as Terrible Mistake" Morning Edition, NPR, original airdate 12 September 2014, located at www.npr.org/2014/09/12/347736999/20-years-later-major-crime-bill-viewed-as-terrible-mistake (last accessed 24 April 2016). Hilary Clinton Quote located in in Michelle Alexander, "Why Hilary Clinton Doesn't Deserve the Black Vote" *The Nation*, 29 February 2016, located at www.thenation.com/article/hillary-clinton-does-not-deserve-black-peoples-votes/ (last accessed 24 April 2016).

18. See Angela Davis, 1998, "What Is the Prison Industrial Complex? Why Does It Matter?" *Color Lines* 1 (2): pp. 1–8; Quote located in Ken Silverstein, "America's Private Gulag" Prison Legal News 1997, located at www.prisonlegalnews.org/news/1997/jun/15/americas-private-gulag/; Wacquant, *Prisons of Poverty*, pp. 58–68.

19. Michael Hallett, 2002, "Race, Crime, and For-Profit Imprisonment: Social Disorganization as Market Opportunity" *Punishment and Society* 4 (3): pp. 369–393, 369.

20. Morgan Reynolds, "Privatizing Probation and Parole" National Center for Policy Analysis, NCPA Policy Report No. 233, June 2000.

21. The SCRAM Systems website has a page titled "Evidence-Based Options in Alcohol Monitoring." It describes how their product can be modified to scale the amount of alcohol consumption to "the client's needs and progress" and to help "reduce recidivism". They use the private language of referring to parolees as clients. They do not provide any evidence on their evidence-based page that this works. The page is located at www.scramsystems.com/products/alcohol-monitoring/options-in-alcohol-monitoring/; Reynolds, "Privatizing Probation and Parole," p. 33.

22. Chris Albin-Lackey, "Profiting from Probation: America's 'Offender-Funded' Probation Industry" *Human Rights Watch*, 5 February 2014, p. 33, 41, pdf located at www.hrw.org/report/2014/02/05/profiting-probation/americas-offender-funded-probation-industry; see Kruse, *White Flight* and Hohle, *Race and the Origins of American Neoliberalism*, Chapter 8 on the long history of privatization in Georgia.

23. Kasey Hendricks and Dania Harvey, *forthcoming*, "Not One but Many: Monetary Punishment and the Fergusons of America" *Sociological Forum*.

24. Myriam Gilles quote located in Jessica Silver-Greenburg and Michael Corkery, "In Arbitration: A Privatization of the Justice System" *New York Times*, 1 November 2015, located at www.nytimes.com/2015/11/02/business/dealbook/in-arbitration-a-privatization-of-the-justice-system.html?_r=0

25. Ibid.

26. Harvey, *The History of Neoliberalism*, 98–104, quote located on 104.

27. Arturo Santa-Cruz, *Mexico-United States Relations: The Semantics of Sovereignty* (New York: Routledge, 2012), pp. 102, 109.

28. Bureau of Justice Statistics, Prisoners in 1994, US Department of Justice, August 1995, NCJ-151654.

29. Michael Hallet, *Private Prisons in America: A Critical Race Perspective* (Urbana and Illinois: University of Illinois Press, 2006), p. 21.
30. Stop and Frisk Data www.nyclu.org/content/stop-and-frisk-data; Matt Apuzzo, "War Gear Flows to Police Departments" *New York Times*, 2 June 2014, located at www.nytimes.com/2014/06/09/us/war-gear-flows-to-police-departments.html

8

DIVERSITY AND FUTURE TRENDS IN RACIST NEOLIBERAL GOVERNANCE

I originally planned to end this book on the topic of diversity in the neoliberal era. Then America went ahead and elected Donald Trump president. Suddenly, I found that I needed to apply my theory that racism is responsible for the origins and expansion of the neoliberal project and that elite whites respond to real instances of black civic inclusion to the first half of 2017. It's not Trump, per se, that matters, but how easily elites can activate a white-private political network by whipping ordinary whites into a racist, nationalist fever. The Trump candidacy itself was straight out of George Wallace's playbook, a strategy consistently adopted by Republicans. Nixon, Reagan, the first Bush, Gingrich, and the second Bush all race-baited their political opponents to link with middle-class white voters. Trump used the language of neoliberalism to rally ordinary whites left behind by the neoliberal turn. He blamed Mexicans and illegal immigrants for stealing white jobs from white people and promised to build an actual wall, paid for by the Mexican government, to keep Mexicans out of America. He stoked the flames of anti-Arab and anti-Muslim sentiment. A white-racist or "alt-right" public assembled to take back their country in relation to the Trump candidacy. The combination of state-sponsored racist voter suppression and the reliable turnout in America's white suburbs in key Midwestern states delivered Trump an electoral college victory. He lost the popular

DIVERSITY AND FUTURE TRENDS

vote. The Trump presidency has followed the white-private/black-public script to the letter. In Trump's first 5 months in office, he attempted to block people from specific Muslim states from entering the United States, backed a proposal to eliminate the Affordable Care Act, reprivatized federal prisons, tampered with FBI investigations into his relations with the Russian government, further deregulated environmental protections to benefit energy companies (e.g., allowing coal companies to dump waste in nearby waterways), cut family-planning services, and nominated an antilabor Supreme Court justice to fill the vacant seat on the bench. I'm expecting white-private tax cuts for businesses and the wealthy coupled with austerity measures for the poor will be the main subjects of his first budget and attempt at tax reform.

My first inclination after the 2016 elections was to scrap this chapter and start over. How could I write on how surface diversity masks systemic racism when Trump shamelessly embraced white nationalism throughout the presidential race like he was Teddy Roosevelt or George Wallace? How could I write how surface diversity masks the growing inequalities within groups alongside inequality between groups when all we saw were white men sheepishly grinning as photojournalists captured the moment Vice President Mike Pence cast the deciding vote to allow states to defund Planned Parenthood? On further reflection, it occurred to me that diversity and neoliberalism are more than just compatible. Whereas racism is the driving force behind the origins and expansion of the neoliberal project, the politics of diversity is the neoliberal project's shield. Neoliberals hide behind the public debate over diversity and identities because diversity is not a threat to elite white power. Discussions around diversity among elites means we never have to address issues of wealth and income inequality, the continued privatization of public life, and the trend of the upward redistribution of resources that have been the hallmark of the neoliberal era.

Neoliberalism Today: A Brief Recap of How We Arrived Here

There is no total neoliberal state. Neoliberalism is neither a linear nor a singular project. A limited but segregated welfare state exists for whites. Blacks and other racial minorities are caught in the throes of our eroding institutional, material, and social infrastructure. The neoliberal project exists in tenacious relationship with the welfare state. Public services and works remain but are not adequate to address social problems or provide a stable safety net for American citizens. Regulations remain to tilt advantages to some businesses over other businesses and ordinary citizens. The wealthy still pay some taxes. Indeed, all one has to do is look to the left and see public parks, public libraries, and public schools to see that some forms of white-public life remain. Then again, you could always look to the right and see the rapidly increasing privatization of education, broadband, aerospace, prisons, and social services to conclude that we are well on our way.

Neoliberalism spreads unevenly but is patterned by a meta history of elite white racism. The composition of elite whites has changed even as their structural base of power has not. The original group of elite whites solidified their power around land ownership and slave ownership but also liberal ideological doctrines of democracy. The emphasis on democracy and citizenship rights masked the material basis of elite white power rooted in a global colonial-slave economy and the numerous devices that denied poor whites the right to vote. The Civil War ended slavery but not elite white control over black labor. Peripheral white violence increased in the former Confederate states. Racist white groups targeted black freedmen during the period of reconstruction. The state took land from Native Americans and gave it to whites. The state gave elite whites land to build railroad infrastructure and ordinary whites land to build homesteads. Black homesteaders received land in the parts of the South where the land was no good for farming. The end of reconstruction began the period of Jim Crow. In general, Jim Crow ensured that public life remained segregated. Southern cities remained in a checkerboard pattern of residential segregation so black women could live by the places they worked: the homes of elite white families. In contrast, northern cities were segregated by neighborhood, ensuring that newly arrived immigrants and migrants remained with their own kind. Nineteenth-century elite whites also endured political challenges from populists and unions. Du Bois noted how the Jim Crow era coincided with the rise of finance and industry, which indicated the consolidation of elite white power at the national level.

The rise of 20th-century progressivism and the continuation of racism resulted in an embryonic white-public welfare state. The white-public welfare state focused on regulating capitalism rather than developing social welfare programs. Progressives like Theodore Roosevelt and his political rival Woodrow Wilson were blatant white supremacists who broke up monopolies, regulated banks and the railroads, imposed income taxes on the wealthy, and ended corrupt social insurance programs. Local state elites rallied ordinary whites to their side around public schools, public pensions, and public sanitation systems while imposing regressive taxation to ensure that blacks paid their fair share. This white-public system was predicated on excluding racial minorities. But elite white power is not hegemonic or absolute. W. E. B. Du Bois helped to organize the Niagara Movement in 1905 and the NAACP in 1909. These civil rights organizations began to dismantle the juridical aspects of racism and pushed for black civic inclusion. The Harlem Renaissance and New Negro Movement, alongside black-owned banks, insurance firms, and retail stores provided an economic and political base to fight for racial equality. The Great Depression erased much of the black economic gains, but the NAACP and other black activists persisted in their goal of civic inclusion. Franklin Delano Roosevelt expanded the white-public welfare state through the 1935 Social Security Act. Ordinary white workers rallied behind Unemployment and Old Age Insurance. The state imposed payroll taxes on employers and citizens. Nonprofit charities all but disappeared. And southern Democrats made sure to exclude blacks from the Social Security Act. Although FDR integrated federal work sites and the military when he signed the 1941 FEPC Act, it did not extend to neighborhood or school integration. Thus, the white-public welfare state was possible because it limited the redistribution of resources to whites and did not threaten elite white power.

The civil rights era is the moment that white-public pivots to white-private. The civil rights movement made and used representations of racially nonthreatening good black citizens to secure citizenship rights. Good black citizenship debunked stereotypes that blacks were biologically, psychologically, and morally unfit to vote, sit next to a white person on a bus, or work side by side with whites in professional fields. Blacks on the margins of segregated black life did not see the civil rights movement addressing the needs of poverty, the overcrowded black ghetto, and the lack of political power that came with being black with the right to vote. In the process, the civil rights movement severed whiteness from American citizenship and black political representation splintered. Elite whites responded to good black citizens differently than racially threatening bad black citizens. The Lyndon Johnson administration did pass the 1964 Civil Rights Act and the 1965 Voting Rights Act. His administration passed Medicare to make sure the poor had health care and changed the formula used to calculate AFDC payments so that poor women could work and still receive childcare and food stamps. History indicates that this was the twilight of the white-public welfare state already on borrowed time.

The language of white-private/black-public originated in the South as whites sought to maintain all-white spaces and institutions. The reason why the language of neoliberalism originated in the South is because that was where the vast majority of blacks lived. School desegregation was a salient issue to whites because it involved their children and their taxes and their communities. The elite white response to the *Brown* decision was to give states the option to privatize public schools. States did not abolish their white-public schools. Instead they transferred public money to white-private schools. There was already a general opposition from agrarians to paying taxes. Ordinary whites viewed tax dollars as white tax dollars and no longer supported integrated public institutions. Regional southern white elites jumped on the various regulations that make up the 1964 Civil Rights Act as proof that the government wanted to steal jobs from white people and give them to black people. As a central part of the white racial frame, good white-private citizenship is the glue that binds heterogeneous white social groups into a unified sense of whiteness. Good white-private citizenship connects probusiness deregulations, reduced public spending on the poor, and elite tax cuts, on the premise that all whites benefit from the neoliberal project.

The pattern of elite whites invoking the language of neoliberalism spread to northern and western cities in the post-civil rights era. Women, gays and lesbians, and antiwar and prodemocracy student movements joined blacks in pushing for structural social change. Nevertheless, the elite white response zeroed in on blacks. Similar to the civil rights era

DIVERSITY AND FUTURE TRENDS

in the South, the language of white-private/black-public arose in urban areas and states with a high proportion of black citizens. There were a few differences. The issue of school privatization endured until the *Milliken* decision limited the use of busing to integrate schools to the municipal level. It opened the doors for suburban white flight. Richard Nixon's southern strategy used George Wallace's platform of linking black-public forced busing and black-public affirmative action to bring more whites to the Republican Party. He also criminalized black poverty to set the stage for mass imprisonment. While the black civil rights movement in general sparked the centralization of white violence into the criminal justice system, the state specifically targeted black political groups working on the local level. The state embedded white-private austerity in drug and alcohol treatment programs as they associated drug use and drug sales with blacks. The welfare mothers' movement secured social citizenship rights for all women, even though it linked black women with black-public welfare. Not surprising, the rhetoric of small government got louder during Reagan's primary run for president as the decade of the 1970s came to a close.

The nationalization of the neoliberal project began in 1979 when the language of white-private/black-public became part of national political policy. White-private/black-public reconfigured the segregated welfare state and created the conditions for the upward redistribution of power. Republican and Democratic elite whites found common political ground in protecting the white-private economy and securing the political consent of middle-class whites. After taking office, the Reagan administration immediately authorized white-private austerity in federal funding for social welfare, deregulated eligibility criteria by eliminating the 30 1/3 rule, and slashed tax rates on high-income earners. This especially hurt the marginalized black community who found an expanding criminal justice system eager to put them in jail. Deindustrialization robbed working-class men and women of their good-paying union jobs. Southern states offered firms tax incentive packages, public money to build custom factories, and right-to-work laws designed to keep their factories union free. Many in the Northeast and Midwest moved down to the southern rim, chasing work related to the housing construction boom made possible by federal banking deregulations. White-private banking deregulations eliminated usury caps and created variable interest rates. SBA deregulations eliminated race as a criterion for SBA support, which essentially transformed black-owned banks into subprime loan centers. The start of the neoliberal economy introduced the world to the double dip recession and how easy it was for corrupt bankers and politicians to profit from the new field of banking regulations. The only thing that kept the American economy from tanking in the 1980s was the increase in defense spending. Spending money on black-public antipoverty programs was bad. Spending money on white-private security was good.

The combination of black civic inclusion and the visibility of black poverty helped assemble a new wave of neoliberalism. The 1992 elections were the first elections that used the majority-minority districts mandated by the 1982 Voting Rights Act. It was also a campaign under the shadow of America's most significant military entry into the Middle East, dubbed Operation Desert Storm, and the Rodney King Riots. Bill Clinton won the presidential election, and the Democrats took control of the House and Senate for the first time since 1976. Pundits called Bill Clinton the first black president. Hoping to build their base, the Democrats passed the 1992 Motor Voter Bill to make it easier for Americans to register to vote. The Republicans viewed the Motor Voter Bill as a strategy to register black voters. Whites responded by supporting the Republicans and their Contract for America in 1994 midterm elections. The business rhetoric of a contract was not coincidental, as there was a renewed and amplified focus on privatization and strategic deregulations. The privatization of social welfare eliminated AFDC and the deregulation of finance eliminated Glass-Steagall. Clinton's neoliberal political platform was established through his third way politics of being socially liberal and economically conservative. Clinton was not too liberal when he expanded the criminal justice system to put more people in jail for a longer period of time, ignored the environment, or supported the Defense of Marriage Act. He was a good neoliberal though, probably the best.

The scope and intensity of neoliberalism escalated in the 1990s. One interesting side effect of racist neoliberal governance was the creation of a white-private market around poverty. This market around poverty was found in states using prisons as economic development and the entry of for-profit firms into social welfare. A for-profit company makes

DIVERSITY AND FUTURE TRENDS

money by purchasing the right to a state's prison or welfare budget. Profits come from gaps between the cost of managing the program and the total value of the budget. The incentive for private social welfare firms is to make money, not to get people out of poverty. Private prisons make money by what seems like never-ending delivery of black and Hispanic bodies to their prisons. Neither should be surprising given that the criminal justice system replaced the labor market in America's black and Hispanic ghettos. Selective public-private investments into metropolitan areas created uneven development that allowed for disparate forms of urbanization to exist side by side: city and rural gentrification, embourgeoisment, downtown redevelopment, hyperghettos, and suburban sprawl. In the 1980s, scholars noted how money began to flow to the second circuit of capital (real estate) to stimulate speculative growth rather than allow for real estate to bottom. The rent gap widened through real estate speculation. Mega-regions developed around global cities in the 1990s as the finance, technology, real estate, and entertainment sectors settled in a handful of cities. Real estate elites began selling a burgeoning white creative class an idealized bohemian urban lifestyle organized around diversity and tolerance and class homogeneity. White racial insecurity drove the assemblage of white-private spaces: security cameras and visible police presence in public spaces, permits to use public space, homeowner associations, and gated communities. Changes in racial segregation coupled with gentrification and racial inclusion into the suburbs by 2010 have not slowed down the conversion of white-public space to white-private space.

The neoliberal reforms of the 2000s included more tax cuts for the wealthy, and the privatization of select institutions associated with blacks and Hispanics. The privatization of prisons and mass incarceration that escalated in the 1990s continued into the 2000s. Mass imprisonment peaked in 2008 but the proportion of nonwhite inmates continued to rise. Despite a very modest dip in the total number of inmates in 2014, the percentage and total number of inmates in federal and state prisons has gotten darker. Hispanic inmates are more likely to be housed in private prisons than whites.[1] In 2013, whites were 33% of the federal and state inmate population, while blacks were 36%, Hispanics were 22%, and the rest of America's racial and ethnic makeup was 8.6%.[2]

Although the number of private prisons seemed to have leveled off, the privatization of the criminal justice system expanded into parole, probation, policing, and arbitration, shifting the financial burden and costs of mass incarceration onto the poor. The privatization of parole and probation harks the spirit of regressive taxation and austerity.

The privatization of schools coupled with a useless and unhealthy obsession with assessment metrics has changed the educational landscape. Charter schools appear primarily in neighborhoods and school districts that are predominantly black. In some areas, they are more segregated than public schools. White families utilize private vouchers to sometimes send their children to white-private schools, but mainly they use vouchers to subsidize the cost of already sending their children to private schools. The federal government does not dictate a national educational curriculum. However, they do dangle a lot of public funding to influence education. Three decades of proausterity and antitax stances by politicians have robbed local schools of their traditional avenues of funding. They can't operate without federal funding. National education policies like No Child Left Behind and Race to the Top combined federal funding with standardized tests to assess learning. There is no problem with using tests in of itself to assess what a child knows and doesn't know. But these tests that rate students on a scale of one to four were designed to weed out bad teachers and bust teachers' unions. This was a stated goal of neoliberal Democrats and Republicans in the early 1980s. White parents who were shocked when the test scores indicated that their children were not as smart as their inflated grades indicated responded by opting out of the tests and demanding that the criteria used to assess their once brilliant child as average change. White parents refused to have their children sit for the tests and if they could afford to, sent their children to expensive private schools that did not use standardized assessment tests. White-private school vouchers may be waiting for them if the neoliberal education reformers get their way.

The neoliberal economy is unstable and not viable without the power of the state to save the white-private economy from itself. Elites used the power of the state and the Federal Reserve Bank to save the white-private economy. Eight years, four months, and four days after Congress passed the Gramm-Leach-Bliley Act in 1999, Bear Stearns sold itself to J. P. Morgan for $10 a share. Almost six months later to the day, Lehman Brothers claimed bankruptcy. Both New York financial giants were victims of the regulatory banking field they supported. They went under because they did not have enough economic capital on hand to cover their losses attributed to the subprime housing market. Elite whites blamed the poor and working class for being irresponsible and borrowing more than they could afford. Elites did not mention how their banks were intimately involved in the subprime and predatory lending that made it impossible for borrowers to pay higher mortgages on variable interest rate loans once the Federal Reserve began raising interest rates to ward off inflation. Elites did not mention that the housing market was a bubble driven by speculation, jumbo loans, and loan repayment terms that accompanied a one-time balloon payment. There was record high inequality in America in 2007. The housing crash erased wealth in the black and Hispanic communities. With the exception of a temporary dip in their investment portfolios, elite whites were fine.

It didn't matter to many elite and ordinary whites that the Barack Obama administration continued the neoliberal project. They couldn't stand the sight of a black man, even if he was half white, in the White House. The Obama era can be described as neoliberal-lite policies. He signed off on continuing the Bush tax cuts but let the tax cuts expire for high-income earners. The signature piece of banking deregulation was the 2010 Wall Street Reform and Consumer Protection Act, commonly known as Dodd-Frank, after Senator Christopher Dodd and Congressman Barney Frank. The logic behind Dodd-Frank was to establish a minimum level of capital for banks to make sure that they could cover investment losses. It did not eliminate the regulatory field defined by Gramm-Leach-Bliley. It did make prospective borrowers prove they had the income to pay back their loans despite this having no causal impact on the housing crisis. Obama's signature piece of domestic policy, the Affordable Care Act (ACA), is a privatized system of national health insurance. The state subsidized millions of uninsured citizens to buy health care in the health-care market from private health-care companies that are also subsidized by the government to offer health-care packages in the insurance market. Neoliberal Republicans rejected a privatized system of health care because it included blacks and Hispanics.

232 DIVERSITY AND FUTURE TRENDS

The Affordable Care Act represents a case study on what happens when there is not white-private pretext to the neoliberal policy. In this case, a tension exists between neoliberal social policy and the association with black. The links between the ACA and black-public occurred by the expansion of Medicaid and the Children's Health Insurance Program to cover the working poor and increased taxes on anyone making over $200,000 a year to help fund the cost of the program. Blacks and Hispanics disproportionately benefited from the ACA because they are most likely to be uninsured. The proportion of blacks aged 18–64 without health insurance fell from about 25% in 2013 to 15% in 2016. White-private redistributes resources back to whites. Whites, many but not all of whom are Republican, rejected neoliberal health care because it was not a white-private health care and the guy who pushed for it was black. White nationalist groups invented conspiracy after conspiracy about Obama to try to question the legitimacy and legality of his presidency. My personal favorite Obama conspiracy theorists were the birthers, a group who believed Obama was actually born in Kenya and was part of some socialist black power movement to overthrow America. The conspiracy theorists couldn't derail Obama. But the Supreme Court could. The Roberts court struck down Section 5 of the Voting Rights Act. In turn, Republican-led states instituted as many devices to prevent blacks from voting as they could. Republicans pledged to repeal Obamacare. The result was a handful of states in the deindustrialized Midwest turning the electoral college vote to Donald Trump and ushering the beginning of neoliberalism 3.0.[3]

Diversity in the Neoliberal Era

America never settled its cultural wars of the 1960s. The cultural wars is an obtuse way of capturing how the social groups anchored on the margins of American society demanded equality while the dominant groups absorbed in tradition, nationalism, and whiteness said no. The cultural wars comprised heterogeneous groups including the black civil rights movement, the anti-Vietnam War protests, feminists, free speech and radical democracy movements, and the gay and lesbian liberation movements, all fighting against the establishment. It was groups of struggle against America's power elite. America's political parties became racially segregated during the 1960s. Upper- and middle-class whites converged on the Republican Party. The groups of struggle found a home in the Democratic Party. The cultural wars reset modernity in America, a modernity defined through relations instead of labor.

Neoliberalism was born out of the elite white strategy to hold on to power in relation to the black struggle for civic inclusion. For elite whites, holding on to power meant maintaining control over the state and the economy. The neoliberal project's relationship with racism and diversity changed as the criteria for inclusion and exclusion changed. Nothing is static. To illustrate, let's return to a paradox I introduced in the introduction of the book: the simultaneous rise of the black middle class and extreme black poverty in the neoliberal era. Elite whites seek to shelter themselves from accusations of racism and white privilege. Even hardened segregationists of the civil rights era tiptoed around making overt racist public statements. They preferred the language of neoliberalism. Khan highlighted how elite boarding schools have deemphasized the notion of entitlement over the last decade or so. Elite white cultures have shifted to meritocratic myths of the value of hard work and embraced diversity as a way to mask the racial and structural privilege of wealth. This cultural change opens up limited opportunities for a limited number of good black citizens. Bad black citizens face increased police brutality as the criminal justice system has replaced the labor market and social welfare system in racially segregated neighborhoods. Thus, elite whites have expanded the neoliberal project in relation to the selective integration of good black citizens. But selective integration does not address the root of elite white power. Instead, racial diversity hides systemic racism by propping up good black citizens as proof of a postracial era defined by individual achievement.

Diversity sits in an easy relationship with neoliberalism. John Skrentny noted that a new practice he characterizes as racial realism has taken root in the private sector of American workplaces. Skrentny defines racial realism as "employer perceptions that workers vary by race in their ability to do certain jobs and contribute to organizational effectiveness, and/or the kinds of signals their racial backgrounds send to customers and citizens." Private and public sector employers have moved away from social justice policies like affirmative action and color-blind workplaces

234   DIVERSITY AND FUTURE TRENDS

to embrace diversity because it benefits the firm. Racial realism is about using diversity to achieve "organizational effectiveness." It does so through racial matching and the belief that diversity will lead to new and better ideas. Firms use racial matching because it creates racial signals that the firm cares about people of color. What you find is a conscious effort to match black physicians and nurses with black patients, black and Hispanic social workers with poor black people and a population more comfortable speaking their native language, black teachers with black students, Hispanic teachers with Hispanic students, and black, Asian, and Hispanic customer service, human resources, and marketing professionals in areas with a high proportion of the matching population.[4]

Racial realism does not challenge the basis of elite white power. Skrentny notes that racial realism benefits whites even if it does not use whiteness to do so. How? Racial realism helps create the impression that elite whites are progressive on issues like race and free of implicit and explicit racial biases. It's a strategy to value racial diversity without threatening the foundation of elite white power. If anything, racial realism reinforces elite white power because elites still control spaces. For example, Frank Dobbin's research shows how organizations used human resources departments to diversify the gender and racial composition of the firm. They made the preemptive move to diversify the firms to prevent the expansion of the Civil Rights Act into the white-private workplace. There is also the question of who gets to diversify these spaces and why. Are they really open to all members of a racial group, or is there a lurking racially nonthreatening citizen behind racial realism? Do black police officers committing police brutality on other black people help justify police brutality? When collection firms hire poor whites and poor blacks to hound poor people crippled by debt, does it justify the financial neoliberal system of forced debt and predatory lending? In short, we have to understand racial realism as another strategy that reproduces elite white power by diversifying the surface while leaving the underlying white-private network intact.[5]

Whites benefit from diversity in places outside the workplace. Whites who have increasingly sought out diversity do so to enhance their own experiences and identities. Diversity is organized around the selective inclusion of good blacks with good whites who share similar cultural tastes. We find this in the threshold of where we live and where we send our children to school. Research on the various forms of gentrification indicates how whites dubbed "social preservationists" want some of the original residents to remain because it enhances *their* sense of authenticity. The presence of white social preservationists does not do much for the original residents enduring the threat of material displacement while experiencing symbolic displacement. White parents will send their children with black and brown children so long as they share the same social class and cultural tastes. Many white parents want to make sure that their children learn to interact with people different from them. It's not the same thing as addressing systemic racism across schools and school districts. And by all accounts, diversity in *good schools* has not closed the racial achievement gap between black and white students.[6]

Would a more diverse class of elites matter? In other words, what would happen if there were more black senators, more women running Fortune 500 companies, and more Latinos on the Supreme Court? Individual case studies suggest that adherence to white-private neoliberal ideology is a major criterion for membership into America's elite. Take Cory Booker for example. Booker was the mayor of Newark, New Jersey, from 2006 to 2013. He was appointed as a US senator to represent the state of New Jersey in 2013. As mayor, he was on the board of Alliance for School Choice with Betsy DeVos and worked closely with New Jersey governor Chris Christie and Facebook CEO Mark Zuckerberg to privatize Newark's schools. He made his commitment to white-private schools as far back as 2000. During one speech to the neoliberal think tank the Manhattan Institute, he stated, "Public education is the use of public dollars to educate our children at the schools that are best equipped to do so—public schools, magnet schools, charter schools, Baptist schools, Jewish schools." As a US senator, Booker refused to criticize the police for acts of blatant police brutality during the 2014 Black Lives Matter protests in Ferguson, Missouri. He did not address the criminalization of poverty and black people. He noted the "complexities of the situation in Ferguson" and urged the US attorney general to investigate how the police handled the journalists who covered the Ferguson protests. Booker's ascendance to the ranks of America's elite has furthered the expansion of the neoliberal project and has not made life better for ordinary blacks.[7]

236 DIVERSITY AND FUTURE TRENDS

Challenges and challengers to the neoliberal project remain on the outside looking in. Elite whites don't embrace black intellectuals like Cornell West, hip-hop artists like Killer Mike, or congressmen like John Lewis like they do Cory Booker and even Barack Obama. In 2016, Lewis led a sit-in on the floor of the House of Representatives to protest anti–gun control legislation. Some 43 years earlier, civil rights leaders censored Lewis's speech during the march on Washington because he criticized the Kennedy administration for wavering in its support for civil rights issues and for addressing the extreme poverty endured by southern blacks. Rival black intellectuals like Michael Eric Dyson dismissed Cornell West as an angry black man for calling Obama a "neoliberal opportunist" and "Rockefeller Republican in blackface." While the latter is definitely harsh, Obama's record of advancing neoliberal policies speaks for itself. Black intellectuals and politicians who speak against neoliberalism and the foundations of elite white power are marginalized and find themselves under the discursive umbrella of bad black citizens.[8]

Diversifying the winners of neoliberal capitalism is not an oppositional strategy to elite white power. The problem with diversity is that it doesn't address the distribution of resources because it can't address who controls the distribution of resources or the mechanism for how resources are distributed. The idea that a black or Hispanic person joining the ranks of America's elite will change the distribution of resources is based on essentialist understandings of race. Even at the height of a white-public culture, elites distributed resources only to the extent that it did not threaten elite white power. Since the civil rights era, the limited inclusions of women, racially nonthreatening black and Hispanics, as well as gender conventional and sexually nonthreatening members of the LGBT community have not slowed down the neoliberal project. This means we have to rethink what we mean by diversity.

Rethinking diversity in the neoliberal era is not the same thing as reducing all social relations to race or social class or inserting race or social class as a foundation variable to build a theory of diversity. The foundational/antifoundational arguments emerged in the 1980s and 1990s to highlight how women and members of the LGBT community faced social oppression in spite of a high socioeconomic status. It was

DIVERSITY AND FUTURE TRENDS 237

a theoretical move against Marxism and the historical exclusion of women from social theory. But you cannot have an adequate account of diversity in the neoliberal era without addressing the relations between racism and wealth. The academic debates and theories of group representations—including intersectionality, performativity, and poststructural approaches to identity—are symptoms of a larger problem on the left: the left has to address the problem of internal and external inequality. There are no difference troubles on the right. The tensions between internal and external inequality shift left-wing politics away from addressing substantive social problems to a battle over identity politics. However, even if we develop a critical approach to diversity that includes social class and addresses substantive social problems, it still leaves the neoliberal project in place. In this regard, diversity is typical of a conservative response to inequality: a strategy to try to fix broken institutions rooted in a belief that the institutions themselves are not part of the problem.

A real opposition to the neoliberal project starts with the state redistributing public resources to those in need. It starts by eliminating regressive taxation by rethinking who and what is taxed and at what levels. It starts by revaluing public life as an antidote to privatization. It starts by eliminating the ability to profit from poverty, which means reworking the social welfare, education, and the criminal justice systems. It starts by ensuring that regulatory fields do not create gross inequalities between actors, especially citizens. And, most important, it means that white America has to finally address the problem of racism. Racism is the cause and expansion of the neoliberal project, and you can't change the effect without changing the causal variable.

Future Trends in Neoliberal Racist Governance

It's impossible to predict the future. All social scientists know that human behavior does not follow a linear pattern. History is rife with black swan events: the unforeseen events and structural changes that make even the best-laid plans and predictions go to waste. The Internet and 9/11 are common black swan events that changed banking, media, social interactions, and US foreign policy. However, some patterns of human relations have been very stable over time. Elite white power and racism represent a meta pattern that cuts through centuries and survived antiracist resistance and anticapitalist challenges. Elite whites have withstood the changing meanings of race, citizenship, and social class. Perhaps the Trump presidency will serve as a rallying point for a movement against neoliberalism. History suggests not. The financial crisis that triggered the Great Recession resulted in the short-lived Occupy Movement. It did not put a dent in elite power. Whites rallied against Black Lives Matter with their own hashtag #bluelivesmatter. It was not just a defense of the police. It was an affirmation of white supremacy, of racial discrimination, of legitimating state violence against marginalized brown bodies. Based on the meta pattern of elite white power, here are some reasonable questions sociologists have to ask regarding future developments in racist neoliberal governance.

Brazil or South Africa or America?

A cultural myth that easily resonates with whites is that the United States is rapidly becoming a majority-minority nation. The US Census projects that by sometime around 2050, whites will become the overall statistical minority. Much of the Census's majority-minority forecast is predicated on the growing population of Hispanics. These projections are like gasoline on the fire of racist whites' fears. White nationalist groups use these projections as proof that they are losing their America. Liberal whites embrace the census projections as a mandate to usher in American multiculturalism and look to the beginning of a real colorblind era of racial relations. Both racist and liberal whites see a change in power relations as an emergent property of demographic changes. Sociologists are skeptical of social change trigged by changing demographics and the criteria used to define the coming white minority in America.

The idea that demographic changes will usher in a majority-minority America is based on a technical definition used to classify race and the assumption that who and what counts as white is, was, and will remain a fixed identity. Richard Alba rejects both assumptions. He noted that the census follows the 'one-drop rule' and classifies any person whose ancestry is mixed race as nonwhite. This includes children from white-Asian, white-Hispanic, white-black, black-Hispanic, Asian-Hispanic, and so on couples. According to Alba, if the census classified these children as white, then whites would make up 75% of the US population by 2050, a very far cry from the majority-minority country predictions based on the one-drop rule. Furthermore, median household incomes for all mixed families are closer to whites than minority families, and a mixed-race person from combinations like white-Asian or white-Hispanic are likely to identify as white, as well as marry a white person. For Alba, this indicates the continued process of assimilation in American society. In this regard, we can understand the process of assimilation, which Alba defines as the external pressure to conform, the method to assimilate, and how the dominant white group responds to another group's claim to whiteness, as an extension of the white racial frame.[9]

The second assumption of a unified and fixed white identity also underlines the assumption of a majority-minority America. Elite whites almost exclusively from an Anglo-Saxon background excluded social groups outside of Northern Europe as white. The boundaries between elite whites and those from Swedish, German, Irish, Italian, and Polish descent weakened and ultimately fell apart as who and what constituted good and bad whites changed in the mid-20th century. The change of who counted as white happened in relation to other racial groups struggling for civic inclusion. The black civil rights movement had more to do with the changing definition of white than a sudden epiphany of tolerance and acceptance among elites. The irony is that as more groups became white, it became easier for elites to cast aside any responsibility for social problems. Bad citizens face economic hardships because they refused to work, have irresponsible spending habits, and make bad decisions. The challenge to who and what counts as white will most likely emerge from selective ethnic threads within the broad identity categories of Asian and Hispanic. Take the identity of Latin American for example. The identity of Latin American was invented by European elites in Argentina in the early 20th century. Latin American connotes ancestry from Spain and Italy. It was the basis to create a racial hierarchy between Europeans, Native Americans, and the descendants of African slaves. The fluid nature and assemblage of the Latin American identities indicates that Hispanics with nonnative features will most likely identify with white and be accepted as white. To put this in a comparative-historical

240 DIVERSITY AND FUTURE TRENDS

context, if white ethnics from predominantly Catholic nations of origin were still defined as nonwhite, America would already be a majority-minority population.[10]

The question of the changing relationship between racial identities and political and economic power is sometimes contrasted as the Brazil or South African model. The Brazil model is based on a large mixed-race population that sits between elite whites who maintain their hold over political and economic power and the marginalized Afro-Brazilian community. The large mixed-race population acts like a petty bourgeoisie, swinging from one political side to the other based on the current political climate. South Africa represents a second model where a small handful of elite whites control the economy while the numerical majority of blacks have political power. American neoliberalism may have created a hybrid model out of Brazilian or South African models. Feagin sees the changing demographics as resulting in modest political gains for blacks and Latinos as they replace liberal whites in political office, but not much changes in terms of elite white control over nondemocratic institutions. Subsequent research on racist neoliberal governance should focus on how specific white-private sequences reconfigure democratic and nondemocratic institutions to protect elite white power.[11]

The changing definition of who is white will most likely preserve elite white power. Elite whites will either use majority-minority demographic projections to arouse the political and economic anxieties of ordinary whites or use selective civic inclusion of racially nonthreatening blacks and Latinos to diversify without having to give up power, or both. But the number of current nonwhites making claims for whiteness will continue to grow. Perhaps even more important is the number of current whites who will be cast aside as bad whites. How will the quantitative expansion of the number of nonwhites combined with the qualitative changes in who and what counts as white impact racist neoliberal governance? Can we have whites without white privilege?

Brown Skin > Black Skin

Decades of American neoliberalism combined with decades of America's aggressive military intervention across the globe has led to a new assemblage of the brown body. As noted above, who counts as white or black, and by extension, who and what counts as good citizenship has always been a fluid classification. After the turn of 21st century, we have witnessed the beginning of a shift from the domestic black body to a global brown body as the figurative focal point for elite whites to expand the neoliberal project. The browning of America may be an overstated myth, but an assemblage of the threatening bad brown body is not. The presentation and audience reception of racialized bodies is important because bodies carry mythologies that are more potent than data-driven facts when influencing political interpretations. Elite whites used the black body primarily to secure tax cuts and scale back the welfare state. Subsequently, a domestic market around poverty developed via the privatization of prisons, parole, and probation and around the privatization of social welfare via housing vouchers and the lack of affordable housing. One unforeseen effect of the market around poverty is that the black body is contained and made invisible via residential and school segregation. Only negative and exaggerated media portrayals of bad black citizens remain to trigger additional waves of neoliberalism. Neoliberalism can't expand without a racial subject. The dangerous and global brown body is emerging as the new black body.

The global brown body adds a layer of flexibility to American racism not readily available to the historic black-white binary. The brown body is always nomadic—a stateless actor. A white framing of security links individual feelings of safety with elite white global hegemony. The visibility of Latino/a bodies connects legal and illegal immigration with global economic insecurity. Latinos steal white jobs. Latinos poison white children with drugs. The assemblage of the Arabs and Muslims as bad brown bodies define the terrorist public that threatens whites' sense of security. Muslims threaten white borders. Their control over the global commodity of oil, especially on the supply side, threatens the white-private economy. Geopolitical battles are about protecting elite white interests abroad but need a bad brown body to link ordinary whites with elite whites. The specific forms of privatization and security that form because of their link to bad brown bodies include privatized immigration detention centers and private companies that manage data for passports and supply body and retina scans at airports. Excess military equipment is passed on to localities for the police to police citizens on the grounds

242 DIVERSITY AND FUTURE TRENDS

that El Salvadoran gangs and Muslim terrorists are coming to a white community near you. This doesn't mean that antiblack racism will disappear. Most likely, blacks will be swept up in antibrown hysteria but will cease to be the dominant racial group driving racist neoliberal governance.

Assessment and Artificial Intelligence

Much of what I've discussed about neoliberalism has dealt with how racism triggers neoliberal reforms. There is still the question of the actual day-to-day operation of neoliberal institutions, especially regarding social welfare programs. The question of the day-to-day operations of neoliberal institutions includes the logic behind the evaluative and decision-making process. The important species of capital necessary to define expertise and the administration of programs will vary based on scale, such as federal versus local, and the populations in need. Lurking behind these decisions is a technical-analytical dispotiff built around the idea of assessment.

Assessment is driving policy goals and programs designed to combat contemporary social problems. Assessment is moving away from a device to see if programs work to defining the program's parameters of success. Policy is designed to fit assessment. In turn, assessment is overtaking goodwilled efforts to fight social problems. For example, we find how assessment drives policy formation in the shift from ensuring all children have access to quality education to fighting bad schools. The bad school is defined in advance, based on ratio of students falling under the metric mark, which is also defined in advance. The lesson plans and pedagogical curriculum are designed to reflect the test, since the test dictates teachers' continued employment, the school's good standing, and how much federal funding the school district receives from the federal and state governments.

The rise of assessment is an indirect expansion of the privatization of social welfare. Privatized social welfare only works when those most in need are excluded from the programs. A system of private health insurance works so long as health insurance companies can exclude sick people. Private prisons work so long as inmates with mental and physical health problems and with a history of violence remain in public prisons.

DIVERSITY AND FUTURE TRENDS

Privatized housing vouchers to fight homelessness work so long as those receiving the vouchers are employed. The state of Massachusetts implemented a system of housing vouchers to replace the costly practice of putting up homeless families in motels. In order for the program to be successful, they cherry-picked the candidates who were most likely to be successful. Massachusetts denied about 50% of all applicants in the first round of white-private deregulations in 2004. A second round of white-private deregulations that gave homeless families housing vouchers for a three-year period was deemed successful on the back of denying 70% of the applicants. Based on the assessment metric of keeping families on the program housed rather than the goal of reducing homelessness, the white-private system of housing vouchers was made to appear successful. The number of homeless continued to rise in the Boston area because of the lack of affordable housing, a problem made worse by a system of white-private housing vouchers that increased the price of rents across the city.[12]

The rise of assessment corresponds with the rise of privatization and the need to make the social welfare programs appear to work in spite of limited budgets. In this sense, assessment acts as the core logic of the neoliberal social welfare programs. It is also a reflection of the rise of what Manuel Castell calls 'the information age' and the importance of data, data processing, data management, data storage, and data analysis in the economy. Financial firms don't make commodities. They make money. They make money by processing and analyzing data. The technology sector also makes money by processing data. Social media giants like Facebook and Twitter, as well as search engine giants like Alphabet (Google's parent company), collect billions of pieces of data on individual likes and dislikes and microinteractions once thought beyond the spectrum of social science methodology. All of this data demands analysis and assessment of the analysts and the quality of their assessment. Public and private social institutions need data analysis and have pushed for universities to train their students in buzzword programs like 'analytics' and 'big data' so they can enter this market of assessment. In turn, the species of capital needed to run states has switched from an informational capital of legal languages monopolized by lawyers to a form of technical and statistical knowledge monopolized by data analysts

244 DIVERSITY AND FUTURE TRENDS

and computer scientists. How will social movements fight for equality when the method of exclusion is defined through assessment instead of the constitutional law?

Artificial intelligence is the future of white-private fixed capital. Companies have invested in fixed capital since the onset of industrial manufacturing. Marx explained that one of the ways that capitalism hides its exploitation of workers is when companies reinvest surplus value back into machines instead of workers. He called the reinvestment of money into machines 'fixed capital'. Fixed capital is about reducing the cost of labor through efficiency and eliminating skilled labor from the labor maker. The period of industrialization featured companies replacing workers with machines. The period of deindustrialization featured companies replacing machines with hydraulics and computation. Artificial intelligence is the next frontier of white-private fixed capital because it will eliminate the need for human labor in the assessment market it created. We already see this in investment banks, which have replaced traders with supercomputers trading in high volume based on algorithms. We see this in how companies are investing in driverless car technology to reduce shipping costs, a potential major blow to truck drivers, taxis, buses, and the future investment in public transportation designed to give everyone access to the city and labor markets. Since the neoliberal state continues to operate on the logic of the upward redistribution of resources, elites, who will continue to be white, will be the main beneficiaries while the labor market erodes and extreme poverty expands.[13]

The future of racist neoliberal governance rests in what appears to be color-blind practices but is actually white-private practices of assessment and artificial intelligence. Can a computer be racist? Phillip K. Dick imagined a world where humans lived with androids, robot servants that are identical to humans, in his science fiction novel *Do Androids Dream of Electric Sheep?*. The main character's new job is hunting down androids that became violent. In essence, the androids are mimicking the human violence that surrounds Dick's postapocalyptic world. Artificial intelligence is designed to reflect or perhaps optimize human intelligence. Human intelligence is a sociological construct, built on a combination of history and linguistic rules of language. It should not be a surprise

DIVERSITY AND FUTURE TRENDS

that computers are also capable of racism even if they lack the intent to be racists. Computers programmers studying machine learning found that computers are quick to learn and then reflect racial and gender biases embedded in the human language. In March 2017, Microsoft unveiled an artificial intelligence chatbot Tay on Twitter. Tay immediately began tweeting racist statements it learned by interacting with other Twitter accounts, stating that Hitler was right and repeating Trump's campaign phrase: "We're going to build a wall and Mexico is going to pay for it." I'm not sure if androids dream of electric sheep, but if they do, they most likely dream of white sheep.[14]

Whites Digging Their Own Graves

The astute reader will have already picked up on the underlying subtext that ordinary whites are not free from the effects of the racist neoliberal project. The neoliberal project has inadvertently led to an increase in social problems for ordinary whites, especially for poor and working-class whites. As Leicht pointed out, "the number of white people classified as poor is almost as big as the total population of African Americans and Latinos." Inequality between whites is greater than inequality between whites and blacks. Median household income for whites has declined since 1999. The life expectancy for working-class whites, defined as whites without a college degree, has also declined since 1999. Monnat has dubbed the increasing social problems of deaths due to suicide, drugs, and alcohol-related causes (e.g., cirrhosis of the liver) in the working-class white community as deaths of despair. The social problem of opioid addiction on a national scale was made possible by the history of white-private health-care acts dating back to the 1970s, white-private pharmaceutical deregulations in the 1990s, the industrial manufacturing of painkillers, and a national infrastructure of white-private doctors, hospitals, and insurance companies to disburse the medications. Assessment of health care is not based on preventive health or even good health. Assessment is based on patients as consumers who need to be satisfied. The physician replaces her question of "What is the matter?" with "Where does it hurt?" An unintended benefit for blacks of racist health-care practices is that whites are more likely to be affected by the current opioid epidemic than blacks.[15]

246 DIVERSITY AND FUTURE TRENDS

The indirect expansion of the neoliberal project, whose racist origins are masked because they are embedded in the normal day-to-day operations of the state and private companies, have ensnared poor whites in the racist web of privatization and deregulations. Recoding social problems as public health problems may spare whites from police brutality and the symbolic violence of the criminal justice system, but it does not address the underlying network causing the social problems. The future expansion of the neoliberal project will claim more white victims. Will anyone declare the increased diversification at the bottom as proof that we've entered a postracial America?

Let's End on the Murder of Yet Another Young Boy

Jordan Edwards was returning home from a house party in Balch Springs, Texas, a suburb roughly 15 miles east of Dallas, when Police Officer Roy Oliver shot Edwards in the back of the head with an assault rifle around 11:00 p.m. It was a Saturday. Edwards was 15 years old. A neighbor called the police because of loud noise at the party. Or was it because of intoxicated teens in the streets? It's hard to tell given the extent that the police lie to cover up a police murder. The police claimed they heard gunfire. The police claimed that a car full of teenagers was backing down the street toward them. The Balch Springs Police Department's official statement was "There was an unknown altercation with the vehicle backing down the road toward the officers in an aggressive manner." None of this was true. Edwards was a passenger in his parents' car. His older brother was the driver. They were driving away when Oliver fired shots from his rifle at the car. The body cameras betrayed the police. The police chief was forced to apologize for lying to the local media: "I unintentionally, incorrect, yesterday [sic] when I said the vehicle was backing down the road. In fact, according to the video that I viewed, the vehicle was moving forward as the officer was approached." He did not apologize for Edwards's death.[16]

The murder of young black children has become a routine police practice of white racialized insecurity. Balch Springs is an inner-ring suburb, where 80% of the Balch Springs Police Department is white while 80% of the residents are black. Should we be surprised that an

DIVERSITY AND FUTURE TRENDS

increase in police brutality and harassment in America's black suburbs today reflects the same patterns of police brutality and harassment in America's black neighborhoods in the 1960s? A discursive battle between the police and the victim's family over Edwards's character took place. The police attempted to establish the black-public crime link. The police detained and handcuffed Edwards's brother and kept him overnight in jail. After Edwards's father arrived at the jail upset and wanting to know about the welfare of his children, the Balch Springs police called the Dallas County Sheriff's Office to restrain Edwards's father "because of his hostile behavior." Edwards's family, friends, teachers, and coaches defended his character. They noted that he was an honor student and well liked at school. Sixty years after the civil rights movement, blacks are still making claims that they are good citizens to get the state to enforce substantive citizenship rights. The neoliberal white-private criminal justice system is not designed to serve and protect its black citizens.[17]

Notes

1. Brett Burkhardt, 2015, "Where Have All the (White and Hispanic) Inmates Gone? Comparing the Racial Composition of Private and Public Adult Correctional Facilities" *Race and Justice* 5 (1): pp. 33–57.
2. US Department of Justice, Prisoners in 2013.
3. Data on changes in the proportion of uninsured in the black and Hispanic population located in Michael E. Martinez, Emily P. Zammitti, and Robin A. Cohen, "Health Insurance Coverage: Early Release of Estimates From the National Health Interview Survey, January–September 2016" Centers for Disease Control (CDC), located at www.cdc.gov/nchs/data/nhis/earlyrelease/insur201702.pdf
4. Skrentny, *After Civil Rights*, xi, p. 11.
5. Frank Dobbin, *Inventing Equal Opportunity* (Princeton, NJ: Princeton University Press, 2011).
6. Japonica Brown-Saracino, 2004, "Social Preservationists and the Question for Authentic Community" *City and Community* 3 (2 June): pp. 135–156; For a good overview of the racial achievement gap and how it persists in good schools see John Diamond and Amanda Lewis, *Despite the Best Intentions: Why Racial Inequality Thrives in Good Schools* (New York: Oxford University Press, 2015).
7. Booker quote located in Dale Russakoff, "Schooled" *The New Yorker*, 19 May 2014, located at www.newyorker.com/magazine/2014/05/19/schooled; also see Dale Russakoff, *The Prize: Who's in Charge of America's Schools* (New York: Houghton Mifflin Harcourt, 2015) for an in-depth look at school privatization in Newark; "Booker Seeks DOJ Probe of Journalist Arrest in Ferguson" Roll Call, located at www.rollcall.com/wgdb/ferguson-journalists-arrested-cory-booker/?dcz=

248   DIVERSITY AND FUTURE TRENDS

8. For West quotes and Michael Eric Dyson's critique of West see Michael Eric Dyson, "The Ghost of Cornell West" *The New Republic*, April 2015, located at https://newrepublic.com/article/121550/cornel-wests-rise-fall-our-most-exciting-black-scholar-ghost

9. Richard Alba, "The Likely Persistence of White Majority" *American Prospect*, 11 January 2016, located at http://prospect.org/article/likely-persistence-white-majority-0

10. David Cook-Martin, *The Scramble for Citizens: Dual Nationality and State Completion for Immigrants* (Stanford: Stanford University Press, 2013); David Scott FitzGerald and David Cook-Martin, *Culling the Masses: The Democratic Origins of Racist Immigration Policy in the Americas* (Cambridge: Harvard University Press, 2015).

11. Joe Feagin, "The Coming White Minority: Brazilianization or South Africanization of US?" Racism Review, 31 August, 2015, located at www.racismreview.com/blog/2015/08/31/the-coming-white-minority-brazilianization-or-south-africanization-of-u-s/

12. Schweid, *Invisible Nation*.

13. For Marx's discussion of fixed capital, see Section G.: Capitalism, Machinery and Automation in Marx's essay The Grundrisse, located in Karl Marx, "The Grundrisse" pp. 221–293 in *The Marx-Engels Reader, 2nd Edition*, edited by Robert Tucker (New York: Norton, 1978).

14. Aylin Caliskan, Joanna J. Bryson, Arvind Narayanan, 2017, "Semantics Derived Automatically from Language Corpora Contain Human-Like Biases" *Science* 356 (6334): pp. 183–186; Elle Hunt, "Tay, Microsoft's AI Chatbot, Gets a Crash Course in Racism from Twitter" *UK Guardian*, 24 March 2017, located at www.theguardian.com/technology/2016/mar/24/tay-microsofts-ai-chatbot-gets-a-crash-course-in-racism-from-twitter

15. Kevin Leicht, 2016, "Getting Serious about Inequality" *The Sociological Quarterly* 57: pp. 211–231, 225; Kevin Leicht, 2008, "Broken Down by Race and Gender? Sociological Explanations of New Sources of Earning Inequality" *Annual Review of Sociology* 34: pp. 237–250; Carmen DeNavas-Walt and Bernadette D. Proctor, "Income and Poverty in the United States: 2014" *US Census Bureau. Current Population Reports*, pp. 60–252 (Washington, DC: US Government Printing Office, 2015); Shannon M. Monnat, 2016, "Deaths of Despair and Support for Trump in the 2016 Presidential Election" The Pennsylvania State University, Department of Agricultural Economics, Sociology, and Education, Research Brief, 2016; Abby Goodnough, "Finding Good Pain Treatment Is Hard: If You're Not White, It's Even Harder" *New York Times*, 9 August 2016, located at www.nytimes.com/2016/08/10/us/how-race-plays-a-role-in-patients-pain-treatment.html?_r=1

16. "'Great Kid' Killed in Officer-Induced Shooting in Balch Springs" 1 May 2017, located at www.wfaa.com/news/local/15-year-old-boy-killed-in-officer-involved-shooting-in-balch-springs/435409090; "Balch Springs Officer Terminated after Death of Jordan Edwards" 3 May 2017, located at www.wfaa.com/news/balch-springs-officer-terminated-after-shooting-and-killing-15-year-old-jordan-edwards/436130282

17. "Balch Springs Police Fire Officer Roy Oliver, Who Fatally Shot Jordan Edwards with a Rifle" *Dallas News*, 4 May 2017, located at www.dallasnews.com/news/dallas/2017/05/02/balch-springs-police-fires-officer-fatally-shot-15-year-old-rifle; "Fatal Force" *The Washington Post*, located at www.washingtonpost.com/graphics/national/police-shootings-2016/?tid=a_inl

REFERENCES

"20 Years Later, Parts of Major Crime Bill Viewed as Terrible Mistake" Morning Edition, NPR, original airdate 12 September 2014, located at www.npr.org/2014/09/12/347736999/20-years-later-major-crime-bill-viewed-as-terrible-mistake (last accessed 24 April 2016).

A Conference on Neoliberalism, October 21–23, 1983, Reston Virginia, Sponsored by the Washington Monthly, Washington, DC.

Alba, Richard. "The Likely Persistence of White Majority" *American Prospect*, 11 January 2016, located at http://prospect.org/article/likely-persistence-white-majority-0

Alexander, Jeffery C. "Citizen and Enemy as Symbolic Classifications: On the Polarizing Discourse of Civil Society" *Where Culture Talks: Exclusion and the Making of Civil Society*, ed. Marcel Fournier and Michele Lamont, 289–308. Chicago: University of Chicago Press, 1992.

Alexander, Michelle. *The New Jim Crow: Mass Incarceration in the Age of Colorblindness.* New York: The New Press, 2012.

Alexander, Michelle. "Why Hilary Clinton Doesn't Deserve the Black Vote" *The Nation*, 29 February 2016, located at www.thenation.com/article/hillary-clinton-does-not-deserve-black-peoples-votes/ (last accessed 24 April 2016).

Alexander, Sandy. *The Properties of Violence: Claims to Ownership in Representations of Lynching.* Jackson, MS: University of Mississippi Press, 2012.

Alexander, Yamiche. "Ben Carson Calls Poverty a 'State of Mind' Igniting a Backlash" *New York Times*, 25 May 2017, located at www.nytimes.com/2017/05/25/us/politics/ben-carson-poverty-hud-state-of-mind.html?mcubz=1&_r=0

Ammons, Lila. "The Evolution of Black Owned Banks in the United States between the 1880s and 1990s" *Journal of Black Studies* vol. 26 no. 4 (1996 March): 467–489.

Anderson, Benedict. *Imagined Communities: Reflections on the Origin and Spread of Nationalism.* London: Verso, 1991.

Anderson, Nick. "Education Secretary Duncan Calls Hurricane Katrina Good for New Orleans Schools" *Washington Post*, 30 January 2010, located at www.washingtonpost.com/wp-dyn/content/article/2010/01/29/AR2010012903259.html

Apuzzo, Matt. "War Gear Flows to Police Departments" *New York Times*, 2 June 2014, located at www.nytimes.com/2014/06/09/us/war-gear-flows-to-police-departments.html

"Balch Springs Officer Terminated after Death of Jordan Edwards" 3 May 2017, located at www.wfaa.com/news/balch-springs-officer-terminated-after-shooting-and-killing-15-year-old-jordan-edwards/436130282

"Balch Springs Police Fire Officer Roy Oliver, Who Fatally Shot Jordan Edwards with a Rifle" *Dallas News*, 4 May 2017, located at www.dallasnews.com/news/dallas/2017/05/02/balch-springs-police-fires-officer-fatally-shot-15-year-old-rifle

Baudrillard, Jean. *Selected Writings*. Stanford: Stanford University Press, 2001.

Baum, Dan. "Legalize It All: How to Win the War on Drugs" *Harper's Magazine*, 18 April 2016, located at https://harpers.org/archive/2016/04/legalize-it-all/

Beauregard, Robert. *When Urban America Became Suburban*. Minneapolis, MN: University of Minnesota Press, 2006.

Beckert, Sven. *Empire of Cotton: A Global History*. New York: Vintage Books, 2014.

Bentele, Keith and Erin O'Brien. "Jim Crow 2.0? Why States Consider and Adopt Restrictive Voter Access Policies" *Perspectives on Politics* vol. 11 no. 4 (2013): 1088–1116.

Berends, Mark. "Sociology and School Choices: What We Know after Two Decades of Charter Schools" *Annual Review of Sociology* vol. 41 (2015): 159–180.

Blakely, Edward J. and Mary Gail Snyder. "Divided We Fall: Gates and Walled Communities in the United States" *Architecture of Fear*, ed. Nan Ellin, 85–99. New York: Princeton University Press, 1997.

Bobo, Lawrence and Cybelle Fox. "Race, Racism, and Discrimination: Bridging Problems, Methods, and Theory in Social Psychological Research" *Social Psychology Quarterly* vol. 66 no. 4 (2003 December): 319–333.

Bolton, Charles. *The Hardest Deal of All: The Battle Over School Integration in Mississippi, 1870–1980*. Jackson, Mississippi: University of Mississippi Press, 2005.

Bonilla-Silva, Eduardo. "More Than Prejudice: Restatement, Reflections, and New Directions in Critical Race Theory" *Sociology of Race and Ethnicity* vol. 1 no. 1 (2015 January): 73–87.

Bonilla-Silva, Eduardo. "Rethinking Racism: Toward a Structural Interpretation" *American Sociological Review* vol. 64 (1996 June): 465–480.

"Booker Seeks DOJ Probe of Journalist Arrest in Ferguson" Roll Call, located at www.rollcall.com/wgdb/ferguson-journalists-arrested-cory-booker/?dcz=

Bourdieu, Pierre and Loic Wacquant. *An Invitation to Reflexive Sociology*. Chicago: University of Chicago Press, 1992.

Bourdieu, Pierre and Peter Collier. *Homo Academicus*. Stanford, CA: Stanford University Press, 1990.

Branch, Enobong. *Opportunity Denied: Limiting Black Women to Devalued Work*. New Jersey: Rutgers University Press, 2011.

Brimmer, Andrew F. "The Black Banks: An Assessment of Performance and Prospects" *The Journal of Finance* vol. 26 no. 2 (1971 May): 379–405.

Brown-Saracino, Japonica. "Social Preservationists and the Quest for Authentic Community" *City and Community* vol. 3 no. 2 (June 2004): 135–156.

REFERENCES

Brubaker, Rogers. *Citizenship and Nationhood in France and Germany*. Cambridge, MA: Harvard University Press, 1992.

Bump, Phillip. "Here's How Rare In-Person Voter Fraud Is", located at www.washington post.com/news/the-fix/wp/2016/08/03/heres-how-rare-in-person-voter-fraud-is/?utm_term=.e29dd86401c0

Bureau of Justice Statistics, Prisoners in 1994, US Department of Justice, August 1995, NCJ-151654.

Burkhardt, Brett. "Where Have All the (White and Hispanic) Inmates Gone? Comparing the Racial Composition of Private and Public Adult Correctional Facilities" *Race and Justice* vol. 5 no. 1 (2015): 33–57.

Bush, Bill. "White Students Disproportionately Use Ohio School Voucher Program" *Columbus Dispatch*, 17 August 2016, located at www.dispatch.com/content/stories/local/2016/08/28/white-students-disproportionately-use-ohio-school-voucher-program.html

Caliskan, Aylin, Joanna J. Bryson, and Arvind Narayanan. "Semantics Derived Automatically from Language Corpora Contain Human-Like Biases" *Science* vol. 356 no. 6334 (2017): 183–186.

Campell, John and Ove Pederson. *The National Origin of Policy Ideas: Knowledge Regimes in the United States, France, Germany, and Denmark*. Princeton, NJ: Princeton University Press, 2014.

Cancio, A. Silvia, T. David Evans, and David J. Maume Jr. "Reconsidering the Declining Significance of Race: Racial Differences in Early Career Wages" *American Sociological Review* vol. 64 no. 4 (1996 August): 541–556.

Casanova, Pascale. *The World Republic of Letters*. Cambridge, MA: Harvard University Press, 2004.

The Center for Research Education Outcomes. "National Charter School Study" Stanford University, 2013, located at http://credo.stanford.edu/documents/NCSS%20 2013%20Final%20Draft.pdf

Chokski, Niraj. "The Most Segregated Schools May Not Be in the States You'd Expect" *Washington Post*, located at www.washingtonpost.com/blogs/govbeat/wp/2014/05/15/the-most-segregated-schools-may-not-be-in-the-states-youd-expect-2/

Churchill, Ward. *'To Disrupt, Discredit, and Destroy': The FBI's Secret War against the Black Panther Party*. New York: Routledge, 2005.

Citizens' Council. Mississippi Department of Archives and History, Jackson, MS, 1954–55.

Citrin, Jack and Frank Levy. "From 13 to 14 and Beyond: The Political Meanings of the Ongoing Tax Revolt in California" *The Property Tax Revolt: The Case of Proposition 13*, ed. George Kaufam and Kenneth Rosen, 1–26. Cambridge, MA: Ballinger Publishing Company, 1981.

Clarity, James R. and Warren Weaver Jr. "Briefing" 6 October 1983, located at www.nytimes.com/1983/10/06/us/briefing-213122.html

Cobb, James. "Somebody Done Nailed Us on the Cross: Federal Farm and Welfare Policy and the Civil Rights Movement in the Mississippi Delta" *Journal of American History* vol. 77 (1990 December): 912–936.

Cook-Martin, David. *The Scramble for Citizens: Dual Nationality and State Completion for Immigrants*. Stanford: Stanford University Press, 2013.

Crespino, Joseph. *In Search of Another Country: Mississippi and the Conservative Counter-revolution*. Princeton, NJ: Princeton University Press, 2007.

Cuyahoga County Medical Examiner's Office, Tamir Rice, located at www.scribd.com/doc/249970779/READ-Full-Tamir-Rice-autospy-report

Davis, Angela. *Are Prisons Obsolete?* New York: Seven Stories Press, 2003.

Davis, Angela. "What Is the Prison Industrial Complex? Why Does It Matter?" *Color Lines* vol. 1 no. 2 (1998): 1–8.

Davis, Martha. "Welfare Rights and Women's Rights in the 1960s" *Journal of Policy History* vol. 8 no. 1 (1996 January): 144–165.

DeNavas-Walt, Carmen and Bernadette D. Proctor. "Income and Poverty in the United States: 2014" *US Census Bureau. Current Population Reports*, 60–252. Washington, DC: US Government Printing Office, 2015.

Desmond, Mathew. *Evicted: Poverty and Profit in the American City*. New York: Crown Publishers, 2016.

Diamond, John and Amanda Lewis. *Despite the Best Intentions: Why Racial Inequality Thrives in Good Schools*. New York: Oxford University Press, 2015.

Dobbin, Frank. *Inventing Equal Opportunity*. Princeton, NJ: Princeton University Press, 2011.

Du Bois, W. E. B. *Black Reconstruction: An Essay toward a History of the Part Which Black Folk Played in the Attempt to Reconstruct Democracy in America, 1860–1880*. New York: Harcourt, Brace and Company, 1935.

Du Bois, W. E. B. *The Philadelphia Negro: A Social Study*. New York: Oxford University Press, 2007.

Dyson, Michael Eric. "The Ghost of Cornell West" *The New Republic*, April 2015, located at https://newrepublic.com/article/121550/cornel-wests-rise-fall-our-most-exciting-black-scholar-ghost

Ehreneich, Barbara and Derek Muhammad. "The Recession's Racial Divide" *New York Times*, 12 September 2009, located at www.nytimes.com/2009/09/13/opinion/13ehrenreich.html

Eskew, Glen. *But for Birmingham: The Local and National Movements in the Civil Rights Movement*. Chapel Hill: University of North Carolina Press, 1997.

"Fact Sheet: Compassionate Conservatism", located at https://georgewbush-whitehouse.archives.gov/news/releases/2002/04/20020430.html

Farrel, William E. "Neoliberals in Need of Constituents" *New York Times*, 24 October 1983, located at www.nytimes.com/1983/10/24/us/neoliberals-in-need-of-constituents.html

Faust, David Gilpin. *The Republic of Suffering: Death and the American Civil War*. New York: Knopf, 2008.

Feagin, Joe. "The Coming White Minority: Brazilianization or South Africanization of US?" Racism Review, 31 August 2015, located at www.racismreview.com/blog/2015/08/31/the-coming-white-minority-brazilianization-or-south-africanization-of-u-s/

Feagin, Joe. *How Blacks Built America: Labor, Culture, Freedom, Democracy*. New York: Routledge, 2016.

Feagin, Joe. *Racist America: Roots, Current Realities, and Future Reparations, 3rd Edition*. New York: Routledge, 2014.

Feagin, Joe. *Systemic Racism: A Theory of Oppression*. New York: Routledge, 2006.

Feagin, Joe. *The White Racial Frame: Centuries of Racial Framing and Counter-Framing*. New York: Routledge, 2013.

REFERENCES

Feagin, Joe R. and Harlan Hahn. *Ghetto Revolts: The Politics of Violence in American Cities.* New York: MacMillan Publishing, 1973.

FitzGerald, David Scott and David Cook-Martin. *Culling the Masses: The Democratic Origins of Racist Immigration Policy in the Americas.* Cambridge: Harvard University Press, 2015.

Florida, Richard. *Cities and the Creative Class.* New York: Routledge, 2005.

"Foster Care Statistics 2014", located at www.childwelfare.gov/pubPDFs/foster.pdf

Frankenberg, Erica, Genevieve Siegel-Hawley, and Jia Wang. *Choice without Equity: Charter School Segregation and the Need for Civil Rights Standards.* Los Angeles, CA: The Civil Rights Project/Proyecto Derechos Civiles, 2010, located at www.civilrightsproject.ucla.edu

Fraser, Nancy and Linda Gordon. "Contract Versus Charity: Why There Is No Social Citizenship in the United States" *The Citizenship Debates,* ed. Gershon Shafir, 113–127. Minneapolis, MN: University of Minnesota Press, 1998.

Freund, David M. P. "Marketing the Free Market: State Intervention and the Politics of Prosperity in Metropolitan America" *The New Suburban History,* ed. Kevin Kruse and Thomas Sugrue, 11–32. Chicago: University of Chicago Press, 2006.

Frey, William. "Melting Pot Cities and Suburbs: Racial and Ethnic Change in Metro America in the 2000s" The Brookings Institute, located at www.brookings.edu/~/media/research/files/papers/2011/5/04%20census%20ethnicity%20frey/0504_census_ethnicity_frey.pdf

Frymer, Paul. *Uneasy Alliances: Race and Party Competition in America.* Princeton, NJ: Princeton University Press, 2010.

Fuquay, Michael W. "Civil Rights and the Private School Movement in Mississippi, 1964–1971" *History of Education Quarterly* vol. 42 no. 2 (Summer 2002): 159–180.

Gabor, Andrea. "The Myth of the New Orleans School Makeover" *New York Times,* 22 August 2015, located at www.nytimes.com/2015/08/23/opinion/sunday/the-myth-of-the-new-orleans-school-makeover.html?_r=0

Galbraith, James K. "The Economy Doesn't Need the Third Way" *New York Times,* 24 November 1999, located at www.nytimes.com/1999/11/24/opinion/the-economy-doesn-t-need-the-third-way.html

Gallup Poll. "In US, Most Reject Considering Race in College Admissions", located at www.gallup.com/poll/163655/reject-considering-race-college-admissions.aspx

Garrow, David. *Bearing the Cross: Martin Luther King, Jr. and the Southern Conference Leadership.* New York, Quill, 1986.

Gates Jr., Henry Louis. "When Candidates Pick Voters" *New York Times,* 23 September 2004, located at www.nytimes.com/2004/09/23/opinion/when-candidates-pick-voters.html?_r=0

Gilens, Martin. *Why Americans Hate Welfare: Race, Media, and the Politics of Antipoverty Policy.* Chicago: University of Chicago Press, 1999.

Glass, Ruth. *London: Aspects of Change.* London: MacKibben and Kee, 1964.

Glickman, Lawrence. "Everyone Was a Liberal" aeon.com, located at https://aeon.co/essays/everyone-was-a-liberal-now-no-one-wants-to-be

Goffman, Irving. *Stigma: Notes on the Management of a Spoiled Identity.* New York: Simon and Schuster, 2009.

Goodnough, Abby. "Finding Good Pain Treatment Is Hard: If You're Not White, It's Even Harder" *New York Times,* 9 August 2016, located at www.nytimes.com/2016/08/10/us/how-race-plays-a-role-in-patients-pain-treatment.html?_r=1

254 REFERENCES

Goodwyn, Lawrence. *The Populist Movement: A Short History of the Agrarian Revolt in America*. Oxford: Oxford University Press, 1978.

Gottdiener, Mark. *Planned Sprawl: Public and Private Interests in Suburbia*. Beverly Hills, CA: Sage Press, 1977.

Gottdiener, Mark. *The Social Production of Urban Space, 2nd Edition*. Austin, TX: University of Texas Press, 1994.

Grafton, Carl and Anne Permaloff. *Big Mules and Branchheads: James E. Folsom and Political Power in Alabama*. Athens, GA: University of Georgia Press, 1985.

Gray, LaGuana. *We Just Keep Running the Line: Black Southern Women and the Poultry Processing Industry*. Baton Rouge: Louisiana University Press, 2014.

"'Great Kid' Killed in Officer-Induced Shooting in Balch Springs" 1 May 2017, located at www.wfaa.com/news/local/15-year-old-boy-killed-in-officer-involved-shooting-in-balch-springs/435409090

Guskin, Emily and Scott Clement. "Poll: Nearly Half of Americans Say Voter Fraud Occurs Often" *Washington Post*, 15 September 2016, located at www.washingtonpost.com/news/the-fix/wp/2016/09/15/poll-nearly-half-of-americans-say-voter-fraud-occurs-often/?utm_term=.38272526c7fe

Hallet, Michael. *Private Prisons in America: A Critical Race Perspective*. Urbana and Illinois: University of Illinois Press, 2006.

Hallett, Michael. "Race, Crime, and For-Profit Imprisonment: Social Disorganization as Market Opportunity" *Punishment and Society* vol. 4 no. 3 (2002): 369–393.

Hanlon, Bernadette. "A Topology of Inner-Ring Suburbs: Class, Race, and Ethnicity in US Suburbia" *City and Community* vol. 8 no. 3 (2009 September): 221–249.

Harvey, David. *The History of Neoliberalism*. New York: Oxford University Press, 2005.

Henderson, Harold Paulk. *Ernest Vandiver, Governor of Georgia*. Athens: University of Georgia Press, 2000.

Hendricks, Kasey and Dania Harvey. "Not One But Many: Monetary Punishment and the Fergusons of America" *Sociological Forum (forthcoming)*.

Hertz, Susan Handley. *The Welfare Mothers' Movement: A Decade of Change for Poor Women?* Washington, DC: University Press of America, 1981.

Hobsbaum, Eric. *Nationalism and Nationalism since 1780: Programme, Myth, Reality*. Cambridge: Cambridge University Press, 1990.

Hochschild, Jennifer L. "Affirmative Action as Culture War" *The Cultural Territories of Race: Black and White Boundaries*, ed. Michèle Lamont, 343–368. Chicago: University of Chicago Press and Russell Sage Foundation, 1999.

Hohle, Randolph. *Black Citizenship and Authenticity in the Civil Rights Movement*. New York: Routledge, 2013.

Hohle, Randolph. "The Body and Citizenship in Social Movement Research: Embodied Performances and the Deracialized Self in the Black Civil Rights Movement 1961–1965" *The Sociological Quarterly* vol. 50 no. 2 (2009): 283–307.

Hohle, Randolph. *Race and the Origins of American Neoliberalism*. New York: Routledge, 2015.

Hohle, Randolph. "The Rise of New South Governmentality: Competing Southern Revitalization Projects and Police Responses to the Black Civil Rights Movement 1961–1965" *Journal of Historical Sociology* vol. 22 no. 4 (2009 December): 497–527.

Howard, Gene. *Patterson for Alabama: The Life and Career of John Patterson*. Tuscaloosa: University of Alabama Press, 2008.

REFERENCES

Hunt, Elle. "Tay, Microsoft's AI Chatbot, Gets a Crash Course in Racism from Twitter" *UK Guardian*, 24 March 2017, located at www.theguardian.com/technology/2016/mar/24/tay-microsofts-ai-chatbot-gets-a-crash-course-in-racism-from-twitter

Hunter, Marcus Anthony. "How the New Voter ID Laws Impede Disadvantaged Children", *The Society Pages*, 2012, located at https://thesocietypages.org/ssn/2012/10/16/how-the-new-voter-id-laws-impede-disadvantaged-citizens/

Hwang, Jackelyn and Robert J. Sampson. "Divergent Pathways of Gentrification: Racial Inequality and the Social Order of Renewal in Chicago Neighborhoods" *American Sociological Review* vol. 79 no. 4 (2014): 726–751.

Hyra, Derek. "The Back to the City Movement: Neighborhood Redevelopment and Processes of Political and Cultural Development" *Urban Studies* vol. 52 no. 10 (2015): 1–21.

Hyra, Derek. "Conceptualizing the New Urban Renewal: Comparing the Past to the Present" *Urban Affairs Review* vol. 48 no. 4 (2012): 498–527.

Hyra, Derek. *The New Urban Renewal: The Economic Transformation of Harlem and Bronzeville*. Chicago: University of Chicago Press, 2008.

Indiana Department of Education, Office of School Finance. "Choice Scholarship Program and Annual Report: Participation and Payment Data" April 2016, located at www.doe.in.gov/sites/default/files/news/2015-2016-choice-scholarship-program-report-final-april2016.pdf

Izadi, Elahe and Peter Holley. "Video Shows Cleveland Officer Shooting 12 Year Old Tamir Rice within Seconds" *Washington Post*, 26 November 2014, located at www.washingtonpost.com/news/post-nation/wp/2014/11/26/officials-release-video-names-in-fatal-police-shooting-of-12-year-old-cleveland-boy/

Jacobs, Jane. *The Death and Life of Great American Cities*. New York: Vintage Books, 1992.

Jacobs, Ronald and Sarah Sobieraj. "Narrative and Legitimacy: Congressional Debates about the Non-Profit Sector" *Sociological Theory* vol. 25 no. 1 (2007): 1–25.

Jasper, James M. *The Art of Moral Protest: Culture, Biography, and Creativity in Social Movements*. Chicago: University of Chicago Press, 1997.

Jim Folsom Papers, Birmingham Public Library.

Katagri, Yasuhiro. *The Mississippi State Sovereignty Commission: Civil Rights and State's Rights*. Jackson, MS: University of Mississippi Press, 2001.

Katz, Michael B. *In the Shadow of the Poor House: A Social History of Welfare in America, 2nd Edition*. New York: Basic Books, 1996.

Keleher, Robert and B. Franklin King. "Usury: The Recent Tennessee Experience" Federal Reserve Bank of St. Louis, July/August, Economic Review, 1978.

Khan, Shamus. *Privileged: The Making of Adolescent Elite at St. Paul's School*. Princeton, NJ: Princeton University Press, 2012.

"Killed by the Cops", located at www.colorlines.com/articles/killed-cops

King Jr., Martin Luther. *Why We Can't Wait*. New York: Harper & Row Publishers, 1964.

Kohler-Hausman, Julilly. "The Attila the Hun Law: New York's Rockefeller Drug Laws and The Making of a Punitive State" *Journal of Social History* vol. 44 no. 1 (2010 Fall): 71–95.

Kruse, Kevin. "The Politics of Race and Public Space: Desegregation, Privatization, and the Tax Revolt in Atlanta" *Journal of Urban History* vol. 31 no. 5 (2005): 610–633.

Kruse, Kevin. *White Flight: Atlanta and the Making of Modern Conservatism*. Princeton, NJ: Princeton University Press, 2005.

Kubal, Timothy. *Cultural Movements and Collective Memory: Christopher Columbus and the Rewriting of the National Myth*. New York: Palgrave Macmillan, 2008.

Lachman, M. Leanne and Deborah L. Brett. "Gen Y and Housing: What They Want and Where They Want It" Urban Land Institute (2014), located at http://uli.org/report/gen-y-housing-want-want/

Lachmann, Richard. *States and Power*. New York: Polity Press, 2010.

Lamont, Michele. *Dignity of Working Men: Morality and the Boundaries of Race, Class, and Immigration*. Harvard: Harvard University Press, 2002.

Lamont, Michele and Virag Monlar. "The Study of Boundaries in the Social Sciences" *Annual Review of Sociology* vol. 28 (2002): 167–195.

Leicht, Kevin. "Broken Down by Race and Gender? Sociological Explanations of New Sources of Earning Inequality" *Annual Review of Sociology* vol. 34 (2008): 237–250.

Leicht, Kevin. "Getting Serious about Inequality" *The Sociological Quarterly* vol. 57 (2016): 211–231.

Levin, Josh. "The Welfare Queen" slate.com, located at www.slate.com/articles/news_and_politics/history/2013/12/linda_taylor_welfare_queen_ronald_reagan_made_her_a_notorious_american_villain.html

Licterman, Paul. *The Search for Political Community: American Activists Reinventing Commitment*. Cambridge & New York: Cambridge University Press, 1996.

Lieberman, Robert. *Shifting the Color Line: Race and the American Welfare State*. Cambridge: Harvard University Press, 1998.

Lipsky, Michael and Steven Rathgeb Smith. "Nonprofit Organizations, Government and the Welfare State" *Political Science Quarterly* vol. 104 no. 1 (1989–1990): 625–648.

Lipton, Eric and Stephen Labaton. "Deregulator Looks Back, Unswayed" *New York Times*, 16 November 2008, located at www.nytimes.com/2008/11/17/business/economy/17gramm.html

Lister, Ruth. *Citizenship: Feminist Perspective*. New York: MacMillan Publishing, 1997.

Lloyd, Richard. "The Neighborhood in Cultural Production: Material and Symbolic Resources in the New Bohemia" *City and Community* vol. 3 no. 4 (2004 December): 343–372.

Lo, Clarence Y. H. *Small Property versus Big Government: Social Origins of the Property Tax Revolt*. Berkeley: University of California Press, 1990.

Loewen, James. *Sundown Towns: A Hidden Dimension of Racism*. New York: Touchtone, 2006.

Logan, John R. "Separate and Unequal in Suburbia" Census Brief prepared for Project US2010, 2014.

Long, Maxine Master. "Trends in Usury Legislation—Current Interest Overdue" *University of Miami Law Review* vol. 34 no. 2 (1980): 325–342.

Loughlin, Ryan and Joie Chen. "Emmett Till's Cousin: Murder Never Crossed My Mind after He Whistled" *America Tonight*, 26 August 2015, located at Aljazeera.com

Loveman, Mara. *National Colors: Racial Classification and the State in Latin America*. New York: Oxford University Press, 2014.

Lublin, David. *The Paradox of Representation: Racial Gerrymandering and Minority Interests in Congress*. Princeton, NJ: Princeton University Press, 1997.

MacClean, Nancy. *Behind the Mask of Chivalry: The Making of the Second Ku Klux Klan*. New York: Oxford University Press, 1994.

REFERENCES

Maloutas, Thomas. "Contextual Diversity in Gentrification Research" *Critical Sociology* vol. 39 no. 1 (2011): 33–48.

Martin, Isaac. "Does School Finance Litigation Cause Taxpayer Revolt? Serrano and Proposition 13" *Law and Society Review* vol. 40 no. 3 (2006): 525–557.

Martin, Isaac. *The Permanent Tax Revolt: How the Property Tax Transformed American Politics.* Stanford, CA: Stanford University Press, 2008.

Martin, Isaac William, Ajay K. Mehrotra, and Monica Prasad. "The Thunder of History: The Origins and Development of the New Fiscal Sociology" *The New Fiscal Sociology: Taxation in Comparative Historical Perspectives,* ed. Isaac William Martin, Ajay K. Mehrotra and Monica Prasad, 1–27. New York: Cambridge, 2009.

Martin, Patricia. "Why Researchers Now Rely on Surveys for Race Data on OASDI and SSI Programs: A Comparison of Four Major Surveys" Social Security Administration, Social Security Office of Retirement and Disability Policy, Research and Statistics, January 2016.

Martin, Patricia P. and John Murphy. "African Americans: Description of Social Security and Supplemental Security Income Participation and Benefit Levels Using the American Community Survey" Social Security Office of Retirement and Disability Policy, Research and Statistics, 2014. Note NO. 2014–01, located at www.ssa.gov/policy/docs/rsnotes/rsn2014-01.html

Martinez, Michael E., Emily P. Zammitti, and Robin A. Cohen. "Health Insurance Coverage: Early Release of Estimates from the National Health Interview Survey" Center of Disease Control January–September 2016, located at www.cdc.gov/nchs/data/nhis/earlyrelease/insur201702.pdf

Massey, Douglas and Nancy Denton. *American Apartheid: Segregation and the Making of the Underclass.* Cambridge: Harvard University Press, 1998.

May, Gary. *Bending toward Freedom: The Voting Rights Act and the Transformation of American Democracy.* New York: Basic Books, 2013.

McGirr, Lisa. *Suburban Warriors: The Origins of the New American Right.* Princeton, NJ: Princeton University Press, 2002.

McKernan, Signe-Mary, Caroline Ratcliffe, Eugene Steuerle, and Sisi Zhang. "Less Than Equal: Racial Disparities in Wealth Accumulation" Urban Institute, 2013, located at www.nsu.edu/Assets/websites/CARPP/Race-and-Ethnicity/RaceEthnicitydoc2(Article).pdf

McMillen, Neil. *The Citizens' Council: Organized Resistance to the Second Reconstruction, 1954–1964.* Urbana: University of Illinois Press, 1971.

McWhorter, Diane. *Carry Me Home: Birmingham, Alabama: The Climatic Battle of the Civil Rights Revolution.* New York: Touchtone, 2002.

Mele, Christopher. *Selling the Lower East Side: Culture, Real Estate, and Resistance in New York 1880–2000.* Minneapolis, MN: University of Minnesota Press, 2000.

Mills, C. Wright. *The Power Elite.* Oxford: Oxford University Press, 1956.

Mink, Gwendolyn. "The Lady and the Tramp: Gender, Race, and the Origins of the American Welfare State" *Women, the State, and Welfare,* ed. Linda Gordon, 92–122. Madison: University of Wisconsin Press, 1990.

Minnite, Lorraine. *The Myth of Voter Fraud.* Ithaca, NY: Cornell University Press, 2010.

Mirel, Jeffery. *The Rise and Fall of an Urban School System: Detroit: 1907–1981, 2nd Edition.* Ann Arbor: University of Michigan Press, 1999.

Monnat, Shannon M. "Deaths of Despair and Support for Trump in the 2016 Presidential Election" The Pennsylvania State University, Department of Agricultural Economics, Sociology, and Education, Research Brief, 2016.

Montgomery Advertiser. "Outlook on School Bills Shaky as Deadline Nears" 1 September 1955.

Montgomery Advertiser. "Special Session to Wipe Out Public School Unlikely Now" 9 September 1954.

Morgan, Kimberly and Monica Prasad. "The Origins of Tax Systems: A French-American Comparison" *American Journal of Sociology* vol. 114 no. 5 (2009 March): 1350–1394.

Munford, Luther. "White Flight from Desegregation in Mississippi" *Integrated Education* vol. 11 (1973): 12–26.

Murphy, David and P. Mae Cooper. "Parents Behind Bars: Happens to Their Children" ChildTrends.org, October 2015, located at www.childtrends.org/wp-content/uploads/2015/10/2015-42ParentsBehindBars.pdf

Nadasen, Premilla. *Welfare Mothers: The Welfare Rights Movement in the United States.* New York: Routledge, 2005.

Norton, Anne Balcer. "Reaching the Glass Usury Ceiling: Why States Ceilings and Federal Preemption Force Low-Income Borrowers into Subprime Mortgage Loans" *University of Baltimore Law Review* vol. 35 no. 2 (Winter 2005): Article 5, 215–238.

O'Learly, Amy. "What Is Middle Class in Manhattan" *New York Times*, 18 January 2013, located at www.nytimes.com/2013/01/20/realestate/what-is-middle-class-in-manhattan.html

Omi, Michael and Howard Winant. *Racial Formation in the United States, 3rd Edition.* New York: Routledge, 2014.

Oshinsky, David. *Worse Than Slavery: Parchment Farm and the Ordeal of Jim Crow Justice.* New York: Free Press, 1996.

Overton, Spencer A. "The Donor Class: Campaign Finance, Democracy, and Participation" *University of Pennsylvania Law Review* vol. 152 (2004): 73–118.

Peterson, Richard L. and Gregory A. Falls. "Impact of a Ten Percent Usury Ceiling: Empirical Evidence" Credit Research Center, Working Paper No. 40, 1981.

The Pew Research Center. "Post Recession and Inequality" 12 December 2014, located at www.pewresearch.org/fact-tank/2014/12/12/racial-wealth-gaps-great-recession/

Pfeffer, Fabian T., Sheldon Danziger, and Robert Schoeni. "Wealth Disparities before and after the Great Recession" *Annual American Academy of Political Science Association* vol. 650 no.1 (2013 November): 98–123.

Pierce, Hester and Stephan Mateo Miller. "Small Banks by the Numbers, 200–2104" Mercatus Center, George Mason University, 2015, located at www.mercatus.org/publication/small-banks-numbers-2000-2014

Pildes, Richard H. "Is Voting Rights Law Now at War with Itself? Safe Election Districts versus Coalition Districts in the 2000s" *University of North Carolina Law Review* vol. 80 no. 5 (2002): Article 2, 1517–1573.

Piven, Frances Fox and Richard Cloward. *Why Americans Still Don't Vote: And Why Politicians Want It That Way.* Boston: Beacon Press, 2000.

Prasad, Monica. "American Exceptionalism and the Welfare State: The Revisionist Literature" *Annual Review of Political Science* vol. 19 (2016 May): 187–203.

Prasad, Monica. *The Politics of Free Markets: The Rise of Neoliberal Economic Policies in Britain, France, Germany, and the United States.* Chicago: University of Chicago Press, 2006.

Preble, Lawrence G. and Thomas K. Herskowitz. "Recent Changes in California and Federal Usury Laws: New Opportunities for Real Estate and Commercial Loans" *Loyola of Los Angeles Law Review* vol. 13 (1980): 1–83.

REFERENCES

Quadagno, Jill. *The Color of Welfare: How Racism Undermined the War on Poverty*. New York: Oxford University Press, 1994.

Rabushka, Alvin and Paul Ryan. *The Tax Revolt*. Stanford, CA: Hoover Institution, 1982.

"Racial Content of FHA Underwriting Practices 1934–1952", located at the University of Baltimore, Langsdale Library, Special Collections Department.

Reynolds, Morgan. "Privatizing Probation and Parole" National Center for Policy Analysis, NCPA Policy Report No. 233, June 2000.

Roberts, Sam. "Income Data Shows Widening Gap between New York City's Richest and Poorest" 20 September 2013, located at www.nytimes.com/2012/09/20/nyregion/rich-got-richer-and-poor-poorer-in-nyc-2011-data-shows.html?_r=0

Rousseau, Max. "Re-Imagining the City Center for the Middle Classes: Regeneration, Gentrification and Symbolic Policies in 'Loser Cities'" *International Journal of Urban Affairs and Regional Research* vol. 33 no. 3 (2009 September): 770–788.

Russakoff, Dale. *The Prize: Who's in Charge of America's Schools*. New York: Houghton Mifflin Harcourt, 2015.

Russakoff, Dale. "Schooled" *The New Yorker*, 19 May 2014, located at www.newyorker.com/magazine/2014/05/19/schooled

The Sam Engelhardt Papers, Alabama Department of Archives, Montgomery Alabama.

Santa-Cruz, Arturo. *Mexico-United States Relations: The Semantics of Sovereignty*. New York: Routledge, 2012.

Schuman, Howard, Charlotte Steeh, and Lawrence Bobo. *Racial Attitudes in America: Trends and Interpretations*. Cambridge, MA: Harvard University Press, 1985.

Schweid, Richard. *Invisible Nation: Homeless Families in America*. Oakland: University of California Press, 2016.

Scott, James. *Seeing Like a State: How Certain Schemes to Improve the Human Condition Have Failed*. New Haven: Yale University Press, 1999.

Seelye, Katharine, "4 Decades After Clashes, Boston Again Debates School Busing" *New York Times*, 4 October 2012, located at www.nytimes.com/2012/10/05/education/new-boston-busing-debate-4-decades-after-fervid-clashes.html

Seidman, Steven. *Beyond the Closet: The Transformation of Gay and Lesbian Life*. New York: Routledge, 2002.

Shaw, Samuel and Daniel Monroe Sullivan. "'White Night': Gentrification, Racial Exclusion, and Perceptions and Participation in the Arts" *City and Community* vol. 10 no. 3 (2011): 241–264.

Shklar, Judith. *American Citizenship: The Quest for Inclusion*. Cambridge: Harvard University Press, 1991.

Shulman, Bruce. *From the Cotton Belt to Sunbelt: Federal Policy, Economic Development, and the Transformation of the State*. New York: Oxford University Press, 1991.

Silver, Christopher. "The Racial Origins of Zoning in American Cities" *Urban Planning and the African American Community: In the Shadows*, ed. June Manning Thomas and Marsha Ritzdorf, 23–42. Thousand Oaks, CA: Sage Publications, 1997.

Silver-Greenburg, Jessica and Michael Corkery. "In Arbitration: A Privatization of the Justice System" *New York Times*, 1 November 2015, located at www.nytimes.com/2015/11/02/business/dealbook/in-arbitration-a-privatization-of-the-justice-system.html?_r=0

Silverstein, Ken. "America's Private Gulag" Prison Legal News, 1997.

260 REFERENCES

Skocpol, Theda. *Protecting Soldiers and Mothers: The Political Origins of Social Policy in the United States*. Cambridge: Harvard University Press, 1992.

Skrentny, John D. *After Civil Rights: Racial Realism in the New American Workplace*. Princeton, NJ: Princeton University Press, 2014.

Skrenty, Jennifer Pierce. "'Racing for Innocence': Whiteness, Corporate Culture, and the Backlash against Affirmative Action" *Qualitative Sociology* vol. 26 no. 1 (2003): 53–70.

Smith, Mitch. "2 Outside Reviews Say Cleveland Officer Acted Reasonably in Shooting Tamir Rice, 12" *New York Time*, 10 October 2015, located at www.nytimes. com/2015/10/11/us/2-outside-reviews-say-cleveland-officer-acted-reasonably-in-shooting-tamir-rice-12.html?_r=0

Smith, Neil. *The New Urban Frontier: Gentrification and the Revanchist City*. New York: Routledge, 1996.

Somers, Margaret. *Genealogies of Citizenship: Markets, Statelessness, and the Right to Have Rights*. Cambridge: Cambridge University Press, 2008.

Somers, Margaret and Fred Block. "From Poverty to Perversity: Ideas, Markets, and Institutions over 200 Years of Welfare Debate" *American Sociological Review* vol. 70 no. 2 (2005): 260–287.

Soss, Joe, Richard C. Fording, and Stanford Schram. *Disciplining the Poor: Neoliberal Paternalism and the Persistent Power of Race*. Chicago: University of Chicago Press, 2011.

Steensland, Brian. *The Failed Welfare Revolution: America's Struggle over Guaranteed Income Policy*. Princeton, NJ: Princeton University Press, 2009.

Strauss, Valerie. "The New Push for School Vouchers at State, Federal Levels" *Washington Post*, 12 February 2014, located at www.washingtonpost.com/news/answer-sheet/wp/2014/02/12/the-new-push-for-school-vouchers-at-state-federal-levels/?utm_term=.6242b019e42e

Surgey, Nick and Katie Lorenze. "Profiting from the Poor: Outsourcing Social Services Puts Most Vulnerable at Risk" 8 October2013, originally published at prwatch.org, locate at www.prwatch.org/news/2013/10/12264/profiting-poor-outsourcing-social-services-puts-most-vulnerable-risk

Tauber, Karl E. and Alma Taeuber. *Negroes in Cities: Residential Segregation and Neighborhood Change*. Chicago: Aldine Publishing Company, 1965.

Theide, Brian C. and Shannon Monnat. "The Great Recession and America's Geography of Unemployment" *Demographic Research* vol. 35 no. 20 (2016): 891–928.

Thernstrom, Abigail and Stephan Thernstrom. "Racial Gerrymandering is Unnecessary" *Wall Street Journal*, 11 November 2008, located at www.wsj.com/articles/SB122637373937516543

Thorton, J. Mills. *Dividing Lines: Municipal Politics and the Struggle for Civil Rights in Montgomery, Birmingham, and Selma*. Tuscaloosa and London: The University of Alabama Press, 2002.

Treaster, Joseph B. "Head of Reagan Panel Apologizes to Puerto Ricans" *New York Times*, 29 May 1982, located at www.nytimes.com/1982/05/29/us/head-of-reagan-panel-apologizes-to-puerto-ricans.html?rref=collection%2Fbyline%2Fjoseph-b.-treaster&action=click&contentCollection=undefined&region=stream&module=stream_unit&version=search&contentPlacement=1&pgtype=collection

Trillin, Calvin. *An Education in Georgia: Charlayne Hunter, Hamilton Homes, and the Integration of the University of Georgia*. University of Georgia Press, 1992.

Tuscaloosa News. "Engelhardt Introduces Bill to Abolish His Macon District" 14 July 1955, 25.

REFERENCES 261

Twain, Mark. *The Adventures of Huckleberry Finn*. New York: Penguin Classic Books, [1884] 1999.

UCLA Civil Rights Project. "Charter Schools, Civil Rights, and School Discipline: A Comprehensive Review" 2016, located at www.civilrightsproject.ucla.edu/resources/projects/center-for-civil-rights-remedies/school-to-prison-folder/federal-reports/charter-schools-civil-rights-and-school-discipline-a-comprehensive-review

The United States Department of Justice Civil Rights Division, United States Attorney's Office Northern District of Ohio. "Investigation of the Cleveland Division of Police" 4 December 2014, located at www.justice.gov/sites/default/files/opa/press-releases/attachments/2014/12/04/cleveland_division_of_police_findings_letter.pdf

United States Government Accountability Office. "Charter Schools: Additional Federal Attention to Help Protect Access for Students with Disabilities" June 2012, GAO-12-543, located at www.gao.gov/products/GAO-12-543

US Census, Boston Public Schools, 2012.

US Census Bureau. "5-Year American Community Survey, Census Track 1017" Cuyahoga County, 2009–2013.

US Department of Health and Human Services. "Privatization of Welfare Services", located at https://aspe.hhs.gov/legacy-page/privatization-welfare-services-review-literature-chapter-ii-current-state-social-service-privatization-147441

US Department of Justice, Bureau of Justice Statistics, Prisoners in 1994.

US Department of Justice, Bureau of Justice Statistics, Prisoners in 2013.

Vandewalker, Ian. "Election Spending 2014: Outside Spending in Senate Races Since Citizens United" Brennan Center for Justice Analysis, New York University School of Law, 2015.

Vann, David. "Oral History Project" conducted 2 February 1995, Birmingham Civil Rights Institute.

Vobejda, Barbara. "Clinton Signs Welfare Bill" *Washington Post*, 23 August 1996, located at www.washingtonpost.com/wpsrv/politics/special/welfare/stories/wf082396.htm

Wacquant, Loic. *Prisons of Poverty*. Minneapolis, MN: University of Minnesota Press, 2009.

Wacquant, Loic. *Punishing the Poor: The Neoliberal Government of Social Insecurity*. Durham, NC: Duke University Press, 2009.

Waters, Sarah. "New Social Movements Politics in France: The Rise of Civic Forms of Mobilization" *West European Politics* vol. 21 no. 3 (1998): 170–187.

Weber, Max. "Politics as a Vocation" *From Max Weber: Essays in Sociology*, 77–128. Oxford: Oxford University Press, 1958.

Weiner, Tim. *Enemies: A History of the FBI*. New York: Random House, 2012.

Whitehurst, Grover J., Richard V. Reeves, and Edward Rodrigue. "Segregation, Race, and Charter Schools: What Do We Know" Brookings Institute, Center on Children and Families, October 2016.

Whittman v. Personhuballah (2016), Oral Arguments, located at www.supremecourt.gov/oral_arguments/argument_transcripts/14-1504_5he6.pdf

Wiese, Andrew. "'The House I Live In': Race, Class, and African American Suburban Dreams in the Postwar United States" *The New Suburban History*, ed. Kevin Kruse and Thomas Sugrue, 99–119. Chicago: University of Chicago Press, 2006.

Williams, Patricia J. "How Could Tamir Rice's Death be Reasonable?" *The Nation*, 2 November 2015, located at www.thenation.com/article/how-could-tamir-rices-death-be-reasonable/

Williams, Richard, Reynold Nesiba, and Eileen Diaz McConnell. "The Changing Significance of Inequality in Home Mortgage Lending" *Social Problems* vol. 52 no. 2 (2005 May): 181–208.

Williams, Timothy and Mitch Smith. "Cleveland Officer Will Not Face Charges in Tamir Rice Shooting Death" *New York Times*, 28 December 2015, located at www.nytimes.com/2015/12/29/us/tamir-rice-police-shootiing-cleveland.html

Wilson, William Julius. *When Work Disappears: The World of the New Urban Poor*. New York: Alfred A Knoff, 1996.

Winant, Howard. "Race and Race Theory" *Annual Review of Sociology* vol. 26 (2000): 169–185.

Wong, Sandy. "Geographies of Medicalized Welfare: Spatial Analysis of Supplemental Security Income in the US, 2000–2016" *Social Science and Medicine* vol. 160 (2016 July): 9–19.

Woodward, David. "The Analysis of Paper and Ink in Early Maps" *Library Trends* vol. 35 (Summer 1987): 85–107.

Wu, Zheng, Feng Hou, and Christoph M. Schimmele. "Racial Diversity and Sense of Belonging in Urban Neighborhoods" *City and Community* vol. 10 no. 4 (2011): 373–392.

INDEX

13th Amendment 55
14th Amendment 35, 55
15th Amendment 55
16th Amendment 84
2000 presidential election 70

affirmative action 87; and good black
    citizenship 89
Affordable Care Act 11, 223, 231–232
Aid to Families with Dependent Children
    (AFDC) (formerly Aid to Dependent
    Children) 109–110, 205; 30 1/3 rule
    119, expansion in the civil rights era
    118–122; 123; Mississippi 128; non-
    profits 126
Alexander v Holmes County 1969 175
American Apartheid 6
American Taxpayer Relief Act (2012) 92
Arizona, and voter ID laws 71
artificial intelligence 243–244
Ashmore, Robert 46
assemblages 23–24, citizenship 35, 38;
    mythology 75
assessment 242–243
Atlanta Project 44

austerity: definition of 172; and schools
    172–173; and social welfare 122–128

Balance Agriculture with Industry
    (BAWI) 86
Balch Springs, Texas 246
Bank of America 102
Bankers' Panic of 1907 93
banking 92–105
Banking Act (1935) 147
Bear Stearns 231
Bearden v Georgia 1983 211
Beatty Plan 168
Bell, John 87
Bill of Rights 35
Birmingham, Alabama 199
Black, Maurice 170
black codes 193, 195
black-owned banks 96–98
black-public: crime 122, 204–214;
    residential segregation 153; social
    welfare 109, 118–122; voting rights 69
Black Panthers 203
black suburbanization: contemporary 2,
    149–152; history of 149

263

INDEX

black women: welfare rights movement 120–122; labor 119–120

Bloody Sunday 57

Bloomberg, Michael 74

Booker, Cory 235

border patrol 215–218

Boutwell, Albert 169

Bratton, William 6, 206

Brazil model of racial social structure 239–240

broken windows theory of policing 205

Brown, Jerry 46

Brown v Board of Education of Topeka Kansas 1954 4, 14, 20, 40, 148, 166, 171

Bryant, Carolyn 4

Bryant, Roy 4

Buchannan, Patrick 82

Buchannan v. Warley (1917) 143

Bush, George H.W. 64, 68, 126, 210

Bush, George W. 47; tax cuts (*see* Bush tax cuts); War on Terror 214

Bush tax cuts *see* Economic Growth and Tax Reconciliation Act (2001); Jobs and Growth Tax Reconciliation Act (2003)

campaign finance reform 72

Campaign Finance Reform Act (2002) 73

Carnegie, Andrew 12, 45

Carter, Jimmy 46

Cato Institute 205

Centex 102

charter schools 180–182; history of 181

Chase Bank 102

Chicago Defender 5

Citizens' Councils 61, 174; privatization of schools 174–175; violence 198

Citizens United v. FEC (2010) 73

citizenship: as an assemblage 35, 38; black authenticity 43–44; civic exclusion 35–40; civic inclusion 29–35, 41–44; good and bad citizenship 29–35, 44–48;

good black citizenship 41–42, 57, 88, 225; economic rights 31; political rights 31; in relation to slavery 36; in relation to systemic racism 29; social rights 31; substantive citizenship 34; symbolic citizenship 33; white-private citizenship 30, 34, 44–49, 226; white-public citizenship 29

Civil Rights Act (1957) 174

Civil Rights Act (1964) 28, 33, 45–46, 48, 50, 69, 83, 87, 226; and funding for schools 173

Civil War 12, 38

Civil War pensions 111–112

Cleveland, Ohio 1–3, 6, 180; school vouchers 184

Clinton, Hillary 206

Clinton, William Jefferson 10, 64, 75, 83, 205, 228

COINTELPRO 200, 202–203

color-blind racism 22

Community Action Agencies (CAA) 119

Conference on Neoliberalism 80–82

Connor, Eugene "Bull" 199

Contract for America 63, 228

convict-lease system 195

Correctional Corporation of America (CCA) 209

cotton 37–38

Countrywide Financial 102

creative class 159

critical race theory 16–17

culture: as ideology 20–21; autonomy of culture 23; definition of 20; culture and symbolic boundaries 21–22

deaths of despair 245

Depository Institutions Deregulatory and Monetary Control Act 1980 (DIDMC) 99

deregulation: banking 94–105, 228; campaign finance reform 72–74; definition of 58; gerrymandering 60–68;

INDEX 265

racial zoning 144–145; the Voting Rights Act 54, 58–60;
derivative trading 99, 102
deserving and undeserving poor, and citizenship 31
devices: contemporary devices (*see* voter ID laws); pre-Voting Rights Act 56
DeVos, Betsy 235
diversity and neoliberalism 223, 232–237
Dixon, Thomas 196
Dodd-Frank Act 11, 104
Dred Scott v. Sandford (1857) 54
drowned body: in *The Adventures of Huckleberry* Finn 4; science of 4
Du Bois W.E.B. 11; black reconstruction 194–195, 224–225; the NAACP 40; the talented 10th 40
Dukakis, Michael 81, 210
Duncan, Arne 180

Economic Growth and Tax Reconciliation Act (2001) 9, 92
Economic Recovery Act (1981) 9, 92, 122
Edwards, Jordan 246
Eisenhower, Dwight 114
electoral college 60; and gerrymandering 60–68
Emancipation Proclamation 55
embodiment 41, 43, 240–242
Engelhardt, Sam 61; and the School Placement Bill 168
English Poor Laws 110
exclusionary zoning 148

Fair Employment Practices Committee (FEPC) 225
Federal Housing Association (FHA) 144; and redlining 145
Federal Reserve Bank 83, 93, 150
Federal Reserve Board 9
Financial Services Modernization Act (1999) 10, 83, 100, 228
Folsom, Jim 14, 168–169

for-profit social welfare firms 126–127
Franklin, Benjamin 45

gated communities 151
gentrification 156; bohemian culture 158–159; demand and supply side approaches 157; in relation with race 157; real estate speculation 156; rent gap theory of 156
Georgia 61; Commission on Education 170; and private parole 212; school privatization 170–171
Georgia v. Ashcroft (2003) 65, 66
gerrymandering 60–68
ghetto: communal ghetto 6, 155; hyperghetto 6, 156; relationship with gentrification 159
Ghetto Informant Program (GIP) 203
Gingrich, Newt 63
Giuliani, Rudolph 6, 206
Goldwater, Barry 58
Grace, Peter 78
Grace Commission 78–80, 82, 169
Gramm, Phil 100
Gramm-Leach-Bliley *see* Financial Services Modernization Act (1999)
Gray Commission 169
Great Depression 10
Great Recession (2008) 83, 131–132; and housing 138
Green v. New Kent County, Virginia (1968) 178
Grubbs v. Bradley (1983) 208
gunshot: ballistic science 3
Gwinn, Ralph 86; and Liberty Amendment to Repeal the 16th Amendment 86

Harding, Warren 12
Hart, Gary 46, 81
Hispanic suburbanization *see* Latino suburbanization
homeowners associations 151

266INDEX

Homestead Acts 38
Horton, Willie 211
Houston, Charles 166

individual-level theories of racism 15
Industrial Development Agencies (IDAs) 160
inner-ring suburbs 150

Jackson, Andrew 39
Jefferson, Thomas 12
Jim Crow: and banking 94; and the criminal justice system 192–193; as a custom 4, 7, 218, 224; and racial zoning 141–143; and schools 167; as a system of laws 4, 6, 12
Jobs and Growth Tax Reconciliation Act (2003) 92
Johnson, Andrew 194
Johnson, Lyndon 57

Kagan, Elena 67
Kelly, Raymond 6
Kemp, Jack 9
Kemp-Roth tax cuts *see* Economic Recovery Act (1981)
Kennedy, Ted 46
Kerik, Bernard 6
Kinsley, Michael 82
Koch, Charles 73
Koch, David 73
Ku Klux Klan 194–197; in Birmingham 199; and *Birth of a Nation* 196

Latino suburbanization 149–150
Little Rock, Arkansas 171
Lohemann, Timothy 2–3
Long, Huey 14
long depression 196
lynching 194

magnet schools 179–187
majority-minority districts 63

Manhattan Institute 6, 205
Marshall, Thurgood 166
Martin Luther King Jr. Day 28
mass imprisonment 204–208, 229; construction of prisons 207
McCain-Feingold *see* Campaign Finance Reform Act (2002)
median net worth and race 103
mesentery tissue 3
Mexico: economic crisis 215; US-Mexico border policy 216
middle-class blacks 6
migration: Mississippi to Chicago 5; rural to urban 140, 176
Milam, J.W. 4
Miller v. Johnson (1995) 64
Milliken v. Bradley (1974) 148, 177
Milliken v. Bradley II (1977) 178
Mississippi: Great Mississippi Flood 5; money 3
Mississippi Legal Educational Advisory Committee (LEAC) 170
Mondale, Walter 46
Monroe Doctrine 214
Morgan, JP 12, 93
mothers' pensions 112–113
Motor Voter Law *see* National Voter Registration Act (1993)

National Housing Act (1934) 144, 146
National Voter Registration Act (1993) 68–70, 228
National Welfare Rights Organization (NWRO) 121
Native Americans 39, 224; and the 1924 Indian Citizenship Act 55
Naturalization Act (1970) 39
neoliberalism: definition of 7; history without race 8–11; recap of history with race 223–232
New Deal 13–14
New Negro Movement 196
New Orleans, Louisiana 180

INDEX

Nixon, Richard 60, 122, 127, 200–201, 204
North Carolina, and racial gerrymandering 64
Northwest Austin Utility District Number One v. Holder (2009) 67

Obama, Barack 10, 66, 70, 131
offender-funded programs and parole 211
Office of Economic Opportunity (OEO) 119
Ohio, and voter ID laws 71
Omnibus Budget Reconciliation Act (1981) 122
O'Neil, Tip 46
Operation Big Vote 70

Pasadena, Texas 53
Pence, Mike 223
Personal Responsibility and Work Opportunity Reconciliation Act (PRWORA) 123–124; privatization of 130–131
Peters, Charles 80
Plessey v. Ferguson (1896) 40 166
police brutality 1–2, 6, 191–192, 206, 246–247
predatory lending 99–101
privatization 7; of health insurance 11; and play 7; of schools 22, 165–188; of social space 145–146; of social welfare 32; 112–113, 117
Professional Air Traffic Controllers Organization 47
Progressive Era 12–13
Project on Fair Representation 67
Pupil Placement Act 169

racial formation theory 16
racial gerrymandering 60–68
racial realism 234–235
racial zoning 141–145
Reagan, Ronald 47, 78, 92, 126, 204
redlining 144–145

Reno v. Bossier Parish School Board (2000) 66
residential segregation 5, 139–146
Revolving Door Ad 210–211
Rice, Tamir 1–3, 15
robber barons 12
Roberts, John 62
Rockefeller, John 12
Rockefeller, Nelson 201–202
Roosevelt, Franklin Delano 13, 114, 225
Roosevelt, Theodore 196
Roth, William 9
Roth IRA 9

Savings and Loan Crisis (1987) 103
School Placement Act 168
school segregation and busing 176–179
school vouchers 183–186, 230; in Cleveland, Ohio, 184; in Florida 184; in Indiana 184; in Milwaukee, Wisconsin 184
segregated welfare state, definition of 108
segregation academies 173–175; as free enterprise schools 174
Selma, Alabama 200
Shaw v. Reno (1993) 64
Shelby, Alabama 53, 66–67
Shelby v. Holder (2013) 66
Sillers, Walter 170
Simmons, William 174
slavery: in relation to citizenship 36; slaves as collateral 36–37
Smith v. Allwright (1944) 166
Social Security Act 114–118, 225; AFDC 116–117; Unemployment Insurance 115–116
South African model of racial social structure 240
Southern Christian Leadership Conference (SCLC) 56; and citizenship schools 57
Southern Reconstruction, and black civic inclusion 55–56

Standard Oil 12, 92
Stanley Plan 169
Student Nonviolent Coordinating
    Committee (SNCC) 199
subprime lending 99–105
suburbanization 146–148
Super Political Action Committee
    (PAC) 73
*Swan v. Charlotte-Mecklenburg County
    Board of Education* (1971) 176
systemic racism 18–19

Tax and Expenditure Limitations (TELs)
    89–90
Tax Reform Act (1986) 92
tax revolts: in Atlanta 90; of the
    marginalized 90; Proposition 4 and
    California 90; Proposition 13 and
    California 90; supply-side tax revolt 89
taxation 83–84; deductions 86; housing
    148; perception of who pays taxes
    84–85, 91; regressive taxation 86, 148;
    tax cuts 9
Temporary Aid to Needy Families
    (TANF) 124–125; privatization of
    126–131
terrorism 217
Thurmond, Strom 87
Till, Emmett 3
Troubled Asset Relief Program
    (TARP) 83
Trump, Donald 222
Tsgonas, Paul 81
Tuskegee, Alabama 61
two-pronged criminal justice system
    192–204; centralization of police
    violence 198–204

United States v. Bhagat Singh Thind
    (1923) 40
urban planning 138, 144; and land
    clearance zones 144
urban race riots 155, 191–92

urban renewal: 1960s 154; 1993–2010 160
US Steel 12, 92
usury caps 94–99, 102

Vann, David 199
vertical zoning 145
Veterans Administration Act (VA) (1934)
    147
Violent Crime Control and Law
    Enforcement Act (1994) 207
Volcker, Paul 9–10
Volcker Shock 150
voter ID laws 71
Voting Rights Act (1965) 28, 33, 48, 50,
    69, 226; history of 54–57; preclearance
    65; section 2 54, 62, 56; section 4 54;
    section 5 54, 60–68
Voting Rights Act (1982) 62–64, 75, 228
Voting Rights Act (2005) 66

Wall Street Reform and Consumer
    Protection Act (2010) 11, 104
Wallace, George 57, 176–177, 200,
    222–223, 227
Walton, Sam 45
War on Drugs 155, 200–203, 208
War on Poverty 119; Work Incentive
    Program (WIN) 119, 204
Warren, Earl 167
Washington, George 12
Watt, Melvin 64
welfare queen: Lillie Harden 123; Linda
    Taylor 123; narrative 123
white ethnics 39
white flight 146–148, 153
white racial frame 22–24; and citizenship
    36, 45
white-private: arbitration 212–214;
    banking deregulations 92–105;
    campaign finance reform 72;
    citizenship 30, 34; 44–49, 226;
    gentrification 159, 162; parole 210–212;
    prisons 208–210; revenue and taxation

83–92; schools 162–166, 180–184, 187–188; social space 145, 151–52, 161; social welfare 112–113, 131

white-private/black public 7, 14, 23–25; and the Gray Commission 78–79

white-public: citizenship 29; disability 132–34; funding for prisons 207; funding for schools 173; racial zoning 143; taxes 84, 86; unemployment insurance 131; the welfare state 108–118

Whitten, Jamie 128

Wilcox Amendment 168

Wilson, Woodrow 93

Wittmann v. Personhuballah (2016) 67

Young Men's Business Community (YMBC) 20